MANHATTAN PREP

Text Completion & Sentence Equivalence

GRE Strategy Guide

This book contains important strategies for tackling Text Completion & Sentence Equivalence questions, two brand-new question formats on the new GRE. Also included is a list of 1,000 likely-to-appear vocabulary words and proven strategies for mastering these words.

guide **8**

MIX
Paper from
responsible sources
FSC® C014174

Text Completion & Sentence Equivalence GRE Strategy Guide, Fourth Edition

10-digit International Standard Book Number: 1-937707-89-X
13-digit International Standard Book Number: 978-1-937707-89-7
eISBN: 978-1-941234-19-8

Layout Design: Dan McNaney and Cathy Huang
Cover Design: Dan McNaney and Frank Callaghan
Cover Photography: Amy Pierce

INSTRUCTIONAL GUIDE SERIES

SUPPLEMENTAL MATERIALS

MANHATTAN
PREP

June 3rd, 2014

Dear Student,

Thank you for picking up a copy of *Text Completion & Sentence Equivalence*. I hope this book provides just the guidance you need to get the most out of your GRE studies.

As with most accomplishments, there were many people involved in the creation of the book you are holding. First and foremost is Zeke Vanderhoek, the founder of Manhattan Prep. Zeke was a lone tutor in New York when he started the company in 2000. Now, 14 years later, the company has instructors and offices nationwide and contributes to the studies and successes of thousands of GRE, GMAT, LSAT, and SAT students each year.

Our Manhattan Prep Strategy Guides are based on the continuing experiences of our instructors and students. We are particularly indebted to our instructors Stacey Koprince, Dave Mahler, Liz Ghini Moliski, Emily Meredith Sledge, and Tommy Wallach for their hard work on this edition. Dan McNaney and Cathy Huang provided their design expertise to make the books as user-friendly as possible, and Liz Krisher made sure all the moving pieces came together at just the right time. Beyond providing additions and edits for this book, Chris Ryan and Noah Teitelbaum continue to be the driving force behind all of our curriculum efforts. Their leadership is invaluable. Finally, thank you to all of the Manhattan Prep students who have provided input and feedback over the years. This book wouldn't be half of what it is without your voice.

At Manhattan Prep, we continually aspire to provide the best instructors and resources possible. We hope that you will find our commitment manifest in this book. If you have any questions or comments, please email me at dgonzalez@manhattanprep.com. I'll look forward to reading your comments, and I'll be sure to pass them along to our curriculum team.

Thanks again, and best of luck preparing for the GRE!

Sincerely,

Dan Gonzalez
President
Manhattan Prep

HOW TO ACCESS YOUR ONLINE RESOURCES

If you...

⊛ **are a registered Manhattan Prep GRE® student**

and have received this book as part of your course materials, you have AUTOMATIC access to ALL of our online resources. This includes all practice exams, question banks, and online updates to this book. To access these resources, follow the instructions in the Welcome Guide provided to you at the start of your program. Do NOT follow the instructions below.

⊛ **purchased this book from the Manhattan Prep online store or at one of our centers**

1. Go to: www.manhattanprep.com/gre/studentcenter.

2. Log in using the username and password used when your account was set up.

⊛ **purchased this book at a retail location**

1. Create an account with Manhattan Prep at the website: www.manhattanprep.com/gre/createaccount.

2. Go to: www.manhattanprep.com/gre/access.

3. Follow the instructions on the screen.

Your online access begins on the day that you register your book at the above URL.

You only need to register your product ONCE at the above URL. To use your online resources any time AFTER you have completed the registration process, log in to the following URL: www.manhattanprep.com/gre/studentcenter.

Please note that online access is nontransferable. This means that only NEW and UNREGISTERED copies of the book will grant you online access. Previously used books will NOT provide any online resources.

⊛ **purchased an eBook version of this book**

1. Create an account with Manhattan Prep at the website: www.manhattanprep.com/gre/createaccount.

2. Email a copy of your purchase receipt to gre@manhattanprep.com to activate your resources. Please be sure to use the same email address to create an account that you used to purchase the eBook.

For any technical issues, email techsupport@manhattanprep.com or call 800-576-4628.

TABLE *of* CONTENTS

guide **8**

Chapter 1 *of*

Text Completion & Sentence Equivalence

Introduction

In This Chapter...

The Revised GRE

Question Formats in Detail

Chapter 1

Introduction

We know that you're looking to succeed on the GRE so that you can go to graduate school and do the things you want to do in life.

We also know that you may not have done math since high school, and that you may never have learned words like "adumbrate" or "sangfroid." We know that it's going to take hard work on your part to get a top GRE score, and that's why we've put together the only set of books that will take you from the basics all the way up to the material you need to master for a near-perfect score, or whatever your goal score may be. You've taken the first step. Now it's time to get to work!

How to Use These Materials

Manhattan Prep's GRE materials are comprehensive. But keep in mind that, depending on your score goal, it may not be necessary to get absolutely everything. Grad schools only see your overall Quantitative, Verbal, and Writing scores—they don't see exactly which strengths and weaknesses went into creating those scores.

You may be enrolled in one of our courses, in which case you already have a syllabus telling you in what order you should approach the books. But if you bought this book online or at a bookstore, feel free to approach the books—and even the chapters within the books—in whatever order works best for you. For the most part, the books, and the chapters within them, are independent; you don't have to master one section before moving on to the next. So if you're having a hard time with something in particular, you can make a note to come back to it later and move on to another section. Similarly, it may not be necessary to solve every single practice problem for every section. As you go through the material, continually assess whether you understand and can apply the principles in each individual section and chapter. The best way to do this is to solve the Check Your Skills and Practice Sets throughout. If you're confident you have a concept or method down, feel free to move on. If you struggle with something, make note of it for further review. Stay active in your learning and stay oriented toward the test—it's easy to read something and think you understand it, only to have trouble applying it in the 1–2 minutes you have to solve a problem.

1

Study Skills

As you're studying for the GRE, try to integrate your learning into your everyday life. For example, vocabulary is a big part of the GRE, as well as something you just can't "cram" for—you're going to want to do at least a little bit of vocab every day. So try to learn and internalize a little bit at a time, switching up topics often to help keep things interesting.

Keep in mind that, while many of your study materials are on paper (including Education Testing Service's [ETS's] most recent source of official GRE questions, *The Official Guide to the GRE revised General Test, Second Edition*), your exam will be administered on a computer. Because this is a computer-based test, you will *not* be able to underline portions of reading passages, write on diagrams of geometry figures, or otherwise physically mark up problems. So get used to this now. Solve the problems in these books on scratch paper. (Each of our books talks specifically about what to write down for different problem types.)

Again, as you study, stay focused on the test-day experience. As you progress, work on timed drills and sets of questions. Eventually, you should be taking full practice tests (available at www.manhattanprep.com/gre) under actual timed conditions.

The Revised GRE

As of August 1, 2011, the Quantitative and Verbal sections of the GRE underwent a number of changes. The actual body of knowledge being tested is more or less the same as it ever was, but the *way* that knowledge is tested changed. Here's a brief summary of the changes, followed by a more comprehensive assessment of the new exam.

The current test is a little longer than the old test, lengthened from about 3.5 hours to about 4 hours. When you sign up for the exam at www.ets.org/gre, you will be told to plan to be at the center for 5 hours, since there will be some paperwork to complete when you arrive, and occasionally test-takers are made to wait a bit before being allowed to begin.

Taking a four-hour exam can be quite exhausting, so it's important to practice not only out of these books, but also on full-length computer-based practice exams, such as the six such exams you have gained access to by purchasing this book (see page 7 for details).

There are now two scored Math sections and two scored Verbal sections. A new score scale of 130–170 is used in place of the old 200–800 scale. More on this later.

The Verbal section of the GRE changed dramatically. The Antonyms and Analogies disappeared. The Text Completion and Reading Comprehension remain, expanded and remixed in a few new ways. Vocabulary is still important, but is tested only in the context of complete sentences.

MANHATTAN
PREP

The Quant section of the new GRE still contains the same multiple-choice problems, Quantitative Comparisons, and Data Interpretations (which are really a subset of multiple-choice problems). The revised test also contains two new problem formats, which we will introduce in this section.

On both Verbal and Quant, some of the new question types have more than one correct answer, or otherwise break out of the mold of traditional multiple-choice exams. You might say that computer-based exams are finally taking advantage of the features of computers.

One way that this is true is that the new exam includes a small, on-screen, four-function calculator with a square root button. Many test-takers will rejoice at the advent of this calculator. It is true that the GRE calculator will reduce emphasis on computation—but look out for problems, such as percents questions with tricky wording, that are likely to foil those who rely on the calculator too much. *In short, the calculator may make your life a bit easier from time to time, but it's not a game changer.* There are **zero** questions that can be solved *entirely* with a calculator. You will still need to know the principles contained in the six Quant books (of the eight-book Manhattan Prep GRE series).

Finally, don't worry about whether the new GRE is harder or easier than the old GRE. You are being judged against other test-takers, all of whom are in the same boat. So if the new formats are harder, they are harder for other test-takers as well.

Additionally, graduate schools to which you will be applying have been provided with conversion charts so that applicants with old and new GRE scores can be compared fairly (GRE scores are valid for five years).

Exam Structure

The revised test has six sections. You will get a 10-minute break between the third and fourth sections and a 1-minute break between the others. The Analytical Writing section is always first. The other five sections can be seen in any order and will include:

- Two Verbal Reasoning sections (20 questions each in 30 minutes per section)
- Two Quantitative Reasoning sections (20 questions each in 35 minutes per section)
- Either an unscored section or a research section

An unscored section will look just like a third Verbal or Quantitative Reasoning section, and you will not be told which of them doesn't count. If you get a research section, it will be identified as such, and will be the last section you get.

Section #	Section Type	# Questions	Time	Scored?
1	Analytical Writing	2 essays	30 minutes each	Yes
2	Verbal #1	Approx. 20	30 minutes	Yes
3	Quantitative #1 (order can vary)	Approx. 20	35 minutes	Yes
10-Minute Break				
4	Verbal #2	Approx. 20	30 minutes	Yes
5	Quantitative #2 (order can vary)	Approx. 20	35 minutes	Yes
?	Unscored Section (Verbal or Quant, order can vary)	Approx. 20	30 or 35 minutes	No
Last	Research Section	Varies	Varies	No

All the question formats will be looked at in detail later in the chapter.

Using the Calculator

The addition of a small, four-function calculator with a square root button means that re-memorizing times tables or square roots is less important than it used to be. However, the calculator is not a cure-all; in many problems, the difficulty is in figuring out what numbers to put into the calculator in the first place. In some cases, using a calculator will actually be less helpful than doing the problem some other way. Take a look at an example:

If x is the remainder when (11)(7) is divided by 4 and y is the remainder when (14) (6) is divided by 13, what is the value of $x + y$?

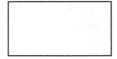

Solution: This problem is designed so that the calculator won't tell the whole story. Certainly, the calculator will tell you that $11 \times 7 = 77$. When you divide 77 by 4, however, the calculator yields an answer of 19.25. The remainder is not 0.25 (a remainder is always a whole number).

You might just go back to your pencil and paper, and find the largest multiple of 4 that is less than 77. Since 4 does go into 76, you can conclude that 4 would leave a remainder of 1 when dividing into 77.

MANHATTAN
PREP

(Notice that you don't even need to know how many times 4 goes into 76, just that it goes in. One way to mentally "jump" to 76 is to say, 4 goes into 40, so it goes into 80…that's a bit too big, so take away 4 to get 76.)

However, it is also possible to use the calculator to find a remainder. Divide 77 by 4 to get 19.25. Thus, 4 goes into 77 nineteen times, with a remainder left over. Now use your calculator to multiply 19 (JUST 19, not 19.25) by 4. You will get 76. The remainder is $77 - 76$, which is 1. Therefore, $x = 1$. You could also multiply the leftover 0.25 times 4 (the divisor) to find the remainder of 1.

Use the same technique to find y. Multiply 14 by 6 to get 84. Divide 84 by 13 to get 6.46. Ignore everything after the decimal, and just multiply 6 by 13 to get 78. The remainder is therefore $84 - 78$, which is 6. Therefore, $y = 6$.

Since you are looking for $x + y$, and $1 + 6 = 7$, the answer is 7.

You can see that blind faith in the calculator can be dangerous. Use it responsibly! And this leads us to…

Practice Using the Calculator!

On the revised GRE, the on-screen calculator will slow you down or lead to incorrect answers if you're not careful! If you plan to use it on test day (which you should), you'll want to practice first.

We have created an online practice calculator for you to use. To access this calculator, go to www.manhattanprep.com/gre and sign in to the student center using the instructions on the "How to Access Your Online Resources" page found at the front of this book.

In addition to the calculator, you will see instructions for how to use the calculator. Be sure to read these instructions and work through the associated exercises. Throughout our math books, you will see the ⬚ symbol. This symbol means "Use the calculator here!" As much as possible, have the online practice calculator up and running during your review of our math books. You'll have the chance to use the on-screen calculator when you take our practice exams as well.

Navigating the Questions in a Section

Another change for test-takers on the revised GRE is the ability to move freely around the questions in a section—you can go forward and backward one-by-one and can even jump directly to any question from the "review list." The review list provides a snapshot of which questions you have answered, which ones you have tagged for "mark and review," and which are incomplete, either because you didn't indicate enough answers or because you indicated too many (that is, if a number of choices is specified by the question). You should double-check the review list for completion if you finish the section early. Using the review list feature will take some practice as well, which is why we've built it into our online practice exams.

The majority of test-takers will be pressed for time. Thus, for some, it won't be feasible to go back to multiple problems at the end of the section. Generally, if you can't get a question the first time, you won't be able to get it the second time around either. With this in mind, here's the order in which we recommend using the new review list feature.

1. Do the questions in the order in which they appear.

2. When you encounter a difficult question, do your best to eliminate answer choices you know are wrong.

3. If you're not sure of an answer, take an educated guess from the choices remaining. Do NOT skip it and hope to return to it later.

4. Using the "mark" button at the top of the screen, mark up to three questions per section that you think you might be able to solve with more time. Mark a question only after you have taken an educated guess.

5. Always click on the review list at the end of a section, to quickly make sure you have neither skipped nor incompletely answered any questions.

6. If you have time, identify any questions that you marked for review and return to them. If you do not have any time remaining, you will have already taken good guesses at the tough ones.

What you want to avoid is surfing—clicking forward and backward through the questions searching for the easy ones. This will eat up valuable time. Of course, you'll want to move through the tough ones quickly if you can't get them, but try to avoid skipping around.

Again, all of this will take practice. Use our practice exams to fine-tune your approach.

Scoring

You need to know two things about the scoring of the revised GRE Verbal Reasoning and Quantitative Reasoning sections: (1) how individual questions influence the score, and (2) the score scale itself.

For both the Verbal Reasoning and Quantitative Reasoning sections, you will receive a scaled score, based on both how many questions you answered correctly and the difficulties of the specific questions you actually saw.

The old GRE was question-adaptive, meaning that your answer to each question (right or wrong) determined, at least somewhat, the questions that followed (harder or easier). Because you had to commit to an answer to let the algorithm do its thing, you weren't allowed to skip questions or to go back to change answers. On the revised GRE, the adapting occurs from section to section rather than from question to question (e.g., if you do well on the first Verbal section, you will get a harder second Verbal section). The only change test-takers will notice is one that most will welcome: you can now move freely about the questions in a section, coming back to tough questions later, changing answers after "Aha!" moments, and generally managing your time more flexibly.

MANHATTAN
PREP

The scores for the revised GRE Quantitative Reasoning and Verbal Reasoning are reported on a 130–170 scale in 1-point increments, whereas the old score reporting was on a 200–800 scale in 10-point increments. You will receive one 130–170 score for Verbal and a separate 130–170 score for Quant. If you are already putting your GRE math skills to work, you may notice that there are now 41 scores possible (170 − 130, then add 1 before you're done), whereas before there were 61 scores possible ([800 − 200]/10, then add 1 before you're done). In other words, a 10-point difference on the old score scale actually indicated a smaller performance differential than a 1-point difference on the new scale. However, the GRE folks argue that perception is reality: the difference between 520 and 530 on the old scale could simply seem greater than the difference between 151 and 152 on the new scale. If that's true, then this change will benefit test-takers, who won't be unfairly compared by schools for minor differences in performance. If not true, then the change is moot.

Question Formats in Detail

Essay Questions

The Analytical Writing section consists of two separately timed 30-minute tasks: Analyze an Issue and Analyze an Argument. As you can imagine, the 30-minute time limit implies that you aren't aiming to write an essay that would garner a Pulitzer Prize nomination, but rather to complete the tasks adequately and according to the directions. Each essay is scored separately, but your reported essay score is the average of the two, rounded up to the next half-point increment on a 0–6 scale.

Issue Task: This essay prompt will present a claim, generally one that is vague enough to be interpreted in various ways and discussed from numerous perspectives. Your job as a test-taker is to write a response discussing the extent to which you agree or disagree and support your position. Don't sit on the fence—pick a side!

For some examples of Issue Task prompts, visit the GRE website here:

www.ets.org/gre/revised_general/prepare/analytical_writing/issue/pool

Argument Task: This essay prompt will be an argument comprised of both a claim (or claims) and evidence. Your job is to dispassionately discuss the argument's structural flaws and merits (well, mostly the flaws). Don't agree or disagree with the argument—simply evaluate its logic.

For some examples of Argument Task prompts, visit the GRE website here:

www.ets.org/gre/revised_general/prepare/analytical_writing/argument/pool

Verbal: Reading Comprehension Questions

Standard five-choice multiple-choice Reading Comprehension questions continue to appear on the revised exam. You are likely familiar with how these work. Let's take a look at two *new* Reading Comprehension formats that will appear on the revised test.

Select One or More Answer Choices and Select-in-Passage

For the question type "Select One or More Answer Choices," you are given three statements about a passage and asked to "indicate all that apply." Either one, two, or all three can be correct (there is no "none of the above" option). There is no partial credit; you must indicate all of the correct choices and none of the incorrect choices.

> **Strategy Tip:** On "Select One or More Answer Choices," don't let your brain be tricked into telling you, "Well, if two of them have been right so far, the other one must be wrong," or any other arbitrary idea about how many of the choices *should* be correct. Make sure to consider each choice independently! You cannot use "process of elimination" in the same way as you do on normal multiple-choice questions.

For the question type "Select-in-Passage," you are given an assignment such as "Select the sentence in the passage that explains why the experiment's results were discovered to be invalid." Clicking anywhere on the sentence in the passage will highlight it. (As with any GRE question, you will have to click "Confirm" to submit your answer, so don't worry about accidentally selecting the wrong sentence due to a slip of the mouse.)

> **Strategy Tip:** On "Select-in-Passage," if the passage is short, consider numbering each sentence (i.e., writing 1 2 3 4 on your paper) and crossing off each choice as you determine that it isn't the answer. If the passage is long, you might write a number for each paragraph (I, II, III), and tick off each number as you determine that the correct sentence is not located in that paragraph.

Now give these new question types a try:

The sample questions below are based on this passage:

> Physicist Robert Oppenheimer, director of the fateful Manhattan Project, said, "It is a profound and necessary truth that the deep things in science are not found because they are useful; they are found because it was possible to find them." In a later address at MIT, Oppenheimer presented the thesis that scientists could be held only very nominally responsible for the consequences of their research and discovery. Oppenheimer asserted that ethics, philosophy, and politics have very little to do with the day-to-day work of the scientist, and that scientists could not rationally be expected to predict all the effects of their work. Yet, in a talk in 1945 to the Association of Los Alamos Scientists, Oppenheimer offered some reasons why the Manhattan Project scientists built the atomic bomb; the justifications included "fear that Nazi Germany would build it first" and "hope that it would shorten the war."

For question #1, consider each of the three choices separately and indicate all that apply.

1.   The passage implies that Robert Oppenheimer would most likely have agreed with which of the following views:

    A   Some scientists take military goals into account in their work
    B   Deep things in science are not useful
    C   The everyday work of a scientist is only minimally involved with ethics

2.   Select the sentence in which the writer implies that Oppenheimer has not been consistent in his view that scientists have little consideration for the effects of their work.

(Here, you would highlight the appropriate sentence with your mouse. Note that there are only four options.)

<u>Solutions</u>

1. **(A)** and **(C)**: Oppenheimer says in the last sentence that one of the reasons the bomb was built was scientists' *hope that it would shorten the war*. Thus, Oppenheimer would likely agree with the view that *Some scientists take military goals into account in their work*. (B) is a trap answer using familiar language from the passage. Oppenheimer says that scientific discoveries' possible usefulness is not why scientists make discoveries; he does not say that the discoveries aren't useful. Oppenheimer specifically says that ethics has *very little to do with the day-to-day work of the scientist*, which is a good match for *only minimally involved with ethics*.

Strategy Tip: On "Select One or More Answer Choices," write A B C on your paper and mark each choice with a check, an *X*, or a symbol such as ~ if you're not sure. This should keep you from crossing out all three choices and having to go back (at least one of the choices must be correct). For example, say that on a *different* question you had marked

    A. *X*
    B. ~
    C. *X*

The answer choice you weren't sure about, (B), is likely to be correct, since there must be at least one correct answer.

---

2. The correct sentence is: **Yet, in a talk in 1945 to the Association of Los Alamos Scientists, Oppenheimer offered some reasons why the Manhattan Project scientists built the atomic bomb; the justifications included "fear that Nazi Germany would build it first" and "hope that it would shorten the war."** The word "yet" is a good clue that this sentence is about to express a view contrary to the views expressed in the rest of the passage.

Verbal: Text Completion Questions

Text Completions can consist of 1–5 sentences with 1–3 blanks. When Text Completions have two or three blanks, you will select words or short phrases for those blanks independently. There is no partial credit; you must make every selection correctly.

> Leaders are not always expected to (i) _____ the same rules as are those they lead; leaders are often looked up to for a surety and presumption that would be viewed as (ii) _____ in most others.

Blank (i)	Blank (ii)
decree	hubris
proscribe	avarice
conform to	anachronism

Select your two choices by actually clicking and highlighting the words you want.

<u>Solution</u>

In the first blank, you need a word similar to "follow." In the second blank, you need a word similar to "arrogance." The correct answers are *conform to* and *hubris*.

Strategy Tip: Do NOT look at the answer choices until you've decided for yourself, based on textual clues actually written in the sentence, what kind of word needs to go in each blank. Only then should you look at the choices and eliminate those that are not matches.

Now try an example with three blanks:

> For Kant, the fact of having a right and having the (i) _____ to enforce it via coercion cannot be separated, and he asserts that this marriage of rights and coercion is compatible with the freedom of everyone. This is not at all peculiar from the standpoint of modern political thought—what good is a right if its violation triggers no enforcement (be it punishment or (ii) _____)? The necessity of coercion is not at all in conflict with the freedom of everyone, because this coercion only comes into play when someone has (iii) _____ someone else.

Blank (i)	Blank (ii)	Blank (iii)
technique	amortization	questioned the hypothesis of
license	reward	violated the rights of
prohibition	restitution	granted civil liberties to

MANHATTAN
PREP

Solution

In the first sentence, use the clue "he asserts that this marriage of rights and coercion is compatible with the freedom of everyone" to help fill in the first blank. Kant believes that "coercion" is "married to" rights and is compatible with freedom for all. So you want something in the first blank like "right" or "power." Kant believes that rights are meaningless without enforcement. Only the choice *license* can work (while a *license* can be physical, like a driver's license, *license* can also mean "right").

The second blank is part of the phrase "punishment or _____," which you are told is the "enforcement" resulting from the violation of a right. So the blank should be something, other than punishment, that constitutes enforcement against someone who violates a right. (More simply, it should be something bad.) Only *restitution* works. Restitution is compensating the victim in some way (perhaps monetarily or by returning stolen goods).

In the final sentence, "coercion only comes into play when someone has _____ someone else." Throughout the text, "coercion" means enforcement against someone who has violated the rights of someone else. The meaning is the same here. The answer is *violated the rights of*.

The complete and correct answer is this combination:

Blank (i)	Blank (ii)	Blank (iii)
license	restitution	violated the rights of

In theory, there are $3 \times 3 \times 3$, or 27 possible ways to answer a three-blank Text Completion—and only one of those 27 ways is correct. In theory, these are bad odds. In practice, you will often have certainty about some of the blanks, so your guessing odds are almost never this bad. Just follow the basic process: come up with your own filler for each blank, and match to the answer choices. If you're confused by this example, don't worry! The Manhattan Prep *Text Completion & Sentence Equivalence GRE Strategy Guide* covers all of this in detail.

Strategy Tip: Do not write your own story. The GRE cannot give you a blank without also giving you a clue, physically written down in the passage, telling you what kind of word or phrase must go in that blank. Find that clue. You should be able to give textual evidence for each answer choice you select.

Verbal: Sentence Equivalence Questions

For this question type, you are given one sentence with a single blank. There are six answer choices, and you are asked to pick two choices that fit the blank and are alike in meaning.

Of the Verbal question types, this one depends the most on vocabulary and also yields the most to strategy.

No partial credit is given on Sentence Equivalence; both correct answers must be selected and no incorrect answers may be selected. When you pick 2 of 6 choices, there are 15 possible combinations of choices, and only one is correct. However, this is not nearly as daunting as it sounds.

Think of it this way: if you have six choices, but the two correct ones must be similar in meaning, then you have, at most, three possible *pairs* of choices, maybe fewer, since not all choices are guaranteed to have a partner. If you can match up the pairs, you can seriously narrow down your options.

Here is a sample set of answer choices:

> A tractable
>
> B taciturn
>
> C arbitrary
>
> D tantamount
>
> E reticent
>
> F amenable

The question is deliberately omitted here in order to illustrate how much you can do with the choices alone, if you have studied vocabulary sufficiently.

Tractable and *amenable* are synonyms (tractable, amenable people will do whatever you want them to do). *Taciturn* and *reticent* are synonyms (both mean "not talkative").

Arbitrary (based on one's own will) and *tantamount* (equivalent) are not similar in meaning and therefore cannot be a pair. Therefore, the *only* possible correct answer pairs are (A) and (F), and (B) and (E). You have improved your chances from 1 in 15 to a 50/50 shot without even reading the question!

Of course, in approaching a Sentence Equivalence, you do want to analyze the sentence in the same way you would a Text Completion—read for a textual clue that tells you what type of word *must* go in the blank. Then look for a matching pair.

Strategy Tip: If you're sure that a word in the choices does *not* have a partner, cross it out! For instance, if (A) and (F) are partners and (B) and (E) are partners, and you're sure neither (C) nor (D) pair with any other answer, cross out (C) and (D) completely. They cannot be the answer together, nor can either one be part of the answer.

The sentence for the answer choice above could read as follows:

> Though the dinner guests were quite _____ , the hostess did her best to keep the conversation active and engaging.

Thus, **(B)** and **(E)** are the best choices.

MANHATTAN
PREP

Try another example:

> While athletes usually expect to achieve their greatest feats in their teens or twenties, opera singers don't reach the _____ of their vocal powers until middle age.
>
> $\boxed{A}$ harmony
> $\boxed{B}$ zenith
> $\boxed{C}$ acme
> $\boxed{D}$ terminus
> $\boxed{E}$ nadir
> $\boxed{F}$ cessation

Solution

Those with strong vocabularies might go straight to the choices to make pairs. *Zenith* and *acme* are synonyms, meaning "high point, peak." *Terminus* and *cessation* are synonyms meaning "end." *Nadir* is a low point and *harmony* is present here as a trap answer reminding you of opera singers. Cross off (A) and (E), since they do not have partners. Then, go back to the sentence, knowing that your only options are a pair meaning "peak" and a pair meaning "end."

The correct answer choices are **(B)** and **(C)**.

Math: Quantitative Comparison

In addition to regular multiple-choice questions and Data Interpretation questions, Quantitative Comparisons have been on the exam for a long time.

Each question contains a "Quantity A" and a "Quantity B," and some also contain common information that applies to both quantities. The four answer choices are always worded exactly as shown in the following example:

$$x \geq 0$$

Quantity A	**Quantity B**
x	x^2

(A) Quantity A is greater.
(B) Quantity B is greater.
(C) The two quantities are equal.
(D) The relationship cannot be determined from the information given.

Solution

If $x = 0$, then the two quantities are equal. If $x = 2$, then Quantity (B) is greater. Thus, you don't have enough information.

The answer is **(D)**.

Next, take a look at the new math question formats.

Math: Select One or More Answer Choices

According to the *Official Guide to the GRE revised General Test*, the official directions for "Select One or More Answer Choices" read as follows:

> Directions: Select one or more answer choices according to the specific question directions.
>
> If the question does not specify how many answer choices to indicate, indicate all that apply.
>
> The correct answer may be just one of the choices or as many as all of the choices, depending on the question.
>
> No credit is given unless you indicate all of the correct choices and no others.
>
> If the question specifies how many answer choices to indicate, indicate exactly that number of choices.

Note that there is no partial credit. If three of six choices are correct, and you indicate two of the three, no credit is given. If you are told to indicate two choices and you indicate three, no credit is given. It will also be important to read the directions carefully.

Here's a sample question:

If $ab = |a| \times |b|$ and $ab \neq 0$, which of the following must be true?

Indicate <u>all</u> such statements.

- [A] $a = b$
- [B] $a > 0$ and $b > 0$
- [C] $ab > 0$

Note that only one, only two, or all three of the choices may be correct. (Also note the word "must" in the question stem!)

Solution

If $ab = |a| \times |b|$, then you know ab is positive, since the right side of the equation must be positive. If ab is positive, however, that doesn't necessarily mean that a and b are each positive; it simply means that they have the same sign.

Answer choice (A) is not correct because it is not true that a must equal b; for instance, a could be 2 and b could be 3.

Answer choice (B) is not correct because it is not true that a and b must each be positive; for instance, a could be −3 and b could be −4.

Now look at choice (C). Since $|a| \times |b|$ must be positive, ab must be positive as well; that is, since two sides of an equation are, by definition, equal to one another, if one side of the equation is positive, the other side must be positive as well. Thus, answer **(C)** is correct.

Strategy Tip: Make sure to fully process the statement in the question (simplify it or list the possible scenarios) before considering the answer choices. That is, don't just look at $ab = |a| \times |b|$—rather, it's your job to draw inferences about the statement before plowing ahead. This will save you time in the long run!

Note that "indicate all that apply" didn't really make the problem harder. This is just a typical Inference-based Quant problem (for more problems like this one, see the Manhattan Prep *Number Properties* guide as well as the *Quantitative Comparisons & Data Interpretation* guide).

After all, not every real-life problem has exactly five possible solutions; why should problems on the GRE?

Math: Numeric Entry

This question type requires the test-taker to key a numeric answer into a box on the screen. You are not able to work backwards from answer choices, and in many cases, it will be difficult to make a guess. However, the principles being tested are the same as on the rest of the exam.

Here is a sample question:

If $x \triangle y = 2xy - (x - y)$, what is the value of $3\triangle4$?

Solution

You are given a function involving two variables, x and y, and asked to substitute 3 for x and 4 for y:

$$x \Delta y = 2xy - (x - y)$$
$$3 \Delta 4 = 2(3)(4) - (3 - 4)$$
$$3 \Delta 4 = 24 - (-1)$$
$$3 \Delta 4 = 25$$

The answer is **25**.

Thus, you would type 25 into the box.

Okay. You've now got a good start on understanding the structure and question formats of the new GRE. Now it's time to begin fine-tuning your skills.

MANHATTAN
PREP

Chapter 2

of

Text Completion & Sentence Equivalence

Text Completion

In This Chapter . . .

Chapter 2
Text Completion

Text Completion questions on the GRE are sentences or paragraphs with one, two, or three blanks for which you must select the appropriate word or words.

Here's an example of the simplest variety of Text Completion, one with a single blank:

> Despite his intense _____, he failed to secure the prestigious university's coveted diploma.

imbibition
lugubriousness
lucubration
magnanimity
character

All single-blank Text Completions have exactly five answer choices, of which exactly one is correct. The answer choices for a given blank will always be the same part of speech.

These questions are very much like some of the questions you probably saw on the SAT.

Your task is to find the choice that **best fits the meaning** of the sentence as a whole.

The best approach will be to **anticipate an answer** before looking at the choices. Many people don't do this. Rather, they just plug in the choices one-by-one, rereading the sentence and stopping when it "sounds good."

Here's how you can tell that many people don't anticipate answers: based on empirical data about the GRE, you know that problems of this type with right answer (A) are, on average, significantly easier than problems with right answer (E). 27% of test-takers got "(A)-problems" wrong, whereas 46% of test-takers got "(E)-problems" wrong—almost twice as many!

Do you think the GRE deliberately creates (E)-problems that are so much harder than (A)-problems? That's very unlikely. What's probably happening is that people are lazy. If you don't predict the answer and just plug in the choices instead—and the correct answer is (A)—then you get lucky. The sentence probably makes sense, and you pick (A). On the other hand, if the right answer is (E), then your lack of good process punishes you. You waste a lot of time plugging in all five choices, then get confused and end up picking the wrong one.

By the way, the GRE doesn't actually label the choices (A), (B), (C), (D), and (E) anymore (as in the example problem above—the choices appear in boxes). To answer a question, you simply click on your choice, and the entire box is highlighted. You get a chance to confirm before submitting that answer. (Also, you're allowed to go back and change answers anytime before the clock runs out.)

Although the real problems don't label the answers with letters, this book still uses that nomenclature, because it is easy to understand what is meant by "answer choice (D)," and because saying "the choice second from the bottom" sounds pretty silly. Try to write "A B C D E" on your paper for each question so that you have somewhere to keep track of which answers you think are wrong, which you think might be right, and which feature words you don't know. (We will revisit the above example shortly.)

Three-Step Process for Text Completions

Take a look at the following example:

> If the student had been less _____, he would not have been expelled from his grade school.

indefatigable
perseverant
refractory
playful
indigent

1. Read only the sentence.

The answer choices will distract you if you read them before you've made sense of the sentence.

2. Find the *target*, *clue*, and the *pivot*, and write down your own fill-in.

The clue and the pivot are the two most important parts of the sentence. **The target is the thing in the sentence that the blank is describing.** Stating the target explicitly can help to locate the clue. Here, the target is simply *the student*.

Note: If the blank represents a missing noun, the idea of a "target" may not apply. That's okay. Targets are very helpful when the blank represents a missing adjective, and can also be useful when the blank represents a missing verb.

The clue is what forces the contents of the blank to be perfectly predictable. In other words, the clue solves the mystery of the blank. Look for dramatic action or emotion. The clue should tell you more about the target (*the student*).

In this case, the clue is *expelled*.

The pivot is what determines the relationship between the blank and the clue. Will the blank agree with the clue? Or will the blank actually disagree with the clue? It depends on the pivot.

The sentence reads "less _____ ... not expelled." So the pivot is *less...not*.

Think about what this means. If the student were *less* <u>such-and-such</u>, then he would *not* have been expelled.

So <u>such-and-such</u> got him expelled. In other words, the blank agrees with *expelled*. *Less* and *not* cancel each other out as negatives.

Finally, **the fill-in is what you predict the answer to be**. At this point, how would you use this blank to describe this student? Write down this adjective or phrase, as well as your (A) through (E).

> badly behaved
>
> A
> B
> C
> D
> E

3. Compare to each answer choice.

Here are the choices again. One at a time, simplify the choices, then see how well your fill-in matches up. Mark down one of the following next to your "A B C D E": Good (✓), Bad (✗), Sort Of (~), or Unknown (?).

> indefatigable = tireless
>
> perseverant = determined
>
> refractory = ??
>
> playful
>
> indigent = poor

So now your paper might look like this:

badly behaved

A ×
B ×
C ?
D ~
E ~

The correct answer is in fact **(C)**, since *refractory* means "rebellious." But even if you didn't know what *refractory* means, you would have a good shot at getting this problem right through process of elimination. Also, notice that you can write a plausible story around some of the wrong answer choices. For example, "If the student had been less *playful*, he wouldn't have been expelled." This could make sense if the student was playing games during a serious lesson. Or maybe, "If the student had been less *indigent*, he wouldn't have been expelled." What an indictment of the school's administration!

You should avoid writing stories when doing Text Completions. What you want for your fill-in is **complete predictability and redundancy**. There should be no surprises in the blank. Remember, there is only one right answer. **No interesting stories!**

Try it again with the example from earlier in the chapter:

Despite his intense _____ , he failed to secure the prestigious university's coveted diploma.

imbibition
lugubriousness
lucubration
magnanimity
character

First, read **only** the sentence. Find the clue (failed to secure the prestigious university's coveted diploma) and the pivot (despite). Write your own fill-in—here, *studying* would be a good choice. Now compare *studying* with every answer choice:

studying

A ×
B ×
C ✓
D ×
E ~

The answer is **(C)**. *Lucubration* means "intense study."

Of course, you may have some question marks due to a lack of vocabulary knowledge, in which case you should make your best guess *without delay*—you have limited time to complete the section, and staring at the words for longer will not suddenly make up for a lack of vocabulary. **Your mastery of a large number of GRE-appropriate words is the biggest single factor that will determine your success on the problem.**

Don't worry—there's a *prodigious* section on learning vocabulary coming up later in this book!

2

How to Write Good Fill-ins

As you try to write good fill-ins, keep in mind the following simple equation:

Fill-in = Clue + Pivot

The fill-in is nothing more interesting than a simple sum, so to speak, of the clue and the pivot. The clue and the pivot tell you something *about* the target.

Take a look at an example:

> In the past decade, the coffee chain has dramatically expanded all across the country, leading one commentator to describe the franchise as _____.

First, find the target. Since the blank comes right after "describe the franchise as," it's pretty clear that the target is *the franchise.*

Next, find the clue. There could be more than one. The clue will tell you something about *the franchise.* The clue is often the most descriptive part of the sentence (e.g., *expelled*). Typically, clues will be the most descriptive or opinionated elements of the sentence.

In the sentence above, *dramatically expanded* is the clue.

Then, find the pivot. Again, the pivot determines the relationship between the clue and the fill-in. The two most common possibilities are these:

1. The fill-in **agrees with** the clue.
2. The fill-in **opposes** the clue. The pivot will express negation or opposition.

The pivot could also indicate a causal relation or some other type, but even then, you can often get away with simply determining whether the fill-in and the clue agree or disagree.

In the sentence above, the words *leading* and *describe* tell you that the fill-in and the clue are in agreement.

So you need a blank that expresses agreement with *dramatically expanded.*

2

Finally, construct the fill-in out of the clue and the pivot. Recycle words if possible. This instinct will keep you from straying too far from the given meaning of the sentence. Feel free to use a phrase.

Your fill-in might be this: having dramatically expanded

Be ready to **change the part of speech**, if necessary.

Or you might have gone just a little further: everywhere

Notice how uninteresting this fill-in makes the sentence. Don't overthink. In real life, you could easily imagine the fill-in taking you substantially further than *having dramatically expanded*. For instance, the commentator may add a negative spin (*overreached*), but the GRE will make the fill-in much more boring in meaning. **Assume as little as possible.**

A likely answer would be something like *ubiquitous*, a GRE favorite.

Pivot Words

Fill in your own word in this sentence:

> Despite his reputation for _____, the politician decided that in a time of crisis it was important to speak honestly and forthrightly.

Did you say something like "not being direct"? The target is *the politician*. The pivot word *despite* indicates an *opposite direction. Honestly and forthrightly* was the clue describing the politician. Since the pivot was negative, the correct answer will need to pivot **away** from *honestly and forthrightly*.

> For all her studying, her performance on the test was _____.

This one relies on an idiom. Did you say something like "mediocre" or "bad"? The expression *for all X, Y* is in play here. *For all* here means "despite." Thus, despite her studying, her performance was *not good*.

> Although he has a reputation for volubility, others at the party didn't find him to be especially _____.

Did you say something like "talkative"? Or did you go for "not talkative"? Notice you have a clue (*volubility*, which means "talkativeness") and a pivot word, *although*. But you also have another pivot—the *not* in *didn't*. Pivoting twice (much like turning 180 degrees twice) is like not pivoting at all. In your blank, you just want another word for *talkative*.

Here are some common pivot words, phrases, and structures:

SAME DIRECTION	OPPOSITE DIRECTION	CAUSAL RELATIONSHIP
; (semicolon)	Although	As a result
: (colon)	Belied	Because
Also	But	Consequently
And	Despite	Hence
Besides	In spite of	So
Furthermore	Nevertheless	Therefore
In addition	On the contrary	Thus
In fact	On the other hand	
Just as … as	Rather than	
Moreover	Still	
Not only … but also	Though	
So … as to be	Whether X or Y	
X, Y, and Z (items in a list)	Yet	

2

Drill: Sentence Analysis

Analyze each sentence for Target, Clue, and Pivot, then fill in the blank in your own words.

2

1. The camp established by the aid workers provided a _____ for the refugees, many of whom had traveled for weeks to get there.

2. While others had given only accolades, the iconoclastic critic greeted the book's publication with a lengthy _____.

3. Though many have impugned her conclusions, the studies on which she based her analysis are beyond _____.

4. The ancient poem's value was more _____ than literary; the highly literal work made no attempt at lyricism, and ended by warning the reader never to lie.

5. French food could be said to be the most _____ of all cuisines, considering the high saturated fat content of the otherwise delectable *bechamels* and *remoulades.*

6. It is unfair and incorrect to _____ about an entire minority group based on the actions of a few people, whether those people are reprobates or model citizens.

7. For all the clamor about bipartisanship, in the end, voting _____ to factional loyalties.

8. While digital media should theoretically last forever, in actuality, there are warehouses full of abandoned computer tape drives and other media that have since been _____ by newer technologies.

9. Chad was the most mercurial of young people, but as an adult was able to _____ his wild fluctuations in personality.

10. The _____ position he adopted on the issue belied his reputation for equivocation.

MANHATTAN
PREP

Answers: Sentence Analysis

1.   This sentence is pretty straightforward—you have the clues that *aid workers* are providing something for *refugees,* who have traveled for a long time to get there. A good fill-in would be *haven* or *sanctuary.*

2.   This sentence has an opposite-direction pivot: *While.* You also have the clue that the critic is *iconoclastic.* Since most critics gave the book *accolades*—and an *iconoclastic* critic would do the opposite—a good fill-in would be something like *condemnation.*

3.   The target is the *studies.* This sentence also has an opposite-direction pivot: *Though.* It seems that this person's conclusions aren't so great. The studies she used, though, *are* pretty great. You want to say something good about the studies, but you have *another* opposite-direction pivot, *beyond.* You want to say that the studies are so good that they are *beyond* something bad. This sentence would almost certainly be completed with the expression *beyond reproach.*

4.   The target is the *poem.* You know that it is *more _____ than literary*—so it's not very literary. You then find out that it's *highly literal* and not even trying to be lyrical—sounds like a really bad poem! It ended by *warning the reader never to lie.* Whoa—that sounds like a *terrible* poem! Maybe the kind that would appear in a children's book. A good fill-in would be *moralistic* or *didactic.*

5.   The target is *French food.* You might be tempted to put *delicious* in the blank, but that would be incorrectly inserting an opinion. The clue clearly says that the French food is full of fat. A good fill-in would be *unhealthy.*

6.   The target is the *entire minority group.* What should you *not _____* about them? The clue is "based on the actions of a few people." A good fill-in might be *make stereotypes* or *generalize.*

7.   The target is *voting.* This sentence depends on an idiom. *For all* here means "despite." The clue is *clamor about bipartisanship* and the pivot is *for all* (meaning *despite*). Thus, the second part of the sentence should indicate that the voting was the opposite of *bipartisan*—that is, *partisan.* Since *factional loyalties* describe a partisan environment, a good fill-in would be *conformed* or *adhered.*

8.   The target is *abandoned computer tape drives and other media.* You have the clue *digital media should theoretically last forever* and the pivot *while.* Thus, the meaning is that digital media does **not** last forever. This tracks with the idea of the computer tape drives being *abandoned.* A good fill-in would be *replaced.* GRE-type words that might appear here would be *supplanted* or *superseded.*

9.   The target is *Chad,* or whatever Chad was able to do to his personality fluctuations. You have a clue about Chad—he was *mercurial,* which matches the idea of *wild fluctuations in personality.* You have a pivot, *but,* indicating that you need to go in the opposite direction. Thus, Chad was able to *hold back* or *moderate* his wild fluctuations. GRE-type words that might appear here would be *temper* or *damp.*

10. The target is the *position.* You know that the person in question has a *reputation for equivocation.* Your pivot is *belied.* Thus, a good fill-in would relate to the opposite of equivocation—something like *firm* or *resolute.*

Double-Blank and Triple-Blank Text Completions

Most Text Completion questions have more than one blank. Consider the following example:

> Twentieth-century America witnessed a nearly (i) _____ ascent to ever greater wealth, leaving its leaders (ii) _____ of publicly acknowledging budgetary limitations.

Blank (i)	Blank (ii)
portentous	chary
pertinacious	opprobrious
unremitting	implicate

In the sentence, the blanks are labeled with lowercase Roman numerals.

Below the sentence, the first column contains the choices—*portentous, pertinacious,* and *unremitting*—for the first blank. The second column contains the choices—*chary, opprobrious,* and *implicate*—for the second blank.

If you took the SAT, or remember the "old" GRE, you'll notice something very different here—*your choice for the first blank is independent of your choice for the second blank.* That is, if you choose *unremitting* for the first blank, that does **not** mean that you have therefore chosen *implicate* for the second blank—you must instead make a separate decision for the second blank.

This means that you cannot "cheat" off one column to make your decision for the other. More importantly: *there is no partial credit.* You must get *both* words right or you receive no credit for your response. Thus, your chance of randomly guessing the correct answer is quite low (1 in 9).

It is very difficult to get these questions right based on incomplete information—you must understand the sentences and you must know all or most of the words. This is why such a large portion of this book is dedicated to vocabulary acquisition.

Fortunately, the fact that you must choose each word independently is somewhat compensated for by the fact that, for each blank, there are only three options, not five (as in single-blank Text Completions),

One more pleasant feature of double-blank and triple-blank problems is that, while they may *seem* harder because they are generally longer, there are also more clues for you to find. Also, having multiple blanks means you get to choose which blank to tackle first…and some blanks are easier to solve than others!

Start with the Easier (or Easiest) Blank

Don't just try to fill in the first blank automatically. Look at all of the blanks and figure out which one has the easiest clue. Then create a fill-in and use that fill-in as an extra clue for the harder blank(s).

MANHATTAN
PREP

Take a look at this example:

> Even seasoned opera singers, who otherwise affect an unflappable air, can be
> (i) _____ performing in Rome, where audiences traditionally view (ii) _____
> performers as a birthright, passed down from heckler to heckler over generations.

Blank #2 is easier. Why? Compare the clues and pivots:

	Clues	**Pivots**	
Blank #1:	*seasoned* *unflappable*	*even…otherwise…*	The pivots express opposition. What is the opposite of *unflappable*?
Blank #2:	*heckler*	none	No pivot = agreement

Your fill-in for #2 should probably be *heckling*. Remember to reuse the given language in the fill-in when you can.

Now you can use that fill-in as another clue. There is no pivot between the two blanks, meaning that the two fill-ins agree in some way. The relationship seems to be causal: the opera performers are going to react to that heckling. A likely fill-in would be *upset by* or *afraid of*.

Your paper might now look like this: afraid of…heckling

Also on your paper, draw a grid so that you can do process of elimination:

Or, if you prefer, write:

A   A
B   B
C   C

Now compare to the answer choices and mark your paper:

Blank (i)	Blank (ii)
intrepid about	extolling
daunted by	lionizing
tempered by	badgering

Here is an example of what a student might have written down for this question. This student wasn't sure about *tempered by,* and didn't know exactly about *lionizing* but felt that it wasn't quite right.

afraid of…heckling

×	×
✓	~
?	✓

Nevertheless, this student picked *daunted by* and *badgering,* which are the correct responses.

Remember, the only way to get credit for the question is to pick BOTH *daunted by* and *badgering.*

Now here's an example with three blanks:

Perceptions of the (i) _____ role of intellectual practices within modern life un-derlie the familiar stereotypes of the educated as eggheads, ideologues, or worse. These negative characterizations may be rooted in a (ii) _____ of the aims of academia, but they are unlikely to be (iii) _____ unless teachers take efforts to address them directly.

Blank (i)	Blank (ii)	Blank (iii)
incongruous	dissemination	espoused
refractory	confounding	dispelled
salubrious	corroboration	promulgated

While this sentence has three blanks instead of two, and is made up of more than one sentence, your method is the same—start with the easiest blank. The easiest blank is often the one surrounded by the most text—that is, the one that is furthest from the other two blanks and thus has the most potential clues located near it. Here, the first blank seems promising:

Perceptions of the (i) _____ role of intellectual practices within modern life un-derlie the familiar stereotypes of the educated as eggheads, ideologues, or worse.

The target is the *role,* and the role *underlies stereotypes* about eggheads "or worse." So the word describing the role should be related to the idea of intellectual = egghead (a mild slang term roughly equivalent to "nerd"). Don't ignore the phrase *within modern life.* A good fill-in would be *irrelevant.* The sentence seems to be saying that people think intellectuals are eggheads because intellectual practices are not a helpful or important part of modern life.

The second sentence mirrors that idea (*These negative characterizations ...*). It seems clear that the speaker is trying to defend academia. A good fill-in for the second blank would be *misunderstanding* or *twisting* (you can't really be sure if the people who think intellectuals are "eggheads" are getting it wrong deliberately or not).

Finally, you have a negative pivot: *unlikely* (and another one, *unless*). Work backwards on this sentence:

> If teachers DON'T address negative stereotypes directly…
>
> the stereotypes will continue
>
> so, the stereotypes are *unlikely to be* **eliminated** *or* **corrected**

On your paper, you might have:

irrelevant   misunderstanding   eliminated

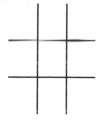

Or, if you prefer:

irrelevant	misunderstanding	eliminated
A	A	A
B	B	B
C	C	C

Consider your choices and mark your paper appropriately:

Blank (i)	Blank (ii)	Blank (iii)
incongruous	dissemination	espoused
refractory	confounding	dispelled
salubrious	corroboration	promulgated

Your notes for this question might look like this:

✓	✗	~
?	✓	✓
✗	✗	✗

The correct answer is **incongruous**, **confounding**, and **dispelled**.

Finally, double-blank and triple-blank questions can sometimes have choices that are phrases rather than single words. These questions tend to be less about knowing difficult vocabulary words than about being able to work out the meaning of the sentence(s).

Try this question:

> (i) _____ subject of the sermon, his words possessed a (ii) _____ quality few could fail to find utterly enchanting. It was only when his conclusion devolved into a (iii) _____ that the congregation began to fantasize about returning to the comfort of home.

Blank (i)	Blank (ii)	Blank (iii)
In spite of the insipid	euphonious	thoroughly fallacious slew of prevarications
Notwithstanding the salubrious	euphemistic	seemingly unending string of divagations
Because of the inauspicious	eulogistic	dubiously sanctified series of assignations

Attack the easiest blank first. That might be the last one, since you have the clues that the sermon's conclusion *devolved* into whatever goes in the blank, and that *the congregation began to fantasize about returning to the comfort of home*. Both clues tell you that you want a fill-in that means something like *bunch of stupid or boring stuff*.

Now that you have mentally completed the last sentence, it might help to paraphrase it before using the information to work backwards and analyze the rest of the sentence. Paraphrase: *It was only when the conclusion became stupid or boring that the people got bored*. The phrase *It was only when* serves as a pivot: before things got stupid or boring, they must have been pretty good, as you can verify from the clue *utterly enchanting*.

The second blank is pretty easy:… *his words possessed a _____ quality few could fail to find utterly enchanting*. That means that nearly everyone finds his words enchanting. In fact, you could recycle that word and put it in the blank—a good fill-in here would be *enchanting*.

Finally, the first blank. It's pretty hard to fill in this one without glancing at the answer choices, but at least try to figure out a general category of what you'll be looking for. There is a blank about the *subject*

2

of the sermon, and then something nice about the words used in the sermon. Either these two things will go in the same direction or in an opposite direction.

You might have something like this on our paper:

something comparing *subject* w/ *words*   enchanting   stupid/boring stuff

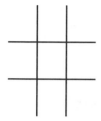

Now try the choices (in any order you prefer).

In the first blank, *In spite of the insipid* makes sense—the meaning is *In spite of the bad quality of the topic, the words of the sermon were enchanting*. In the second option, *notwithstanding* is similar to *in spite of*, so you would expect something bad to come after, but *salubrious* means *healthy*. Since the third choice begins with *because*, you would expect something positive to come after it (*Because of some good quality of the sermon, the words were enchanting*). But *inauspicious* means *likely to be unsuccessful*. Only *In spite of the insipid* works.

In the second blank, only *euphonious* works. The root *eu* means *good*, but that's not too helpful here, since all three words use that root. However, *euphemistic* (substituting inoffensive words in for more explicit or hurtful ones) doesn't make sense, and *eulogistic* (full of praise, especially for a deceased person) also doesn't match the idea of *enchanting*.

Finally, the only phrase that means anything like *stupid/boring stuff* is *seemingly unending string of divagations* (*divagations* are tangents, or instances of going off-topic). *Prevarications* are falsehoods, and *assignations* are romantic meetups.

The answer is **In spite of the insipid**, **euphonious**, and **seemingly unending string of divagations**.

Tricky Aspects of Text Completion Sentences

Take a look at this example:

> Although Paula claimed not to be _____ that she was not selected for the scholarship, we nevertheless worried that our typically sanguine friend was not entirely _____ by the decision.

This sentence is just chock-full of switchbacks. Count the oppositional pivots: *Although... not... nevertheless... typically... not entirely....*

It's easy to lose your way in a thicket of **double-negative pivots**, especially under exam pressure. How many wrongs make a right?

When you face a situation such as this…

Break It Down

2

Chop up the sentence and process it in small chunks. Start with the earliest or the most concrete part of the story. Then add one chunk at a time. Change complicated pivots to simple words, such as *but* and *so*.

As you go, emotionally punctuate each part of the story. Exaggerate the switchbacks in your mental voice, as if you were telling a story you really cared about. Finally, as you think about the whole, discard unnecessary elements, so that you don't have to hold everything in your head at once.

For the sentence above, the breakdown might go like this:

Our friend Paula is *typically* sanguine = optimistic ☺

She was not selected for a scholarship ☹

She claimed NOT to be _____

BUT

We still worried ☹

that she was NOT entirely _____ by the decision.

The fill-ins should be pretty easy to generate now: *upset/saddened* ☹ for the first blank, and *unaffected* for the second.

It looks like a lot of work, but your brain can generate this train of thought in seconds. Give it a try.

Other tricky aspects of the sentence yield to the same basic medicine: **Break it down**.

Now break down a few more challenging sentence types.

Unfamiliar Style or Content

That such a _____ of precedent would be countenanced was itself unprecedented in the court, a bastion of traditionalism.

The sentence starts with a *that* clause, a hallmark of a very academic writing style. Moreover, the content is about a legal matter. These two factors combine with difficult vocabulary (*precedent, countenanced, bastion*) to make the sentence forbidding.

MANHATTAN
PREP

The meaning of the sentence is something like, "That such a _____ of previously established examples would be tolerated was a surprising instance of a very traditional court going against tradition."

A good fill-in here would be something like *rejection*.

Red Herring Clues

A "red herring" is something that seems to be a clue, but is actually only there to confuse you. Such traps occasionally appear on Text Ccompletion questions, so be careful that all the clues you're using are *actually* clues.

> By rigorously observing social behavior, anthropologists _____ strict, though implicit, codes of conduct.

A few "clues" might not really be clues. ("Red herring" is an expression for something that seems like it's going to be important, but turns out to be just a distraction. The expression arose when criminals started rubbing herring—a type of fish—on trails to distract the hunting dogs chasing after them.)

Here, the word *strict* turns out to be less important to the answer than *implicit*. Decoy answers might be *undermine* or *challenge* (somehow dealing with the *strict* element, but introducing too much new information in the fill-in). The real meaning of the sentence is based on the idea that, because the behavior is implicit (hinted at or unspoken), anthropologists have to be rigorous in their observations in order to detect or decode it. A good fill-in would be something like *reveal* or *make explicit*.

Blanks in Tough Spots

> If these managers (I) _____ the purported advantages of the new deep-sea recovery methodology to be (ii) _____ ,then it will rapidly be judged less useful than current alternatives by the broader business community.

Some blanks are positioned in such a way that it's hard to hold the sentence in your head. The gaps occur early or in strategic places. For instance, in the sentence above, the verb of the first clause is missing.

A completed version of this sentence would read something like, "If these managers <u>find</u> the purported advantages... to be <u>lacking</u>, then..."

The main thing to remember is that, no matter how complex or awkward the sentence, you have to make sense of it. The best way to do that is to **break it down into pieces**. Start at the easiest-to-understand chunk and work outwards from there.

Drill: Sentence Analysis with Multiple Blanks

Analyze each sentence for Target, Clue, and Pivot, then fill in the blanks in your own words. Here, you're just practicing the first two steps of the strategy. You'll practice complete problems soon.

2

1. The radio host claimed to have preternatural powers that allowed her to (i) _____ future events, from cataclysms and illnesses to global booms and personal (ii) _____.

2. After Alexander Graham Bell invented the telephone, he was greeted not with (i) _____ but with a barrage of ridicule. The *London Times* called the invention the latest American "humbug," disbelieving electricians declared the machine a (ii) _____, and prominent capitalists—always with an eye out to make a profit—all (iii) _____ to buy Graham's patent.

3. Louis Armstrong rose to (i) _____ in the 1920s as an innovative cornet and trumpet player. A(n) (ii) _____ influence in jazz, he is largely credited for shifting focus from a style based on group improvisation to one based on solo performance—such as his own distinctive, even (iii) _____, solos.

4. For years, the idea that blind people can hear better than sighted people was considered something of an old (i) _____. However, functional brain imaging has recently uncovered the fact that a brain region called V1, which (ii) _____ at the back of the skull and which normally responds only to light, has been rewired in the brains of blind people and now processes auditory information in what could be termed a stunning example of the brain's (iii) _____.

5. Throughout the history of human thought, virtually every thinker has (i) _____ of the mind as a unitary entity. (ii) _____, in the 1960s, Roger Sperry conducted his famous studies working with epileptics who had been treated via the cutting of the *corpus callosum,* or division between the two hemispheres. During the studies, Perry was able to observe that each half of the brain could gain new information independently, and that one hemisphere could be entirely unaware of what the other had learned or experienced. Truly, our brains are not unitary, but (iii) _____.

6. The company president was not just (i) _____ but positively (ii) _____; his subordinates lived in perpetual fear of his reproof.

7. Marissa's date was neither (i) _____ nor (ii) _____; he was surly to the waiter and expatiated at great length about mechanical engineering, a topic Marissa finds quite tedious.

8. While many people think of migraines simply as bad headaches, migranes are actually neurological events that can include numbness, slurred speech, and ringing in the ears, with or without headache. Even doctors are (i) _____ to this mischaracterization, thus leading to frequent (ii) _____; these mistakes can lead to instances where both patients with migraines and patients whose disorders are confused with migraines end up getting treatment that may be ineffective or even (iii)_____.

9. We ought not (i) _____ our leaders; it is our (ii) _____ and foibles that make us human, and only by humanizing the greatest among us can we fully understand those whose achievements we admire.

10. In her later years, the artist (i) _____ the wild, chaotic imagery of her early work and instead embraced a prim, highly (ii) _____ formalism.

Answers: Sentence Analysis with Multiple Blanks

1. The clue for the first blank is *preternatural powers*. A good fill-in is *predict*. The clue for the second blank is *from cataclysms and illnesses to global booms*. A *from… to…* structure will have to set up opposites. Furthermore, you can expect that the comparison will fit a predictable pattern (otherwise, how could the GRE expect you to know what to put in the blanks?). A *cataclysm* is a big, bad thing, and *illnesses* is a smaller, bad thing. *Global booms* are a big, good thing, so you're looking for a smaller, good thing. A good fill-in might be *windfalls* or *strokes of luck*.

2. For the first blank, you have an opposite-direction pivot (*not with _____ but with ridicule*). Thus, *praise* would be a good fill-in for the first blank. The clue about the electricians is *disbelieving,* so a good fill-in for the second blank would be *hoax*. The third sentence is perhaps the trickiest. If read in isolation, the sentence would seem to indicate that capitalists *always with an eye out to make a profit* would want to *buy* the patent. However, this item is part of a list of ways in which Graham was *ridiculed*. Thus, a correct fill-in for the third blank would indicate that the capitalists did NOT want to buy the patent. A word like *declined* would fit nicely.

3. If Armstrong *rose,* then you're looking for a word describing a high position—something like *prominence* would be a good fill-in for the first blank. For the second blank, simply recycle *influence* and fill in something like *influential* (a nice GRE word might be *foundational*). For the third blank, you want something even more distinctive than *distinctive*—something like *showy, flashy,* or *ostentatious.*

4. The opposite-direction pivot in the second sentence (*However*), followed by news of a recent discovery, indicates that whatever was thought *for years* has turned out to be incorrect. Thus, a good fill-in for the first blank would be *folk tale* or *urban legend*. A more GRE-type word would be *canard*. The second blank should simply say something like *located*. The third blank needs to sum up the idea that part of the brain that normally only responds to light has actually been repurposed to do something else. Thus, a good fill-in would be something like *versatility* or *plasticity*.

5. The first blank should simply be a verb like *thought* or *conceived* (both words that can be followed by *of*). You learn from the first sentence that the traditional way to think of the mind is *as a unitary entity*. The next sentence describes the mind acting in a very non-unitary way (a binary way, actually). So, the word in the second blank should be something like *however*. Finally, the third blank simply needs to be the opposite of *unitary*—perhaps *modular* or *decentralized.*

6. The clue is that the subordinates lived in fear. You also have an important sentence pattern: *not just _____ but positively _____*. This pattern indicates that the second thing should be a more extreme version of the first. Good fill-ins might be *bossy* and *domineering* or even *bossy* and *terrifying.*

7. Notice again the structure: two things are compared to two things. There must be a logical pattern. In this case, the first blank is the opposite of *surly*, so *nice* would be a good fill-in. The second blank is the opposite of *expatiating* on a *tedious* subject, so you could go with something like *interesting.*

8.   Most people make mistakes in how they think of migraines—*even doctors*. From that clue, a good fill-in for the first blank would be *prone* (or something else indicating that the doctors also make this mistake). Following this idea, the second blank should say something like *misdiagnoses* (this idea is supported by the phrase "whose disorders are confused with migraines"). Finally, there is an important pattern in the final sentence: *that may be ineffective or even* _____. The *even* indicates that you want something even worse than *ineffective*. A good fill-in would be *harmful*.

9.   The phrase *only by humanizing the greatest among us can we fully understand those whose achievements we admire* is a big clue—that's a strong statement that gives you a very good idea of the point of the sentence. You have an opposite-direction pivot (*not*), so a good fill-in for the first blank would be *idealize*. The second blank is matched up with *foibles,* so it will probably mean something very similar, perhaps *flaws.*

10.   Since the later years are being contrasted with the early years, the first blank should contain something like *cast off* or *eschewed*. In the second blank, you can simply recycle *prim* or *formal*—she cast off her old, wild style to pursue *a prim, highly formal formalism.*

Traps to Avoid During Elimination

In this section, you're going to learn about some traps that you might see in harder Text Completion questions.

Theme Trap

Give the following problem a try:

> The event horizon (or boundary) of a black hole represents both (i)_____ and intangibility; space travelers would pass through this literal "point of no return" so (ii)_____ that the precise moment at which their fate was sealed would almost certainly not be registered.

Blank (i)	Blank (ii)
constellation	indiscernibly
irrevocability	universally
infallibility	cosmically

Which is the easier blank?

Most would agree that the second blank is easier. The clue is *the precise moment ... certainly not be registered*, and the lack of a pivot tells you that the fill-in agrees with the clue. So you might fill in something like *without registering* (again, recycling language from the sentence itself).

Turning to the first blank, you can see that the *without registering* fill-in lines up with *intangibility*, while the first blank lines up with "point of no return." So you might fill in *no return* for the first blank.

Now you match to the answer choices. Only *indiscernibly* fits *without registering*. Only *irrevocability* fits *no return*. *Irrevocability* and *indiscernibly* are the correct responses.

A *theme trap* in a wrong answer choice shares a theme or field (such as medicine, sports, etc.) with the sentence. As a result, the choice sounds okay on its own and somehow "together" with the sentence, even though it doesn't really fit the blanks.

Notice the trap language in the choices: *constellation, universally, cosmically*. These words all relate to space, but they have no actual relation to the meanings you want for your blanks. Have the mental discipline to *follow the strategy every time*, and you won't fall for traps like this!

Close But Not Close Enough Trap

Now try this problem:

Marie was nettled by her sister's constant jocularity and preferred a _____ approach to life.

miserable
indignant
waggish
staid
sycophantic

It was probably pretty easy for you to identify the clues (*nettled, jocularity, preferred*) and to see that Marie is against *jocularity,* or joking behavior. A fill-in might be *serious.*

Now, imagine that you go through the answer choices. *Miserable* and *indignant* both "sort of" match, but they both seem a little off, too. Just because Marie doesn't like her sister's constant joking, that doesn't mean she's *miserable* or *indignant* in her outlook on life. Perhaps you don't remember what *waggish* or *staid* mean, and you don't totally remember *sycophantic* either, but you're sure it doesn't mean *serious.*

So your paper might look like this:

serious

A ~
B ~
C ?
D ?
E ×

You can now identify another trap. You don't like *miserable* or *indignant,* but you don't know the other words, so you find yourself reluctant to choose (C) or (D). Unfortunately, you're falling into a trap…

The *Close But Not Close Enough Trap* occurs when a wrong answer choice is "in the ballpark" but something is off in the meaning—however, the word is familiar, so it's attractive.

You might be afraid to pick a word you don't know. **Overcome this fear.** As it turns out, the correct answer is *staid,* which means "serious, sedate by temperament or habits."

You will also see **reversal traps** (you miss a pivot or mix up a negative). This is a matter of attention to detail in the moment.

Finally, there are **vocab traps**. *Conversant* doesn't mean *talkative* (it means *knowledgeable*), *factitious* does not mean *factual* (it means the opposite!), and *ingenuous* can look a lot like *ingenious* if you're not reading carefully. To avoid these traps, you're going to need to really know your vocab!

Text Completion Recap

Three-Step Process	1.	Read only the sentence.
	2.	Find the clue and pivot, and write down your own fill-in.
	3.	Compare to each answer choice.

Principle for Writing Fill-Ins

Fill-in = Clue + Pivot   The clue describes the target. Reuse material from the sentence when writing a fill-in.

Principle for Two or Three Blanks

Start with the easier/easiest blank. Work outwards from the part of the sentence that is easiest to understand.

Things to Watch Out For

- **Double Negative Pivots**, which create **Reversal Traps**
- **Unfamiliar Style/Content**, which can confuse you and cause you to abandon your process
- **Red Herring Clues**
- **Blanks in Tough Spots**
- **Theme Traps**, where wrong answers are thematically related to the stem
- **Close But Not Close Enough Traps**, where wrong answers have the right spin (positive or negative), but are incorrect in degree or detail
- **Vocab Traps**, where the GRE takes advantage of visual similarities between words to trick you into thinking one word has a similar meaning to some other word it happens to look like

Drill: Easy Questions

Here is the first of three 20-question Text Completion drills. Remember to follow the strategy! Look for clues and pivots, write down your own fill-in on separate paper, write A B C D E or make a grid, and use process of elimination.

You won't get any more reminders after this, so it's important that you make a vow to yourself to maintain the mental discipline to use this strategy and not simply revert back to what most people do (look at the question and pick the choices that "seem best").

You will also want to make a list of vocabulary words to look up later (if you haven't been making such a list already). Even after you've done these drills, you could still spend quite a long time just learning the words in these 60 problems (and then going over the problems again—another reason to work on separate paper and not in the book).

If your current vocabulary is extremely limited, here's another idea: go through the following 20 questions looking at the answer choices only, without reading the sentences. Make flashcards for all new words (look words up on dictionary.com, m-w.com, thefreedictionary.com, etc.). Learn all of the words, *then* come back and attack these questions.

1. Although it appeared to be _____ after its stagnation and eventual cancellation in 1989, *Doctor Who* returned to the BBC in 2005, becoming the longest-running science-fiction show in history.

lackluster
ascendant
unflagging
defunct
sated

2. _____ against China's record on environmental protection has become a ubiquitous pastime at energy summits, especially among those already inclined to invective on such topics.

Inveigling
Speculating
Needling
Ranting
Lauding

3. In 1345, the brothers of Queen Blanche of Namur, Louis and Robert, were appointed _____ to her spouse, conveying upon them the protection of King Magnus Eriksson in exchange for their homage and fealty.

protégés
vassals
vanguards
precursors
partisans

4. Social critic Neil Postman identified what he saw as a sort of intellectual _____ when he wrote, "What Orwell feared were those who would ban books. What Huxley feared was that there would be no reason to ban a book, for there would be no one who wanted to read one."

pondering
mulishness
degeneration
cerebration
banishment

5. The doctor's presentation went into great detail about the supposed _____ of the treatment, but failed to discuss any way of obviating damage to auxiliary structures.

diagnosis
mien
prognosis
costs
benefits

6. Richardson's (i) _____ handling of the (ii) _____ scandal successfully prevented what seemed poised to become the spectacular devastation or ruination of his coalition.

Blank (i)	Blank (ii)
penitent	fretful
adroit	looming
heterogeneous	ecumenical

2

7. The (i) _____ forces were just barely held at bay by a loyalist battalion
    (ii) _____ by its allies' reinforcements.

Blank (i)	Blank (ii)
revolting	obviated
outclassed	bolstered
fascistic	sapped

8. While it would be lovely if what he said were true, many of the shareholders are afraid he
    is _____ liar, based on observations made during his long tenure at the company.

a libelous
an inveterate
a nullified
an unverified
a forfeited

9. In determining the defendant's sentencing, the jury will take into account whether
    he acted on _____ motives, or, as he claims, acted primarily to shield himself and
    others in the restaurant from harm.

ulterior
resolute
pathological
lucrative
violent

10. During years of mismanagement by the Socialist Party, Burma drifted into economic
    _____ and isolation, a far cry from the power and influence exerted by the coun-
    try at the peak of the Toungoo Dynasty in the 16th century.

monotony
opulence
nonchalance
feebleness
recriminations

11. As the new government revealed itself to be far more authoritarian than the people
    ever could have guessed, and curfews and roadblocks threatened the _____ of
    citizens, the public houses began to fill with whispers of a possible coup d'état.

insolence
epitome
belligerence
recidivism
autonomy

12. He is the most hubristic individual his colleagues have ever met, and never passes up an opportunity for _____.

hedonism
augmentation
profit
jubilation
bombast

13. (i)_____ by circumstance, the entrepreneur once known for his overweening (ii) _____ was now seen by others as the possessor of a broken spirit and timid demeanor.

Blank (i)	Blank (ii)
Unaffected	pretension
Humbled	liberality
Exalted	wealth

14. Though she had made attempts to adopt a more (i)_____ lifestyle, she was not above indulging her proclivities towards fattening, (ii) _____ dishes.

Blank (i)	Blank (ii)
truculent	odious
salutary	edible
frugal	unwholesome

15. The discovery that exposure to allergens through the mother's diet during the last trimester could lead to complications during the first year after birth (i) _____ the U.K. Department of Health to (ii) _____ dietary recommendations for expecting mothers.

Blank (i)	Blank (ii)
prompted	intuit
instigated	codify
lulled	officiate

16. Fearful of being seen as (i)_____ , the Bieber Appreciation Society took pains to include (ii) _____ voices in its monthly newsletter.

Blank (i)	Blank (ii)
enthusiasts	conciliatory
detractors	critical
toadies	tantamount

17. The fact that bringing together criminals and their victims for a moderated conversation has been shown to vastly reduce rates of (i)_____ might be explained by the fact that those who commit crimes can only do so by convincing themselves their actions have no (ii) _____ .

Blank (i)	Blank (ii)
violence	inconsistencies
recidivism	aberrations
malfeasance	ramifications

18. The (i) _____ of monks and abbots in Eastern Christianity were typically of plain black modest cloth, indicating their spiritual indifference to matters of this world in favor of a commitment to a (ii) _____ mindset. In this regard, the contrast with the (iii) _____ garments of Buddhist monks is striking.

Blank (i)	Blank (ii)	Blank (iii)
vestiges	mundane	iridescent
habiliments	dogmatic	drab
paragons	transcendent	flowing

19. In many criminal trials, it emerges that the defendant (i) _____ some kind of abuse as a child. However, these biographical revelations should not have any effect on how the jury apportions (ii) _____. An excuse is not a justification, and the criminal justice system wasn't constructed to help balance the (iii) _____ of someone's life.

Blank (i)	Blank (ii)	Blank (iii)
appreciated	culpability	ledger
exploited	history	imprisonment
suffered	insanity	verdict

20. The university president argued that top universities should not (i) _____ education as an academic (ii) _____; discouraging our brightest students from pursuing teaching careers does a disservice to the next generation of students by (iii) _____ them of the opportunity to learn from the cream of the crop.

Blank (i)	Blank (ii)	Blank (iii)
disdain	recommendation	denigrating
proscribe	tome	degenerating
circumvent	discipline	divesting

Drill: Medium Questions

1. O'Neill's Irish _____ was so incomprehensible to the Royal visitors, accustomed to speaking in formal Queen's English, that they struggled to complete the negotiation.

fortitude
patois
equanimity
diffidence
consternation

2. Traditional upper class _____ such as fox hunting and cricket have largely given way to more egalitarian amusements over the course of the last century.

stereotypes
disportments
vocations
canards
professions

3. Professor Honeycutt was known as a probing questioner of her students; she always wanted to get to the _____ of any intellectual matter.

emotions
academics
pith
periphery
examination

4. Seeing its only alternative to be a (i) _____ diplomacy unbecoming of political visionaries—as members of the so-called National Liberation Organization saw themselves in those days—the militant branch veered toward a policy of (ii) _____ aggression against its perceived ethnic rivals.

Blank (i)	Blank (ii)
wheedling	supine
freewheeling	unremitting
verdant	superfluous

MANHATTAN
PREP

5. A (i)_____ ran through the crowd of protesters chanting slogans and threats when the queen made the sudden announcement—only a fortnight after vowing not to give in to the popular demands for her departure—that she would abdicate the throne, (ii) _____ a period of disorder and confusion.

Blank (i)	Blank (ii)
frisson	marring
murmur	precipitating
panegyric	diluting

6. After Bismarck's cunning leadership helped the Prussians overcome years of infighting, they were able to turn the aggression outwards, becoming known and feared across Europe for their (i)_____ .

ennui
extravagance
opulence
covetousness
truculence

7. A perfectionist in all things, Joseph expected to immediately become a (i)_____ and was downtrodden indeed when he remained (ii) _____ despite his best efforts.

Blank (i)	Blank (ii)
hack	novel
musician	inane
virtuoso	inept

8. (i) _____ is unlikely to serve someone (ii) _____ by liars and fabulists.

Blank (i)	Blank (ii)
Credulity	foresaken
Duplicity	brooked
Ingenuity	beset

2

9. The idea, espoused by such heavyweights as Peter Singer, that each sentient being deserves fair treatment on a par with human beings clashes with the ecological in-sight that _____ some members of a species is occasionally necessary to prevent the devastating effects of overpopulation.

protecting
culling
murdering
reintroducing
depleting

10. While she was known to all her friends as quite the (i) _____ , legendary for humorous stories from her years spent driving a taxi, her private behavior belied this (ii) _____ image.

Blank (i)	Blank (ii)
sage	belligerent
prevaricator	pedantic
raconteur	genial

11. The common opinion at the court had it that her droll utterances as often as not (i) _____ attitudes unbecoming of a lady. This reputation cost her the attentions of some gentlemen, above all thanks to their fear of being bested by her (ii) _____ .

Blank (i)	Blank (ii)
eluded	subtlety
derided	doggerel
evinced	repartee

12. While courage is an important virtue to teach—and his character is indeed (i) _____—a cartoon mouse with a (ii) _____ for excessive violence is hardly an appropriate mascot for a children's charity.

Blank (i)	Blank (ii)
mettlesome	penchant
impetuous	kinship
heady	largess

13. The double-dealing ambassador's political (i) _____ and backpedaling looked all the worse when compared to the (ii) _____ straightforwardness of his Australian counterpart.

Blank (i)	Blank (ii)
plutocracy	occlusive
bugaboo	ostensible
sleight of hand	intransigent

14. The most (i)_____ puzzle was in determining how to deliver the antisense strand to the right place at the right moment, after the virus had penetrated the cell, but before it had replicated and escaped to infect other cells. To accomplish this, the synthetic strand had to be potent enough to be effective and to resist rapid (ii)_____ inside the body, allowing it time to accomplish its task.

Blank (i)	Blank (ii)
recalcitrant	desiccation
pedestrian	degradation
monolithic	compunction

15. It takes only a (i) _____ of dry shrub for an errant spark to turn into a destructive (ii) _____.

Blank (i)	Blank (ii)
surfeit	conflagration
scintilla	incendiary
pallet	havoc

16. The Russo-Turkish war (i) _____ Albanians, placing before them the (ii) _____ prospect of a division of their lands among competing powers. This, above all, served to bring Albanian nationalism surging out of its former (iii) _____, culminating in a successful bid for independence only a few decades later.

Blank (i)	Blank (ii)	Blank (iii)
rankled	evanescent	latency
enervated	pernicious	insularity
debased	transient	lucidity

2

17. Though she acknowledges that modern farming practices are more (i)_____ than traditional agriculture, she nonetheless argues that this difference represents no real (ii) _____. Perhaps more worrying, however, is her insistence that similar claims can be advanced regarding the treatment of farmers by an often (iii) _____ social hierarchy.

Blank (i)	Blank (ii)	Blank (iii)
expensive	progress	iniquitous
efficient	disincentive	halcyon
polluting	countermand	stratified

18. The (i)_____ of the word *assassin* is (ii) _____ in philological circles, as the word comes from a sect of brutal killers believed to have smoked the drug hashish before going on a mission. The topic is equally attractive to historians, as the (iii) _____ of the sect, which dates to before the First Crusade in the 11th century, remains a mystery.

Blank (i)	Blank (ii)	Blank (iii)
introduction	notorious	provenance
derivation	unheralded	legend
circumlocution	enigmatic	bane

19. Statistics often need to be (i)_____ for their real meaning: in the last decade, while both the population and the amount of meat eaten annually in the nation remained (ii) _____, the growing gap between rich and poor meant that the wealthy few were eating more meat than ever, while the masses suffered from a (iii) _____ of foodstuffs of all kinds.

Blank (i)	Blank (ii)	Blank (iii)
plumbed	plastic	deceleration
calculated	static	dearth
designed	demographic	glut

20. Although Cage supported the expanded reliance on electronically produced (i) _____ , most of his early music is surprisingly (ii) _____ . His "Music for Marcel Duchamp," a prepared-piano work from 1947, never rises above mezzo-piano, offering instead (iii) _____ melody that maintains its softness throughout.

Blank (i)	Blank (ii)	Blank (iii)
timbre	deleterious	a noisome
murmur	auspicious	an undulating
clangor	subdued	an erstwhile

Drill: Hard Questions

1. After renouncing the significant advantages of his noble birth, he wandered from village to village as a lowly _____ ; this reliance on alms, he maintained along with other members of his religious order, was the life best suited to one who wished to see both the miserliness and the generosity of humanity.

abettor
mendicant
rube
anachronism
malefactor

2. The serial comma is _____ of many grammarians, who consider it an unnecessary addendum to a perfectly clear sentence structure; obviously, they're wrong, because the serial comma is critical to conveying the correct meaning.

a crotchet
an awl
an apogee
a nadir
an opus

3. In contrast to American social conventions regarding neighborly relations, in which families or individuals residing in close proximity often interact on a familiar basis, residential _____ does not necessarily imply intimacy (or even amity) among the English.

commodiousness
amiability
reciprocity
propinquity
cordiality

4. It is quite dangerous to _____ unnecessarily through the city these days, when explosions shake the buildings to their foundations without letup; it is best to conduct only essential errands, and to do so with haste.

bop
traipse
circumambulate
sidle
reconnoiter

2

5. The tokens given by the aristocrat, while (i) _____ , still served as a reminder that the power of the Crown continued to be held in some esteem even in such (ii) _____ political times.

Blank (i)	Blank (ii)
sardonic	mercurial
nugatory	jocund
sumptuous	magisterial

6. Having built up to a (i)_____ , the shelling stopped as suddenly as it had begun; gazing at the drooping barrels, one might be forgiven for thinking they were rendered (ii) _____ by the pathetic sight of their (iii) _____ targets.

Blank (i)	Blank (ii)	Blank (iii)
pique	sidereal	ethereal
crescendo	woebegone	effulgent
euphony	erroneous	haggard

7. Despite having engineered and overseen the return of several stray dioceses that had broken away under his predecessor's (i) _____ , the bishop had a modest and open quality that (ii) _____ the (iii) _____ of his position.

Blank (i)	Blank (ii)	Blank (iii)
diligence	construed	tenuousness
epaulet	belied	audacity
laxity	derided	eminence

8. The (i) _____ of "surds"—irrational roots—with the Pythagoreans' faith that all phenomena in the universe could be expressed through harmonious ratios of whole numbers led the cult to (ii) _____ any mention of their existence to the uninitiated.

Blank (i)	Blank (ii)
absurdity	condone
incongruity	proscribe
imperilment	palliate

9. Architectural (i) _____ such as Koolhaas recognized Hadid's talents early and encouraged their development. By 1977, only a few years after their initial encounter, she had perfected her (ii) _____ style, inspired equally by such disparate styles as Malevich's sparse constructivism and the flowing calligraphy of her native Arabic.

Blank (i)	Blank (ii)
cognoscenti	fungible
fledglings	malleable
neophytes	heteromorphic

10. Aleister Crowley, despite being given to wildly fantastic claims—he insisted, for instance, that the founding book of his religion was dictated to him by a divine being who visited his hotel room wearing sunglasses and a trench coat—had his share of (i) _____ followers. These were likely spurred on more than dissuaded by the (ii) _____ cast on him by the popular press, whose dubbing him "the wickedest man in the world" was, to be fair, hardly (iii) _____ given the relative harmlessness of his eccentricities.

Blank (i)	Blank (ii)	Blank (iii)
sycophantic	disadvantages	glib
sordid	gauntlets	peevish
skeptical	animadversions	condign

11. The Biblical portrayal of (i)_____ times preceding the great deluge stands in stark contrast to the ancient Greek representation of the (ii) _____ past as a Golden Age from which humanity has slowly descended into godless chaos. Such observations can easily give rise to the notion that stories about the past are less faithful attempts at reconstruction than (iii) _____ , expressing both our cultural fears and hopes.

Blank (i)	Blank (ii)	Blank (iii)
flagitious	proximate	allegories
dubious	antediluvian	equivocations
rustic	obscure	platitudes

12. Seeing (i) _____ as perhaps the most significant cause of preventable illness, such twelfth-century physicians as Moses Maimonides aimed the bulk of their (ii) _____ pamphlets at the prescription of medieval dietary regimens, offering advice that often appears (iii) _____ to modern sensibilities.

Blank (i)	Blank (ii)	Blank (iii)
costiveness	didactic	disingenuous
bathos	maleficent	risible
convalescence	tenable	burgeoning

13. Uncertain whether his (i) _____ attire could impress the suave, nattily-dressed executive—despite her frequent affirmations of a fondness for rural life—Francis reduced himself to near (ii) _____ through new wardrobe acquisitions. If only he had known that the executive was secretly ashamed of her (iii) _____ showboating, which she only indulged to conceal her financial ruin.

Blank (i)	Blank (ii)	Blank (iii)
georgic	penury	bombastic
natty	malaise	runic
exclusive	lethargy	sartorial

14. (i) _____ is unlikely to gain a reputation for reliability; Garth's poorly disguised excuses, however, were improbably interpreted by his (ii) _____ , hypochondriac employer as a sign of great foresight and (iii) _____ .

Blank (i)	Blank (ii)	Blank (iii)
An embezzler	casuistic	insipidity
A malingerer	imposing	sagacity
A pilferer	trepidatious	temerity

15. History has (i)_____ the movement's leader to the extent that his quite considerable moral shortcomings—his (ii) _____ misogyny, for example—are rarely discussed and, if mentioned at all, are seen as no more than (iii) _____ .

Blank (i)	Blank (ii)	Blank (iii)
lionized	risqué	malefactions
narrativized	incorrigible	peccadilloes
impugned	waggish	trespasses

16. The new film, though a chronicle of exploitation and iniquity, nevertheless is deeply concerned with notions of (i) _____ , eventually showcasing the elimination of all the protagonist's abusers, granting the audience the (ii) _____ they've been awaiting for two hours. Despite the satisfying upheaval, however, the plodding plot en route to this (iii) _____ leaves much to be desired.

Blank (i)	Blank (ii)	Blank (iii)
fairness	catharsis	embellishment
slavery	relief	denouement
injustice	inconclusiveness	platitude

17. Although (i) _____ is frequently used to give otherwise insubstantial work (ii) _____ of profundity, even Wallgot's most charitable readers were known to sneer at the breadth of his references.

Blank (i)	Blank (ii)
stringency	an iota
insularity	a veneer
eclecticism	a medley

18. He rarely bothered to (i) _____ his lengthy tomes, but their surprising popularity with the public empowered him to avoid editorial complaints through (ii) _____ threats to sign a contract with a different publisher.

Blank (i)	Blank (ii)
emend	impuissant
allay	peremptory
edify	toothsome

19. In future discounting, subjects place a lower value on events in the distant future than on (i) _____ ones, explaining the common tendency to (ii) _____ present pleasures even at the expense of a likely (iii) _____ of future detriments.

Blank (i)	Blank (ii)	Blank (iii)
atavistic	avert	malady
remote	rescind	proliferation
proximate	protract	buttressing

20. She claims it is possible to deduce matters of fact from logic and, with just as little (i) _____ , aims to derive ethical and economic truths as well. The laws of logic, in her opinion, (ii) _____ her proclamation that "existence exists," which is very much like saying that the law of thermodynamics is hot.

Blank (i)	Blank (ii)
epigram	license
warrant	occlude
fallacy	galvanize

Solutions: 20 Easy Questions

1.   **Defunct.** The show stagnated and was canceled, so afterward it might appear to be "dead" or "gone." *Defunct* (no longer existing) is a good match. A *lackluster* (dull) show might be cancelled, but it doesn't make sense that Doctor Who appeared to be dull **after** it was cancelled, and this would clash with the fact that the show returned in 2005 and had success. A canceled show is unlikely to appear in a positive light, such as *ascendant* (upwardly moving) or *unflagging* (not tiring; steady and unrelenting). *Sated* (fully satisfied, maybe too much) doesn't make sense in this context.

2.   **Ranting.** "Inveighing" (expressing disapproval; railing against) would fit, but *inveigling* (winning over by flattery) is a trap. The clues are that this is an action done "against" China's record and "already inclined to invective (insulting or harsh language)." *Speculating* is too neutral, and *lauding* (praising) is too positive. *Needling* (teasing or provoking) can be negative, but would be done to someone or to some group, not something that could be done "against China's record."

3.   **Vassals.** The queen's brothers became something to her spouse, the king. This gave "them the protection of King Magnus Eriksson in exchange for their homage (publicly expressed respect) and fealty (loyalty)". By definition, a *vassal* is a person loyal or in service to a feudal lord. *Proteges*, *vanguards*, *precursors*, and *partisans* are all roles that people could serve on a king's behalf, but the sentence does not provide clues that indicate any of these meanings.

4.   **Degeneration.** Postman's quote talks about a society in which no one wants to read books anymore. This suggests an intellectual weakening or decline (these are good suggestions for filling in the blank). *Degeneration* is a good match; its primary definition is "a decline." *Pondering* (thoughtful consideration) and *cerebration* (thinking about something) are near-synonyms that are too positively intellectual, and thus the opposite of what the blank requires. *Mulishness* (unreasonable stubbornness) and *banishment* (condemnation to exile) are unrelated to the clues in the sentence.

5.   **Benefits.** The pivot here is "but," and the clue is that the doctor "failed to discuss any way of obviating (anticipating and preventing) damage." Thus, the doctor went into great detail about only "supposed" good things about the treatment, and only *benefits* works. *Diagnosis* (determination of disease) and *prognosis* (forecast of medical outcome, chances of recovery) both relate to the medical theme, but neither fits in the blank. *Mien* (appearance, bearing) is unrelated.

6.   **Adroit, looming.** His handling of the scandal was "successful" or "skillful," so *adroit* (skilled, adept) fits best. Neither a *penitent* (sorry for sin) nor *heterogeneous* (mixed; composed of differing parts) "handling of the ... scandal" is supported by clues in the sentence. The scandal seemed poised to ruin things—that is, it hadn't done so already. What makes the most sense here is that the scandal itself hadn't quite broken yet—it was only *looming* (taking shape as an impending event). Someone might be *fretful* (worried) over a scandal, but *fretful* doesn't make sense as a description of the scandal itself. There are no indications in the sentence that the scandal was *ecumenical* (worldwide in scope).

7.   Revolting, bolstered. One good clue to the first blank is the word "loyalist." Those fighting the loyalists would likely be the rebels. You don't have any indication that the forces were *fascistic* (totalitarian, led by dictator). *Outclassed* (surpassed in quality) is irrelevant here, so *revolting* fits best. Don't be thrown off by the dual meaning of *revolting*—certainly *revolting* can mean disgusting, but it can also mean engaging in a revolt, such as against a government. The loyalist battalion was helped or strengthened by "its allies' reinforcements," so only *bolstered* (supported) makes sense. *Obviated* (anticipated and made unnecessary) isn't indicated by any clue in the sentence. *Sapped* (weakened, especially of energy) conflicts with the idea that allies would help the loyalists.

8.   Inveterate. The "while" and the hypothetical "if what he said were true" in the first part of the sentence indicate that he is actually a liar. This is based on his long track record, so a good fill-in might be "an established" liar. *Libelous* is a trap answer—libel is lying in print for the purpose of damaging someone's reputation. *Libelous* liar would actually be redundant—and, of course, you have no indication that the lying was done in print. *Nullified* (invalidated, voided), *unverified* (unconfirmed), and *forfeited* (lost as a result of crime or fault) all don't quite work as a description of a liar; to the extent that they do, they cast doubt on his ability to lie, a doubt this sentence doesn't support. *Inveterate* (long-established and unlikely to change) is the correct answer.

9.   Ulterior. The pivot here is "whether … or"—you are looking for a characterization of "motives" that would make them negative, namely the opposite of "primarily to shield himself and others in the restaurant from harm." If he truly was acting in defense of himself and others, he would likely get a lighter sentence than if he had *ulterior*, or hidden, (generally selfish) motives. *Resolute* (determined; steady) is unrelated. *Pathological* (related or due to physical or mental disease; compulsive) and *lucrative* (producing large profit) introduce themes of illness and money, respectively, that are not indicated by any clues in the sentence. *Violent* is a theme trap.

10. Feebleness. You know that Burma was being mismanaged, so you want something bad (and appropriate to describe an economy). The blank and "isolation" are contrasted with "power and influence." Just as isolation and influence are (somewhat) opposite ideas, you can expect the blank to oppose power: something like "not powerful" or "not strong." *Feebleness* (weakness) is a good match. *Monotony* (lack of variety, tedious repetition) is negative, but no clues in the sentence indicate this meaning. Opulence (wealth, abundance) is opposite of the desired meaning. Both *nonchalance* (casual lack of concern) and *recriminations* (counteraccusations) don't make sense following "economic."

11. Autonomy. What would an authoritarian government threaten with roadblocks and curfews? Most likely, something like "independence." *Autonomy* is more or less a synonym of independence. Though citizens might need to be belligerent to stage a coup, the blank describes what the citizens would lose that would **initially** cause people to just begin to utter "whispers" of a "possible" coup. *Belligerence* (aggressively hostile attitude) doesn't work in this context. Likewise, *insolence* (rude and disrespectful behavior) does not work in the blank. The remaining choices, *epitome* (a perfect example of something) and *recidivism* (tendency to relapse to previous behavior, often criminal), are not indicated by clues in the sentence.

2

12. Bombast. "Hubristic" means arrogant—a "hubristic" person would never decline an opportunity for bragging, or *bombast. Augmentation* (the action of making or becoming greater in size or amount) is not quite right; greater "size or amount" is not exactly indicated by the "hubristic" clue. *Hedonism* (the devotion to sensual pleasures and their pursuit) and *jubilation* (the state of rejoicing) are off-topic. Finally, while an arrogant person might desire *profit*, so might anyone else. The sentence would need to include a clue more specifically about money for *profit* to be the right answer.

13. Humbled, pretension. The clue is that the entrepreneur is now "the possessor of a broken spirit and timid demeanor"—thus, he must have been the opposite of that before the change. A good fill-in for the second blank might be "confidence." The accompanying adjective "overweening" means conceited, or just excessive, so the entrepreneur was previously known for his "confidence, to an extreme degree," so look for a negative choice for the blank. *Pretension* fits best; *liberality* (giving or spending freely; open-mindedness) is positive and not overweening, and *wealth* adds an idea that is not indicated in the sentence. Moving on to the first blank—a good fill-in might be "brought down." The only answer that is a match is *humbled. Exalted* (held in high regard; in a state of extreme happiness) is the opposite of what the blank requires, and *unaffected* is too neutral to explain the change in how the entrepreneur is seen by others.

14. Salutary, unwholesome. Start with the second blank. Most people would not indulge in a "proclivity" (inclination or predisposition) toward dishes that are *odious* (extremely unpleasant) or *sodden* (soaked); the correct word must be *unwholesome* (not conducive to health), which also agrees with the clue "fattening." The first word should contrast with this because of the pivot "though." The best bet is salutary (conducive to health). *Truculent* (ferocious, cruel, or savage) and *frugal* (economical in the spending of money or resources) do not work.

15. Prompted, codify. A discovery that pregnancy complications are being caused and can be avoided would *prompt* action—specifically, *codifying,* or "systematizing," the recommendations. For the first blank, *instigated* (urged, goaded, provoked, or incited) has a somewhat negative spin, and *instigating* is generally something that people do; it is odd to say that a "discovery" instigated a group of people to do something. *Lulled* (deceptively caused to feel safe) is the opposite of what the discovery of the allergen/complications link would do to the Department of Health. For the second blank, *intuit* (understand or solve by instinct) and *officiate* (act as an official in charge) are not right, though the latter represents a bit of a theme trap related to a government agency.

16. Toadies, critical. The Bieber Appreciation Society clearly exists to appreciate all things Bieber, but it seems that the society has become "fearful" of being seen in a certain way. What way? Keep reading—they "took pains" to include a certain kind of voice. *Tantamount* (equivalent) doesn't make sense in the second blank, and *conciliatory* would be positive towards Bieber (so why would the Bieber Appreciation Society have trouble finding such voices?). Only *critical,* which in this context means "involving careful evaluation and judgment," works. If the societies is struggling to include *critical* voices, it seems that they fear being seen as not having balanced views—that is, they fear being seen as *toadies*; making them nothing but a group of servile flatterers. There is very little danger of an appreciation society (or fan club, booster organization, or any similar group) being seen as *detractors* of their namesake. *Enthusiasts* and "Appreciation" agree in degree of positivity, so that's not something the group would fear, either.

MANHATTAN
PREP

17. Recidivism, ramifications. The people in question are already criminals, so the issue isn't one of bringing down crime or violence in general, but of repeat offenses, that is, *recidivism*. What meeting victims must convince the criminals of is that their actions have consequences—or *ramifications*.

18. Habiliments, transcendent, iridescent. The first blank is referring to something made of cloth, which is contrasted with the garments of Buddhist monks. You are looking for something that means garments or clothes; *habiliments* (clothes associated with a particular profession or occasion) is the only choice that fits. The second blank is looking for a description of a spiritual reality beyond this one; only *transcendent* (above and beyond the limits of material existence) fits. *Mundane* (earthly, rather than heavenly or spiritual) agrees rather than contrasts with "matters of this world." *Dogmatic* (inclined to present opinion as unassailable truth) is unrelated. The third blank is looking for a contrast with the "plain black modest cloth" outfits of the first sentence segment; *iridescent* (colorful, lustrous, or brilliant) is the only option that directly contrasts. *Drab* actually agrees with "plain black modest cloth." *Flowing* is not necessarily the opposite of garments "of plain black modest cloth," which may or may not be *flowing*.

19. Suffered, culpability, ledger. The first blank is a good place to start. Obviously, no one *appreciates* abuse. *Exploited* is trickier, but the text never implies that the abuse is being used to exploit the system. The best choice is *suffered*. For the second blank, you only need to know what a jury does: they apportion blame, which is a synonym of *culpability*. Finally, the third blank only makes sense with *ledger* (you can't balance *imprisonment* or a *verdict*).

20. Disdain, discipline, divesting. The semicolon in this sentence is a clue that the two parts of the sentence agree—the first part should mirror the meaning that "the brightest students … pursuing teaching" would be a good thing. For the first and second blanks, universities should therefore not "put down" education as an academic "area" or "pursuit." Don't fall for trap answers; *proscribe* (ban) and *circumvent* (avoid via circuitous means) add extra meaning to the idea of "put down." Only *disdain* fits the first blank. *Discipline* is the closest match for the second blank (*tome* means "book, especially a large, academic book"). The third blank needs something that explains the "disservice" done to future students, namely, something like "depriving" them of the chance to learn from the best. The best choice is the synonym *divesting*; don't fall for the traps of *denigrating* (defaming; belittling) and *degenerating* (deteriorating; declining). Both trap choices work with the theme, but don't fit into the blank.

Solutions: 20 Medium Questions

1. Patois. Since the negotiators find O'Neill "incomprehensible," there must be something in his speech, not the tone or content of that speech, that is confusing them. *Patois* is a regional dialect, in contrast to the official language spoken by the negotiators (Queen's English). The Royal visitors would not find any of the other characteristics—*fortitude* (courage, resilience), *equanimity* (composure, mental calmness), *diffidence* (hesitance or resistance to speak), *consternation* (amazement or dismay that leads to confusion)—"incomprehensible," nor do any of these relate to the clue about speech.

2

2. **Disportments.** Fox hunting and cricket are not professional activities for the upper class (the clue is "amusements"); they are hobbies, amusements, or diversions, that is, *disportments*. *Vocations* and *professions* both contradict the idea of these activities as "amusements." Fox hunting and cricket are not examples of *canards*, which are unfounded rumors or stories, so that choice does not fit. *Stereotypes* is a trap, since stereotypes of the upper class might have them constantly engaging in such *disportments*.

3. **Pith.** A "probing questioner" is looking for the central point of a matter. That it is an "intellectual matter" suggests a word other than *emotions* for the blank, as does that choice's failure to relate to the "probing questioner" clue. *Periphery* is the opposite of central. *Examination* doesn't fit at all. *Academics* is a theme trap. The only answer that means "core or central point" is *pith*.

4. **Wheedling, unremitting.** What would seem to be unbecoming of political visionaries is to attempt to convince someone (rather than, say, commanding or dictating terms), especially in a flattering way. That's exactly what *wheedling* means. *Freewheeling* (acting without concern for rules or consequences) is not indicated by any clues in the sentence, and *verdant* (green, covered in vegetation) is totally unrelated to diplomacy. You have no indication that the aggression undertaken was *superfluous* (unnecessary); if so, why would they undertake it? A "policy of *supine* (passive; apathetic) aggression" would be contradictory. Rather, it was persistent or relentless (*unremitting*).

5. **Frisson, precipitating.** The protesters are getting what they want: the queen is suddenly abdicating (giving up) the throne. "Thrill" or "excitement" may work well for the first blank, and *frisson* fits. *Murmur*, while possible, doesn't capture the sense of excitement one would expect. A *panegyric* (formal speech or composition in praise of someone or something) is not something that would "run through the crowd," certainly not in praise of the very queen the crowd wishes to depose. For the second blank, one might expect a period of disorder to begin following a political upheaval; *precipitating* is the only possibility. *Marring* (damaging, disfiguring) and *diluting* (making weaker by adding other elements to it) aren't really things that could be done to "a period" of time.

6. **Truculence.** The blank is referring to something that makes the Prussians feared, and something that has led to internal fighting. *Truculence*—aggression or belligerence—is the best fit here. Neither *ennui* (listlessness arising from boredom) nor *covetousness* (envious desire to possess something) are indicated by any clues in the sentence, and neither would really inspire fear. *Extravagance* and *opulence* (both mean lavishness) aren't especially threatening.

7. **Virtuoso, inept.** Since Joseph is a perfectionist, he probably expected to become "perfect," or at least "good," and was disappointed when he remained something like "unskilled" or "bad." *Virtuoso* (highly skilled, especially in music or art) and *inept* match the fill-ins well. Beware of choosing answers by comparing the options for each blank. Someone who is inept, particularly a writer who is inept, could be called a *hack* (a dull, unoriginal writer), but this is the opposite of what is called for in the first blank. In turn, *hack* might present a theme trap to someone mistakenly thinking of the noun definition of *novel* (book) in the second blank. For the second blank, all the options are adjectives, and *novel* (new) and *inane* (silly) don't work as contrasts to "perfectionist."

8.   Credulity, beset. For the first blank, you are looking for a trait that is unhelpful in dealing with "liars and fabulists" (fabulists are just very creative liars). Duplicity and ingenuity would be actively helpful, so the answer must be *credulity* (a tendence to believe people too easily). For the second blank, you are looking for a participle describing "someone," that is, you can read it as "someone (who is) *foresaken/brooked/beset* by liars and fabulists." It wouldn't be that bad to be *forsaken* (abandoned) by liars—at least they would leave you alone. *Brooked* (tolerated) by liars doesn't make as much sense; it is the liars that would need to be tolerated by others. But someone who is *beset* (surrounded) by liars would have a problem, and would not be well served by *credulity*.

9.   Culling. The discussion is about doing something to "some members of a species … to prevent the devastating effects of overpopulation." Something like "removing" or "getting rid of" would work in the blank. *Protecting* and *reintroducing* don't make sense; they are theme traps. *Depleting* can apply to a resource, but not to individuals. *Murdering* and *culling* are both types of killing, but *culling* is the better option since it is a technical term for killing individual members to avoid overpopulation. (Bonus: if you understand this sentence, you've got a handle on one of the key debates among environmentalists.)

10. Raconteur, genial. The sentence indicates that she was "legendary for humorous stories" from a certain set of life experiences. A *raconteur* is someone who tells amusing stories, but she wouldn't be "known to all her friends" as a *sage* (wise or learned person) or a *prevaricator* (someone who tells false stories) just based on that clue. In the last part of her sentence, "belied" indicates that "her private behavior" is at odds with her public reputation, but the blank refers to her image, so it agrees with the first blank. Someone who tells amusing stories would be considered *genial* (friendly and cheerful), but not *belligerent* (hostile and aggressive) or *pedantic* (overly concerned with small details or rules).

11. Evinced, repartee. The opinion about her is clearly negative, so her utterances don't *deride* (ridicule) negative utterances or *elude* (avoid) them, but rather demonstrate (*evince*) them. One isn't likely to fear being bested by *doggerel* (triviality) or—usually—*subtlety* (if you're bested by *subtlety*, you're likely not the sort of person who notices), but clever, quick, and witty replies (*repartee*) are threatening indeed!

12. Mettlesome, penchant. You are looking for another word for "courageous," but one that doesn't carry negative connotations (the "indeed" in front of the blank indicates that the spin will be the same as the spin of "virtue"). *Mettlesome* means spirited or courageous, but *impetuous* (impulsive) and *heady* (intoxicating; exhilarating) do not match the fill-in. But the cartoon mouse seemingly engages in excessive violence, so it has a tendency toward, or a *penchant* for, violence, not a *kinship* (blood relationship) or *largess* (generosity) for violence.

13. Sleight of hand, ostensible. The ambassador is "double-dealing" (duplicitous) and "backpedaling" (retreating from a position). A good fit in the first blank would be something like "deceitfulness," so *sleight of hand* (skillful deception) works. There is no indication that the ambassador had political *plutocracy* (government by the wealthy) or political *bugaboo* (something causing fear). The Australian counterpart is straightforward, and compares favorably with the ambassador mentioned first, so expect a positive adjective that can describe "straightforwardness" for the second blank. *Occlusive* (tending to close off) would conflict with being straightforward, and *intransigent* (uncompromising, obstinate) is too negative. Only *ostensible* (supposedly true, but not necessarily true) is neither too negative nor at odds with any clue, and works in a sentence about how politicians "looked," not necessarily about how they really were.

14. Recalcitrant, degradation. The puzzle sounds quite complicated—delivering an antisense strand to the right place at just the right moment. Only *recalcitrant* (stubborn) is appropriate to describe a complicated puzzle; *pedestrian* (commonplace, uninspired) conflicts with the clue and *monolithic* (inflexible, unchanging) is not indicated by any clue. The strand must be strong enough to resist rapid (something), "allowing it time to accomplish its task." The clue is that the strand needs time to work, so it needs to resist something like "not being able to work." *Dessication* (drying out) is probably bad, but there is no indication in the sentence that drying out would prevent the strand from working, and *compunction* (uneasiness due to guilt) doesn't apply to strands. However, *degradation* (deterioration; breakdown) is something the strand would have to resist in order to work on the virus.

15. Scintilla, conflagration. The clue "only" indicates that you are looking for something that means "small amount" in the first blank. *Surfeit* (excessive amount) is an antonym, but *scintilla* (minute quantity, trace, or bit) is a perfect fit. *Pallet*, which means either "straw mattress" or "platform for storage, stacking, and moving of goods" (such as those often lifted by forklifts), doesn't follow the "only" clue, so beware of the possible straw/dry shrub theme trap. A *havoc* is destructive, but has nothing to do with fire (which is what "spark" would lead you to expect). An *incendiary* does, but it is not quite appropriate in this spot—an *incendiary* is more of a fire-starter, like dynamite. A *conflagration* is specifically a destructive fire.

16. Rankled, pernicious, latency. The war clearly didn't weaken (*enervate*) Albanians, since it encourages them to strive for independence. And while some features of the war might have *debased* them, the prospect of division of their lands didn't do this. However, it might have angered, vexed, or caused bitterness for them, that is, *rankled* them. The "prospect of a division of their lands" would not be a good thing for the Albanians, so expect a negative word in the second blank. Also, the sentence indicates that "a successful bid for independence" happened a few decades later. *Pernicious* (greatly destructive, deadly, injurious, or harmful) works well, but *evanescent* (fleeting; tending to vanish like vapor) and *transient* (quickly coming into and passing out of existence; transitory) aren't negative enough and both have short-term meanings that conflict with the long time frame indicated by the clue. The Albanian's nationalism surged out—it wasn't already clear (*lucid*), and whether it was *insular* before or after doesn't seem to make much of a difference; but if it emerged out of *latency*, that would explain why it suddenly became a force that could lead to independence.

17. Efficient, progress, iniquitous. There is a difference between modern farming practices and traditional agriculture. "She nonetheless argues that this difference represents no real" *progress*, the only choice for the second blank that makes sense. *Disincentive* means "deterrent" and *countermand* as a noun means "order that revokes a previous order." *Progress* in turn provides an additional clue for the first blank: she is arguing that the difference is not really progress, even though modern farming is more (something) than traditional farming, so the blank must be something positive like "advanced." While more advanced practices could be expensive, more expensive practices would not be thought of as progress, so *expensive* doesn't fit in this context. *Polluting* is negative, so *efficient* must be the answer in blank (i). The last blank is referring to something bad about the social hierarchy and how it treats farmers. *Stratified* describes the hierarchy, but doesn't say anything negative about it (aside from the fact that it is a hierarchy!). Since *halcyon* (calm, peaceful, or tranquil) is positive, *iniquitous* or unjust is the only fit.

18. Derivation, notorious, opacity. The first sentence links the word *assassin* with "hashish," so the first blank is addressing the *derivation* of the term. It says nothing about its *introduction*, since you are only told where the word originates, not how it was introduced. *Circumlocution* (roundabout or evasive speech; use of more words than necessary) represents a theme trap. Since the derivation is known, it follows that it isn't *enigmatic*; but it is *notorious* given the shadiness involved in the derivation. Nothing in the sentence indicates that the derivation is *unheralded* (unannounced, unsung). Something about the sect presents a mystery, and because the sentence discusses how it "dates to before the First Crusade in the 11th century," you can expect a word that means something like "origin" (*provenance* is a synonym). The *legend* of the sect must not be much of a mystery, given that it is summarized in this sentence. The sentence indicates nothing about the *bane* (curse; affliction) of the sect being a mystery, or even whether such a problem existed for the sect.

19. Plumbed, static, dearth. The "growing gap between rich and poor" and the second "while" indicate a contrast in how much meat is consumed by different groups. The "wealthy few were eating more meat than ever," so the masses must have suffered from a "lack," or *dearth,* of foodstuffs. *Glut* (excessive supply) is the opposite, and *deceleration* (slowing down) could happen to the production/harvest of foodstuffs, but not to foodstuffs themselves.

The second blank is a bit trickier: the truth is that the rich are eating more meat and the poor less, but the statistics, on their face, don't make that clear. Thus, the statistics indicate that the amount of meat eaten "remained the same," or was *static*. *Plastic* (artificial; flexible) has some definitions that are unrelated and others that are somewhat opposite the fill-in. *Demographic* (related to structure of a population) is a theme trap.

Finally, consider the surprising "growing gap" and the initial clue that "statistics … need to be _____ for their *real* meaning" (emphasis added). Only *plumbed,* or "examined closely," works in the first blank.

20. Clangor, subdued, an undulating. Cage's early music is "surprisingly" (something), in contrast to something "electronically produced." Music is the main clue that the first blank is something like "music" or "sound." *Clangor* (loud racket or sustained noise) is a type of noise that could be electronically produced, and contrasts nicely with the later clues about the earlier works having "melody" and "softness." *Timbre* (unique combination of qualities distinguishing a sound from others) is a quality of a sound, not a sound itself; this is a theme trap. *Murmur* (soft, indistinct sound) typically refers to human-generated sound, not "electronically produced," and also fails to contrast with "softness" as it should. *Clangor* serves as additional clue for the second blank: Cage's early music is surprisingly "not clangorous" or "soft." *Subdued* (quiet, soft) works perfectly, while *deleterious* (harmful; unhealthy) and *auspicious* (promising or propitious) are unrelated to the sentence. If "'Music for Marcel Duchamp' … never rises above" some level of volume, only *undulating* (rising or falling in pitch, volume, or cadence) works in the last blank. *Noisome* (noxious, harmful, or dangerous) and *erstwhile* (former, in the past, previous) are unrelated to the sentence. Don't be distracted by the superficial similarity between *noisome* and "noise."

Solutions: 20 Hard Questions

1. **Mendicant.** The clues are that he "wandered" and was "lowly" and lived by a "reliance on alms," which is a reliance on charity, as did the "other members of his religious order." A *mendicant* is sometimes just a "beggar," but it can have a specifically religious connotation. The other choices all introduce meanings that the rest of the sentence doesn't suggest. Both *abettor* (a person who supports an action, typically wrongdoing) and *malefactor* (evildoer) introduce the unsupported idea that he was bad. *Rube* (unsophisticated or naive person) and *anachronism* (person or object out of its proper time) do not follow from the clues either.

2. **Crotchet.** These answer choices are killer nouns! The fill-in shouldn't be too hard: something like "peeve" or "concern." A *crotchet* is a perverse or unfounded belief. The others are all nonsensical: an *awl* is a hole-punching tool, an *apogee* is a climax or high point, a *nadir* is a low point, and an *opus* is a musical or literary composition.

3. **Propinquity.** You are told that, for Americans, familiarity follows from close proximity. The blank should be a synonym for proximity, and *propinquity* is. The other answer choices all deal with comfort or friendliness, and thus are theme traps drawing on associations with "neighborly": *commodiousness* (spaciousness), *amiability* (friendliness), *reciprocity* (relationship with mutual exchange of favors or benefits), and *cordiality* (amity).

4. **Traipse.** The answer choices are all difficult; all of them mean "walk" or "travel" in some way, so nuance is key. Both *bop* (move or travel energetically) and *sidle* (walk timidy) carry strange spin. *Circumambulate* means "walk all the way around," which would avoid the city, the explosions, and, presumably, the danger. *Circumambulate* also conflicts with "through." *Reconnoiter* (make a military observation of a place) carries an unhelpful militaristic spin. *Traipse* (walk casually or needlessly) agrees with the clue "unnecessarily" and properly contrasts with "conduct only essential errands."

5. **Nugatory, mercurial.** The "while" in front of the first blank suggests that the items given by the aristocrat are valuable *only* as reminders: that is, they have no real value in themselves. *Nugatory* means "of no value," while *sumptuous* (very costly, luxurious, or lavish) implies real value, and also conflicts with the "tokens" clue. *Sardonic* (scornfully or derisively mocking) is unrelated. The "power of the Crown continued to be held in esteem"—you are looking not just for political conditions that are bad or dangerous, but conditions that are changeable. *Mercurial* means "frequently changeable or changing." *Jocund* (cheerful, merry) political times are not indicated by any clues. *Magisterial* (having great authority; dictatorial) is a theme trap, and doesn't follow the pivot "even." The Crown "still ... continued to be held in some esteem" even in political times when the esteem attributed to the Crown must have decreased.

6.   Crescendo, woebegone, haggard. The shelling is building up to something like a "peak," or *crescendo* (climax; loudest point). *Pique* (passing feeling of irritation at a perceived slight) sounds the same as "peak," but is unrelated to the shelling. *Euphony* (pleasing sound) is positive, a meaning not indicated by this sentence. The pieces of artillery seem like they are "sad," since that would be an apt response to a pathetic sight. Only *woebegone*—extremely sad or full of woe—fits; *sidereal* (relating to the stars or constellations) and *erroneous* (wrong) are unrelated. Their targets aren't likely to be *effulgent* (radiant, brilliantly shining, or splendid) or *ethereal* (light, airy; heavenly, celestial) since neither of these is "pathetic." The targets are most likely *haggard*—worn out.

7.   Laxity, belied, eminence. The predecessor had some quality that allowed "several stray dioceses" to break away. *Laxity* (looseness; leniency) is the only choice that works; *diligence* (perseverance; attentiveness) is the opposite of what is needed. *Epaulet* (shoulder ornament, typically worn on military uniforms) would only make sense—if at all—in an extremely metaphorical sense. The third blank refers to the (something) of the bishop's position. There is no indication of *tenuousness* (uncertainty) or *audacity* (recklessness, daring), but *eminence* (high rank, station, or status) would apply to a leader's position. You can now turn to the second blank: you don't expect someone with a position of *eminence* to be "modest and open," so his openness seems to misrepresent (*belie*) that *eminence*. *Construed* (deduced; explained) and *derided* (mocked, ridiculed) don't work.

8.   Incongruity, proscribe. For the first blank, "with" is important: *absurdity* (ridiculousness) and *imperilment* (endangerment) are not things that would happen "with the Pythagoreans' faith," but surds do seem to have an *incongruity* (lack of agreement) with their faith in "harmonious ratios of whole numbers." For the second blank, the seriousness of the problem would seem to suggest that the Pythagoreans wouldn't want to *condone* (accept, allow) the spreading of this information; they might want to *palliate* (alleviate, diminish) the impact of the information, but forbidding, or *proscribing*, any mention of it outright fits better.

9.   Cognoscenti, heteromorphic. People such as Koolhaas "recognized ... and encouraged" Hadid's talents, which sounds like the work of a mentor. For the first blank, look for "someone in the know," or *cognoscenti* (people well informed about a subject). *Fledglings* (young, immature, or inexperienced people) and *neophytes* (beginners) are the opposite. Hadid's style mixes at least two diverse inspirations, so you would not expect it to be replaceable by something else (*fungible*) or easily changeable (*malleable*), but simply to exhibit a plurality of forms: *heteromorphic*.

10. Sycophantic, animadversions, condign. Followers are rarely *skeptical* and you have no reason to think they were particularly *sordid* (morally degraded, base, or vile), since you don't know what sorts of activities Crowley engaged in, short of making "wildly fantastic claims." But followers, especially those of clearly eccentric figures, do tend to be *sycophantic* (fawning, obsequious, or servile). The press is saying something bad about him, not casting *disadvantages* or *gauntlets* (open challenges) on him, so *animadversions* (strong criticisms) fits best. The criticism seems excessive or undeserved in light of his "relative harmlessness," so the criticism was hardly *condign* (appropriate, deserved). Neither *glib* (fluent to the point of insincerity) nor *peevish* (discontented; ill-tempered) works in this context.

11. Flagitious, antediluvian, allegories. The first blank gives you a "stark contrast" with the Greek representation of these times as a Golden Age, so it should be something bad, even starkly bad. *Dubious* (warranting uncertainty or doubt) doesn't necessarily mean bad, and *rustic* (rural; lacking refinement) isn't anywhere near as negative as *flagitious*, which means "marked by vice." The ancient Greek myths are about the "distant" or "remote" past. *Antediluvian* is the correct fit (don't be misled into thinking of *antediluvian* as a trap—it does literally mean "before the flood," and thus doesn't apply to the Greek myths, but it also means "extremely ancient," which is what you're looking for). The stories about the past—in the third blank—would be *equivocations* if each of them contained a mixed message; but instead it looks like the mix comes only if you are comparing Biblical with Greek stories. *Allegories*, or stories with a moral or political meaning, are the right contrast for "faithful attempts at reconstruction" and correctly match "expressing ... fears and hopes." *Platitudes* (dull, banal, trite statements or remarks) introduces a connotation of banality not indicated by the text.

12. Costiveness, didactic, risible. *Convalescence* (a period of recovery from illness; recuperation) might seem reasonable, but it is a theme trap. *Convalescence* would follow an illness, not cause it. The topic is medieval medicine, with an emphasis on diet, so the correct choice is *costiveness*, which is a fancy way of describing constipation. *Bathos* (anticlimax) does not fit. The pamphlets are seemingly designed to tell people what to eat; they are educational, or *didactic*. There is no indication that the pamphlets are *maleficent* (malicious; intending or producing harm or evil) or *tenable* (able to be maintained; credible). The dietary regimens might have been *tenable*, but there is no indication that the pamphlets were, and it's worth checking the second blank against the third blank and sentence ending. Since dietary and health views are quite different today from those held by medieval doctors, "modern sensibilities" are likely to find their advice funny, or *risible*. Both *disingenuous* (insincere; hypocritical) and *burgeoning* (growing rapidly; flourishing) add meaning that isn't supported by any clues in the sentence.

13. Georgic, penury, sartorial. His attire has something to do with "rural life"; *georgic* means "agricultural or related to rural life." *Natty* means sharp or stylish and is the opposite of what is required in the first blank; Francis was uncertain about whether he could impress a "nattily-dressed" person, or a person dressed in *natty* clothes. When *exclusive* is used to describe a commodity, it means "not obtainable elsewhere," and is generally used in a positive sense. Out of concern, Francis "reduced himself ... through new wardrobe acquisitions." It sounds like Francis spent a lot of money on clothes—spending a lot of money could reduce someone—especially someone with *georgic* means—to near poverty (*penury*). *Malaise* (vague, general sense of unease or mental discomfort) and *lethargy* (state of sluggishness, inactivity, laziness, or indifference) are near-synonyms, and neither follows from the clues. The executive to whom he devoted his attentions, on the other hand, was concealing "her financial ruin." But how did she ruin herself? Given that she was nattily-dressed, she probably also spent her money on clothes. *Sartorial* means "relating to clothes or style," so fits the third blank perfectly. *Bombastic* (pompous, pretentious) and *runic* (mysterious) both add meaning that isn't indicated by any clues.

14. A malingerer, trepidatious, sagacity. The first blank options all involve some sort of unreliability, but the clues is that Garth's behavior was "improbably" well-received by his boss, who is a hypochondriac. Since stealing (*embezzler* or *pilferer*) has nothing to do with health, *malingerer* (someone who fakes illness) fits best.

The second blank asks for something similar to "hypochondriac." The boss may be *casuistic* (practicing clever but unsound reasoning) or *imposing* (grand and impressive in appearance), but it's only his *trepidatious*, or "in a state of fear that something may happen," character that ties well with hypochondria. The last blank is a word similar to "foresight"; only *sagacity* fits. *Insipidity* (boringness; dullness) and *temerity* (excessive confidence; audacity) don't agree with "foresight."

15. Lionized, incorrigible, peccadilloes. The leader's "moral shortcomings" are overlooked or ignored. This isn't because he was *impugned* (disputed; called into question), but quite the opposite: he has been *lionized* (given public attention and approval). *Narrativized* (presented in a story) is too neutral; it doesn't address the second part of the sentence. His misogyny, if it is a "considerable moral shortcoming," can't be *waggish* (humorous; mischievous) or *risqué* (indecent; sexually suggestive). Only *incorrigible* (inveterate; irredeemable) fits. Finally, his moral failures are "seen as no more than" small or insignificant sins, or *peccadilloes*, not as such larger failures as *malefactions* (crimes) or *trespasses* (sins).

16. Fairness, catharsis, denouement. There is a contrast between "exploitation and iniquity" and what the film is actually concerned with: the first blank must be the opposite of exploitation or iniquity, that is, *fairness*. *Slavery* and *injustice* are theme traps in agreement with "exploitation and iniquity"; both don't fit considering the pivots "though" and "nevertheless." The film showcases "the elimination of all the protagonist's abusers," which grants the audience something like "closure." The audience hasn't been waiting for *inconclusiveness*. Maybe it has been waiting for *relief*, but *catharsis* is a better fit, since it refers specifically to purging of built-up emotions. Finally, the plot is building up to a resolution, or *denouement*. A *platitude* (trite saying) might leave "much to be desired," but wouldn't provide a "satisfying upheaval." There is no indication that the conclusion of the film was an *embellishment* (an untrue detail added to a story to make it more interesting).

17. Eclecticism, a veneer. You are looking for something that could make a work look less "insubstantial" and that has to do with "breadth"; *insularity* (the narrow point of view resulting from life in a closed, isolated community) and *stringency* (tightness or strictness) imply the opposite of breadth, but *eclecticism* (drawing on a wide variety of sources) fits. *Eclecticism* doesn't give a work a little bit (*iota*) or a mixture (*medley*) of profundity, which means "deep insight"; *eclecticism* gives a work a surface appearance (*veneer*) of profundity.

18. Emend, peremptory. For the first blank, you are looking for something the writer could do to his lengthy tomes that would appease editors; something like "edit," "redact," or "change" seems to fit, and *emend* is a synonymous verb that often has a text as its object (as it does here). He avoids editorial complaints through threats, which are certainly not delicious (*toothsome*) and don't seem to be powerless (*impuissant*)—rather, they prevent complaints from publishers in advance; *peremptory* fits this role.

19. Proximate, protract, proliferation. The first blank asks for a contrast with "distant future"; *remote* is a synonym trap, and *proximate* fits. *Atavistic* (manifesting or reverting to ancestral characteristics) events don't make sense in context. Future discounting involves placing more of a premium on present than on future events, and pleasures are desirable while detriments are not. It follows that subjects will tend to want to promote or prolong (*protract*) present pleasures, not *avert* (avoid by turning away or aside) or *rescind* (revoke) them. This is the common tendency "even at the expense of" a rapid increase in or a large number of (*proliferation*) "future detriments." Neither *malady* (illness) nor *buttressing* (reinforcing) fits in this context.

20. Warrant, license. It is clear from "claims" and the generally derisive tone of the sentence that the author does not think it is possible to deduce matters of fact from logic (that would be pretty silly, come to think about it). Thus, the "she" who is the subject of the text has little *warrant* (justification) for doing this, and just as little *warrant* for using logic to inappropriately derive other "*truths*." A *fallacy* is a "mistaken belief, especially one based on unsound argument"—she has lots of *fallacies*, not the dearth of *fallacy* indicated by "just as little." An *epigram* is a "witticism" or "quip," an extra meaning not indicated by any clues. *License* is similar to *warrant* and serves the same function in the second sentence. The "laws of logic" do not *occlude* (close, cover, or obstruct) or *galvanize* (spur to action) "her proclamation."

MANHATTAN
PREP

Chapter 3
of
Text Completion & Sentence Equivalence

Sentence Equivalence

In This Chapter...

Chapter 3
Sentence Equivalence

Sentence Equivalence questions on the GRE are very similar to single-blank Text Completion questions, with one twist—there are six answer choices, and two of them are correct. For example:

> The judge dismissed Steffen's lawsuit, ruling that since Steffen had been the first to _____ the contract, the company he was suing was no longer obligated to uphold the provisions of the original agreement.
>
> ☐ forswear
> ☐ transmute
> ☐ breach
> ☐ abrogate
> ☐ vituperate
> ☐ slake

Note that the answer choices are marked not with letters (as in, choices A–F), but with checkboxes. Throughout the exam (in math, too), the GRE uses circular radio buttons for questions with one correct answer and square checkboxes to indicate questions with more than one correct answer.

To get a Sentence Equivalence question correct, you must select **both** correct answers—there is no partial credit. In the question above, the correct answer is **breach** and **abrogate**, which both mean "fail to do what is required by."

Take a look at what Educational Testing Service (ETS) has to say about the approach for this question type before revisiting this question.

According to ETS:

> *Like Text Completion questions, Sentence Equivalence questions test the ability to reach a conclusion about how a passage should be completed on the basis of partial information, but to a greater extent they focus on the meaning of the completed whole. Sentence Equivalence questions consist of a single sentence with just one blank, and they ask you to find two choices that both lead to a complete, coherent sentence and that produce sentences that mean the same thing.*

Success on a Sentence Equivalence question sometimes depends on hard vocabulary words in the answer choices, sometimes depends on hard vocabulary words or complex sentence construction in the sentence itself, and sometimes hinges on both of these things at once.

Although the idea of "two correct answers" is an interesting test-making twist, it doesn't actually make the questions any harder for you. In fact, it opens up the strategic tool of Answer Choice Analysis, which will be explained in this chapter.

Many of the skills you have already learned for Text Completion still apply here, such as looking for clues and pivots, and filling in your own word in the blank.

There are two main methods of attack for a Sentence Equivalence question, both of which will be reviewed in the pages that follow:

1. Sentence analysis
2. Answer choice analysis

Sentence Analysis

Like Text Completion questions, Sentence Equivalence questions ask you to fill in a blank based on the information contained in the text around it.

As with Text Completions, it is very important to remember that the sentences are not anything like sentences pulled from a newspaper, with a few words blanked out. In such a real-life case, you might not be able to fill in the missing word—what if the sentence didn't provide any context for figuring out what word should go in the blank?

On the GRE, things have to be much more concrete. In order to construct a Sentence Equivalence question that has two objectively correct answers and four objectively incorrect answers, *the test makers have to specifically construct sentences that have clues planted in them for you to find.*

The clue is always there.

There are four questions you should ask yourself for each Sentence Equivalence question:

1. What is the blank referring to? Call this the "target." To find the target, ask which of the nouns in the sentence the blank is describing, or who is doing the action in the blank and to what.

Note: If the blank represents a verb, you might have two targets. In "The ornery critic _____ the play," the *critic* is performing the action and the *play* is receiving the action. In such a case, think of the target as the relationship between the subject and object. Ask "What happened to the play?" or "What did the critic do to the play?"

2. What does the sentence tell you about the target? This is the "clue." **Do not guess, assume, or use outside information.** The clue will be physically present in the sentence.

3. Does the sentence have a "pivot"? Pivots indicate whether the blank is on the same side as or the opposite side from the clue.

4. What word would you use to fill in the blank in your own words (a "fill-in"), based on the clue?

Remember the four parts: *target, clue, pivot, fill-in*.

Here's an example:

The village's water supply had been _____ ___ by toxic industrial by-products that had seeped into groundwater.

- ☐ adumbrated
- ☐ vitiated
- ☐ abashed
- ☐ adulterated
- ☐ truncated
- ☐ abridged

The blank is about the water supply. Thus, "water supply" is the target. What do you know about it? That "toxic" substances seeped into it. There is no pivot (like "but" or "however") that sends you in the opposite direction. So you are looking for a pair that means something like "contaminated."

The answer is **adulterated** and **vitiated**. *Adulterated* means "contaminated," and *vitiated* means "spoiled, made defective, corrupted." (Of the incorrect answers, *truncated* and *abridged* are similar in meaning, and *adumbrated* and *abashed* are unrelated.)

Try one more:

Unlike the more genial researchers, who often went out together after work, the _____ Dr. Spicer believed that socializing was nothing more than a distraction, and thus made few friends at the lab.

- ☐ sedulous
- ☐ baneful
- ☐ standoffish
- ☐ partisan
- ☐ glacial
- ☐ assiduous

3

The blank is about Dr. Spicer. He or she is the target. The primary clue is the word "unlike," which sets up a comparison between "the more genial X" and "the _____ Dr. Spicer." The rules of a comparison tell you that the blank should be something that means "less genial." Thus, you are looking for a word in the blank that means "unfriendly."

The answer is **standoffish** and **glacial**. Both words can mean "emotionally cold and distant." (*Glacial* can also mean slow, physically cold, or pertaining to glaciers.) *Sedulous* and *assiduous* mean hardworking or persistent. *Baneful* means harmful, and *partisan* means biased, in favor of only one's own side or party.

Drill: Sentence Analysis

Analyze each sentence for target, clue, and pivot, then fill in the blank in your own words. (This drill is kept succinct, as a similar practice set appears in the Text Completion chapter; the skill is the same for both question types.)

1. The biography was neither encomium nor condemnation, but rather a _____ look at a life, its facts verifiable and delivered without commentary.*

2. After her friends betrayed her, she vowed never to trust anyone again, becoming a virtual _____ .

3. While several months of progress had been made on the new highway plan in the early part of the year, it was now questionable whether the plan would ever re-emerge from its current state of _____ , its funding held up while politicians bickered about the changing state of the economy.

4. Josh's generally lackadaisical attitude towards his work caused his boss to suspect that his "moral objection" to the task was really just a way to _____ his duties.

5. In isolation, the data may seem _____ , but when the context is supplied, trends can indeed be isolated.

* In situations where "a" or "an" comes before the blank, the "a" or "an" will often be included with each answer choice rather than in the sentence itself so that some of the answer choices can begin with vowels and some with consonants.

Answers: Sentence Analysis

1. The target is the "biography." What you know about it is that it is neither "encomium nor condemnation." Even without knowing the word "encomium," you could probably figure out from the "nor" that the phrase means "neither praise nor criticism." Thus, the biography must be neutral or in the middle. "Its facts verifiable and delivered without commentary" corroborates this. A good word to fill in the blank would be something like **an objective**, **a disinterested**, or **an unbiased**.

2. The target is the subject of the sentence ("she"). Since her friends "betrayed" her and she has "vowed never to trust" again, a good word to fill the blank would be something like **recluse** or **hermit**.

3. The target is the "highway plan." "While" is an opposite-direction pivot, indicating that the fill-in should be on the opposite side of making progress. Indeed, you are given the clue that the project's funding is held up (tied up or delayed). A good fill-in would be something like **gridlock**, **deadlock**, or simply **not moving**.

4. The target is both "Josh" and his "duties"—or, the relationship between Josh and the duties. The clues are that the boss "suspects" (which has a negative connotation) that Josh's "moral objections" (the quotes in the original sentence also indicate suspicion) are motivated by something else. One more clue fills in the blank for us—the fact that Josh is "lackadaisical" (casual or lazy). A good fill-in would be **avoid** or **shirk**.

5. The target is the "data." You know that, "with context," trends can be found. So your blank should disagree with the notion that one can find trends in something. A good fill-in would be **random** or **chaotic**.

Answer Choice Analysis

When Educational Testing Service introduced the Sentence Equivalence format, most people's natural response was, "So we pick a pair of synonyms, right?" ETS officials insist that the two correct answers don't have to be
synonyms:

> Do not simply look among the answer choices for two words that mean the same thing. This can be misleading for two reasons. First, the answer choices may contain pairs of words that mean the same thing but do not fit coherently into the sentence, and thus do not constitute a correct answer. Second, the pair of words that do constitute the correct answer may not mean exactly the same thing, since all that matters is that the resultant sentences mean the same thing.

Hmmn. When the two correct answers are inserted into the sentence, the resulting sentences mean the same thing? Sounds like those words would have to be pretty close, right?

Theoretically, the GRE could give a question like this one:

Miriam broke up with John because he was _____ .

- ☐ boring
- ☐ handsome
- ☐ limber
- ☐ unintelligent
- ☐ kind
- ☐ fun

Since Miriam "broke up" (your clue) with John (your target), you are looking for something bad. There are only two matches: **boring** and **unintelligent**. These two words certainly are not synonyms, although each makes sense in the sentence.

However, there is little evidence for this type of "loose construction" on the GRE. A question like the one above, in which the correct choices really aren't synonyms, would have to have answers that fall into pretty easily distinguishable categories (e.g., "something bad"). Most of those questions would fall on the easy side.

What seems to be going on is that the GRE is being overly respectful of the English language. To quote the famous science-fiction writer Theodore Sturgeon, "There are no synonyms." In other words, subtleties of meaning separate **any** two words you find listed in any individual entry in a thesaurus. *Deluge* and *flood* **don't** mean the exact same thing (a *deluge* is, by definition, a **severe** flood), and the GRE wants you to recognize that the two words you pick will likely differ in terms of some similar nuance. However, unless you are trying to write some very stylish and precise prose, the difference between *deluge* and *flood* doesn't really matter.

On the actual GRE, it is almost always the case that the two correct answers are pretty close to being synonyms. Here's an example:

> Many people at the dinner party were inordinately interested in questioning the _____ new guest, who refused to reveal his profession or even the origin of his exotic accent.
>
> ☐ acerbic
> ☐ mysterious
> ☐ insightful
> ☐ trenchant
> ☐ intrepid
> ☐ inscrutable

Look for clues. The blank describes the new guest. You know that this guest is very cagey about himself. You're looking for a word like *secretive* or *mysterious*.

As it turns out, **mysterious** and **inscrutable** are the correct answers. *Inscrutable* means "not able to be scrutinized" and often indicates hiding emotions. It's not exactly the same thing as *mysterious*, but there's a substantial overlap in their meanings.

You've discovered that most correct answer pairs are at least as closely related as these two. For the purposes of this book, call them "near-synonyms."

Finding Near-Synonym Pairs

Most Sentence Equivalence questions have a built-in secret strategy: answer choice analysis. This is because most sets of answer choices are "two by two"—that is, among the six choices there are two pairs of synonyms and two "loose," unrelated words.

Typical "two by two":

> horrible
> nice
> pleasant
> impoverished
> terrible
> dying

Horrible and *terrible* are a pair. *Pleasant* and *nice* are a pair. *Impoverished* and *dying* are unrelated.

Here is a weaker variant of a "two by two":

> wicked
> healthful
> evil
> qualified
> gifted
> well-practiced

Wicked and *evil* are a pair. *Gifted* and *well-practiced* are "sort of" a pair—that is, *gifted* implies an ability that comes from within, whereas *well-practiced* implies an ability that comes from, obviously, practice. However, both are different paths to the same goal (being talented or skilled). They're a weak pair.

In any sentence, it should be pretty easy to tell whether *wicked/evil* or *gifted/well-practiced* is the more appropriate match. However, *in the case that a set of choices provides a closely related pair and a less closely related pair, the more closely related pair is more likely to be the answer.*

Occasionally, three words will seem to match up (a "triplet"). Usually, in this case, two are really synonyms, and the other is off in terms of spin or strength. For instance, in the case of *excoriate, admonish,* and *castigate*, the real pair is *excoriate* and *castigate*—both mean to criticize or scold very harshly, and *admonish* means to scold mildly. (Note that if all three "triplets" really were synonyms, they would necessarily all be wrong as a result, since there can only be two correct answers. However, this is unlikely.)

False triplet:

> determined
> talkative
> hapless
> unsuccessful
> unlucky
> resolute

Determined and *resolute* are a pair. *Hapless, unsuccessful,* and *unlucky* seem to be a "triplet." (*Talkative* is not related to the others.)

However, *hapless* really does mean *unlucky* ("hap" is actually a rarely used Old English word for "luck" or "lot"). A person can be unsuccessful without being unlucky. *Hapless* and *unlucky* are the true pair.

It is also possible to have just one pair, or three.

Only one pair:

> pale
> flexible
> hidden
> celebrated
> equitable
> fair

Equitable and *fair* are a pair. The other four words are unrelated.

Three pairs:

> candid
> latent
> ingenuous
> inimical
> dormant
> hostile

Candid and *ingenuous* are a pair. *Latent* and *dormant* are a pair. *Inimical* and *hostile* are a pair.

While all of these answer choice patterns are possible, the most common by far is the "two by two."

When to Use Answer Choice Analysis

To use Answer Choice Analysis as your main tool for Sentence Equivalence questions, you can actually proceed to the choices first, before even reading the sentence. For instance:

*Blah blah blah blah blah blah blah blah blah blah blah blah blah
_____, blah blah blah blah blah blah blah blah blah.*

- ☐ myrmidons
- ☐ aesthetes
- ☐ tyros
- ☐ lackeys
- ☐ anchorites
- ☐ novices

Go straight to the words and attempt to make pairs: *myrmidons* and *lackeys* are subordinates who follow without question. *Tyros* and *novices* are both beginners. An *aesthete* loves or studies beauty, and an *anchorite* is a recluse, especially a religious hermit, and thus those two words are not related.

Therefore, the answer must be *myrmidons/lackeys* or *tyros/novices*. The only question you need to ask is, "Does the sentence call for a 'suck-up' or a 'beginner?' Here is the complete problem:

> It may be true that everyone likes flattery, but a good manager is not unduly persuaded by it, and thus not taken in by _____ , who use wheedling and fawning to get ahead.
>
> ☐ myrmidons
> ☐ aesthetes
> ☐ tyros
> ☐ lackeys
> ☐ anchorites
> ☐ novices

Of course, the question is calling for **myrmidons** and **lackeys**.

This approach can be very effective in cases where you know all of the words in the choices. However, since most test-takers don't have strong enough vocabularies to be able to complete the Answer Choice Analysis consistently, Sentence Analysis will probably be a first line of attack for many people, and Answer Choice Analysis a backup plan.

Drill: Answer Choice Analysis

For each set of choices, match up the "pairs." Most, but not all, sets of choices consist of two pairs of near-synonyms and two other, unrelated words. A few will have one or three sets of near-synonyms.

1. verbose
   turbid
   diffident
   prolix
   self-effacing
   pious

2. amicable
   pithy
   scholarly
   arcane
   succinct
   esoteric

3. distend
   traduce
   alienate
   flatter
   slander
   complement

4. auxiliary
   cardinal
   principal
   ordinal
   collateral
   prefatory

5. hawkish
   cogent
   turgid
   eloquent
   bombastic
   intelligible

6. pellucid
   transparent
   rustic
   sedulous
   assiduous
   earthy

7. eclecticism
   aberrance
   deviation
   idiosyncrasy
   adulation
   eccentricity

8. bevy
   modicum
   paucity
   excess
   surfeit
   bunch

9. machicolation
   epitome
   scruple
   apothegm
   contumely
   maxim

10. pique
    slake
    quench
    succor
    fructify
    stimulate

MANHATTAN
PREP

Answers: Answer Choice Analysis

1.   2 pairs: **Verbose** and **prolix** are a pair, each meaning "talkative." **Diffident** (lacking confidence) and **self-effacing** (putting oneself down) are a pair; they are not perfect synonyms, but they are close enough for Sentence Equivalence questions on the GRE. *Pious* and *turbid* have no relationship.

2.   2 pairs: **Pithy** and **succinct** both mean "short and to the point." **Arcane** and **esoteric** both mean "obscure or specialized, known to only a few" (of information). *Amicable* and *scholarly* are not related.

3.   1 pair: **Traduce** and **slander** are a pair, meaning "tell malicious lies about." **Complement** and **flatter** are a TRAP—*complement* (to complete, to make up a whole with) is NOT the same word as *compliment* (to say something nice about). *Distend* and *alienate* are also unrelated.

4.   2 pairs: **Auxiliary** and **collateral** mean "secondary, off to the side." **Cardinal** and **principal** (first, main) are actually synonyms with each other *and* antonyms with auxiliary and collateral. *Ordinal* and *prefatory* are not related.

5.   2 pairs: **Turgid** and **bombastic** are a pair. *Bombastic* means "pompous, overinflated" and is used to describe speech. While *turgid* can simply mean "swollen," when it is applied to speech, it has the same meaning of "overinflated, showing off." **Eloquent** and **cogent** are a weak pair—*eloquent* means beautiful and articulate (of speech), and *cogent* means compellingly persuasive. *Intelligible* and *hawkish* are not related.

6.   3 pairs: **Pellucid** and **transparent** are a pair (see-through), as are **rustic** and **earthy** (primitive, of the earth, undeveloped), and **assiduous** and **sedulous** (hardworking).

7.   2 pairs: **Aberrance** and **deviation** are a pair (being different from the normal). *Eclecticism, idiosyncrasy* and *eccentricity* may all seem similar. However, **idiosyncrasy** and **eccentricity** (harmless personal oddness) are a true pair. *Eclecticism* (having mixed, wide-ranging tastes) is somewhat different, and is also unrelated to *adulation*.

8.   2 or 3 pairs: **Bevy** and **bunch** are a pair, as are **surfeit** and **excess**. **Modicum** and **paucity** are questionable as a pair because they differ in spin—*modicum* means a little, and *paucity* means not enough.

9.   1 pair: **Apothegm** and **maxim** are a pair (proverb, pithy statement). *Machicolation, epitome, scruple,* and *contumely* are unrelated.

10. 2 pairs: **Pique** and **stimulate** are a pair. **Slake** and **quench** (satisfy, especially of thirst) are a pair. *Succor* (provide comfort or relief) might seem related the second pair, but one *succors* a person, and one *slakes* or *quenches* a desire. *Fructify* is unrelated.

What If I Don't Know the Words?

It almost seems as though this new question type on the GRE was designed to prevent lucky guesses. On a typical multiple-choice question with choices A–E, a test-taker has a 1/5 chance of randomly guessing the correct answer. On a Sentence Equivalence, a random guess of two out of the six answers has only a 1/15 chance of being correct.

If you know *one* of the correct choices and randomly guess on the other, your chance of getting the question correct is 1/5.

Thus, it is very important that you assiduously augment your vocabulary, which is why so much of this book is dedicated to learning words.

That said, a little answer choice analysis can be helpful in making a good guess.

Most Sentence Equivalence questions match the "two-by-two" format; that is, the answer choices contain two pairs of near-synonyms and two other "loose" words. Thus, if you can find a single pair of synonyms in the choices, there is about a 1/2 chance that that pair is correct (it is only "about" one-half, since not all sets of choices follow a "two-by-two" format). Here is an example:

- ☐ agog
- ☐ akimbo
- ☐ obeisant
- ☐ dyspeptic
- ☐ kowtowing
- ☐ crotchety

If you were able to pick out that *dyspeptic* and *crotchety* were a pair—or that *obeisant* and *kowtowing* were—then you should test that pair in the sentence and pick it if it seems to be a good match. (As will be the case in most questions, the two remaining words, *agog* and *akimbo*, have no relationship.)

If the pair that you are able to find is not a fit for the sentence, cross off both words. You now have a 1/6 chance of guessing correctly.

If you cannot find a synonym pair, you are unlikely to get the question correct. Accept that fact and don't waste time. Your strategy here is simply to make a guess and move on, conserving time for questions that you will be able to answer later.

Although the new GRE allows you to move around within a section and come back to questions you previously left blank or wish to reconsider, keep in mind that, **if you don't know the words, you won't do any better by attempting the question twice**—you'll only waste time and lower your overall score.

If you don't know the words, **do not leave the question blank**. Make your best guess and move on. Don't waste time coming back—spend that extra time on Reading Comprehension or other vocabulary questions that you are able to answer more effectively.

In sum: learn the words!

MANHATTAN
PREP

Why It Is Important to Learn Words in Context

Educational Testing Service tells you not only to check that the two answers you select for a question create sentences that mean the same thing, but also to make sure that each one "produces a sentence that is logically, grammatically, and stylistically coherent."

Hmm. Asking test-takers to check that the completed sentences are "grammatically coherent" implies that some of the choices will create sentences that are not. Here's an example:

> Education advocates argued that the free school lunch program was vital to creating a school environment _____ to learning.
>
> ☐ conducive
> ☐ inimical
> ☐ substantial
> ☐ appropriate
> ☐ beneficial
> ☐ hostile

"Education advocates" are certainly in favor of learning; your fill-in might be something like *helpful*.

Looking at the choices, *conducive*, *appropriate*, and *beneficial* all seem to be matches.

However, if you place each word into the sentence, one choice creates an incorrect idiom. "Conducive *to*" works, and "beneficial *to*," but "appropriate to learning" is not a correct idiom —instead, you would say "appropriate *for* learning."

Thus, it is important not only to memorize dictionary definitions of words, but also to be able to use those words in context, in a grammatically correct way.

Here's another example:

> He's a _____ fellow, always grandstanding and deploying his formidable lexicon for oratorical effect.
>
> ☐ declamatory
> ☐ grandiloquent
> ☐ didactic
> ☐ florid
> ☐ titanic
> ☐ cabalistic

The target is "he" and the clue is "grandstanding and deploying his formidable lexicon for oratorical effect"; that is, he speaks in a pompous way, as though showing off his vocabulary for an audience.

The word *florid* seems appropriate—it means "flowery" and often applies to speech, as in "florid poetry." But wait! *Florid* applies to writing, speech, decor, etc.—not the people who produce those things! (Actually, you can apply *florid* to people, but in that context it means "flushed, ruddy," as in having rosy cheeks, which is not appropriate here.)

The answer is **declamatory** and **grandiloquent**, both of which describe pompous orators (that is, people who make speeches) or the speech of such people.

Memorizing that *florid* means "flowery" is better than nothing, but doesn't really tell you what kinds of things to describe with that word, or how to use it metaphorically. Once again, it is important to learn words in context.

There are several ways to do this. Manhattan Prep's GRE vocabulary flashcards provide example sentences for all 1,000 words. Many online dictionaries provide quotes from literature in which the word being defined is used in context. In some cases, it is fruitful to simply Google a word to see how different writers are using it.

Whatever your process, your goal is to be able to do two things for any given word. First, to define it in a concise and straightforward way. Second, to be able to use it in a sentence in a descriptive way (such that someone reading the sentence would understand what it meant from the context).

You want to be comfortable when seeing a word used in any legitimate way. For instance, you would have no trouble if the word "darkness" were used metaphorically ("While she at first resisted going on antidepressants, she ultimately decided that she would do anything that might lift the darkness"), or if the word "enthusiastic" were used sarcastically ("As enthusiastic as I am about unnecessary surgery, I will have to decline your offer to appear on an extreme makeover reality show").

To perform excellently on the GRE, that's how well you want to know your new words: inside and out. You want to be *flexible* in how you use and interpret those words. The "Learning Vocabulary" chapter of this book provides more guidance for formidably augmenting your lexicon.

Drill: 20 Easy Questions

1. The children's story—seemingly a simple tale of animals gathering for a picnic in the forest—took a _____ turn at the end, admonishing readers to always be honest.

   ☐ magnanimous
   ☐ beneficent
   ☐ didactic
   ☐ garrulous
   ☐ moralistic
   ☐ futile

2. Floodwaters had already breached the library's walls, but hopeful volunteers in hip boots worked tirelessly to _____ the damage.

   ☐ mitigate
   ☐ exacerbate
   ☐ abase
   ☐ bolster
   ☐ forestall
   ☐ flummox

3. The candidate campaigned on a platform of willingness to cooperate with the members of other political parties, yet many commentators were nevertheless surprised that he indeed turned out to be less _____ than his predecessor.

   ☐ irate
   ☐ divisive
   ☐ impulsive
   ☐ wily
   ☐ infuriated
   ☐ combative

4. When Sven got angry, whether it was during an argument with his family or with just a coworker, it proved almost impossible to _____ him and thereby return him to his normal demeanor.

   ☐ condemn
   ☐ pacify
   ☐ judge
   ☐ incense
   ☐ mollify
   ☐ influence

5. The graduate student's experiment yielded results as surprising as they were promising; her next step was to pursue additional data that would _____ her findings.

    - ☐ undergird
    - ☐ buttress
    - ☐ gainsay
    - ☐ undermine
    - ☐ eschew
    - ☐ lecture

3

6. There is no fundamental difference between a person who quietly _____ a bigoted viewpoint to a friend and one who spews chauvinist vitriol on television.

    - ☐ eschews
    - ☐ espouses
    - ☐ professes
    - ☐ denies
    - ☐ reneges
    - ☐ substantiates

7. A 1957 lawsuit against the U.S. Department of Agriculture regarding aerial pesticide spraying was the _____ for Rachel Carson to begin the writing of her environmentalist manifesto *Silent Spring*, though she had become concerned about and started researching the practice years earlier.

    - ☐ stimulus
    - ☐ conspiracy
    - ☐ atrocity
    - ☐ impetus
    - ☐ catastrophe
    - ☐ climate

8. A commentator with a more _____ worldview would not find it so easy to divide up the nation into good guys and bad guys.

    - ☐ belligerent
    - ☐ subtle
    - ☐ philosophical
    - ☐ aberrant
    - ☐ peaceful
    - ☐ nuanced

9. James Joyce's *Finnegan's Wake*, written in a stream of consciousness style full of convo-
    luted puns and obscure allusions, has a deserved reputation for linguistic _____ .

    - ☐ caprice
    - ☐ opacity
    - ☐ meaninglessness
    - ☐ informality
    - ☐ uniqueness
    - ☐ inscrutability

10. The financial situation in many European nations is _____ enough that
    even a small incident could lead to catastrophe.

    - ☐ drab
    - ☐ unstable
    - ☐ illegitimate
    - ☐ unsafe
    - ☐ precarious
    - ☐ churlish

11. While the argument for global warming may not be _____ by the record
    low temperatures reported this year, this data does not undermine the overall trend
    of steadily higher global temperatures.

    - ☐ bolstered
    - ☐ fortified
    - ☐ subverted
    - ☐ defined
    - ☐ supplanted
    - ☐ subordinated

12. The debate coach expected some gravitas from her team, arguing that pithy quips
    and gibes, while sometimes effective, had no place in a _____ argument.

    - ☐ polite
    - ☐ shallow
    - ☐ competitive
    - ☐ serious
    - ☐ cantankerous
    - ☐ substantive

13. Last year it was discovered that *South Park* writers _____ part of its *Inception* spoof from a similar *College Humor* sketch.

   ☐ amalgamated
   ☐ filched
   ☐ indulged
   ☐ combined
   ☐ poached
   ☐ assumed

14. Some critics view Abstract Expressionism, which is characterized by geometric shapes and swathes of color, as a _____ of realist painting.

   ☐ rejection
   ☐ manifestation
   ☐ renunciation
   ☐ memento
   ☐ commemoration
   ☐ vindication

15. The nascent United States' first spy, Nathan Hale, was captured by the British when he attempted to _____ British-controlled New York City to track enemy troop movements.

   ☐ thwart
   ☐ penetrate
   ☐ infiltrate
   ☐ permeate
   ☐ research
   ☐ conquer

16. Romantic comedies of the 1950s were characterized more by sexual _____ than the straightforward vulgarity that characterizes dialogue in today's "rom-coms."

   ☐ conversation
   ☐ blatancy
   ☐ insinuation
   ☐ illusion
   ☐ innuendo
   ☐ rapport

17. Inflation isn't dead, only _____; as the economy turns around, the purchasing power of the dollar is likely to fall again.

- [ ] paralyzed
- [ ] dormant
- [ ] indigent
- [ ] itinerant
- [ ] problematic
- [ ] inactive

18. Some boxers talk about trying to access their more _____ selves in order to counter the fact that civilized people generally don't punch each other in the face.

- [ ] seething
- [ ] barbaric
- [ ] irate
- [ ] insidious
- [ ] dynamic
- [ ] primitive

19. Many people assume that creative work is less _____ than manual labor, but they underestimate the difficulty of being entirely self-motivated (as well as writing one's own paychecks).

- [ ] inventive
- [ ] collaborative
- [ ] serious
- [ ] arduous
- [ ] taxing
- [ ] grave

20. The education debate is only getting more _____ as politicians demonize teachers unions and every special interest group jumps into the fray.

- [ ] vehement
- [ ] overt
- [ ] heated
- [ ] problematic
- [ ] tired
- [ ] unavoidable

Drill: 20 Medium Questions

1. While many individual religions insist on the primacy of their particular deity, syncretism advocates the _____ of multiple religious beliefs, attempting to reconcile even opposing principles and practices.

☐ exclusion
☐ marriage
☐ commingling
☐ division
☐ transgression
☐ schism

2. The ambassador was invested with _____ power by his government and hence was able to draft and finalize the agreement unilaterally, without first consulting with even the president.

☐ tertiary
☐ consummate
☐ enigmatic
☐ tyrannical
☐ complete
☐ dictatorial

3. Sometimes it seems that today's politicians will exploit any opportunity to _____ their views to the world, no matter how sordid or partisan.

☐ declaim
☐ invoke
☐ disparage
☐ parrot
☐ adduce
☐ trumpet

4. The many chapters of the organization decided that a mandatory national _____ would be necessary to reconcile what had become a haphazard and often chaotic set of bylaws and regulations.

☐ introduction
☐ acclamation
☐ intervention
☐ colloquium
☐ symposium
☐ mediation

MANHATTAN
PREP

5. Though it seems implausible that one could be a great writer without some experi-
    ence of life, many famous authors have led a _____ and solitary existence.

    ☐ idiosyncratic
    ☐ cloistered
    ☐ susceptible
    ☐ enigmatic
    ☐ sheltered
    ☐ cryptic

6. Though he wasn't particularly well-known as a humanitarian, his deep sense of
    responsibility for those who were suffering was real, and was belied by an outward
    appearance of _____ .

    ☐ concern
    ☐ sagacity
    ☐ mirth
    ☐ felicity
    ☐ nonchalance
    ☐ indifference

7. Excessive patriotism is by definition _____ , as the elevation of one
    country to the rank of quintessential on Earth necessarily requires some amount of
    demonization of other people.

    ☐ minatory
    ☐ xenophobic
    ☐ unethical
    ☐ bigoted
    ☐ nationalistic
    ☐ truculent

8. One possible explanation for the mandatory debauchery of most bachelor parties is
    that if the husband-to-be is able to practice _____ in those circumstances,
    he must be ready for marriage.

    ☐ forbearance
    ☐ gentility
    ☐ fiat
    ☐ tenacity
    ☐ temperance
    ☐ autonomy

9. Jon Stewart's "Rally to Restore Sanity" was purportedly organized to prove that it was possible to discuss politics humorously but civilly, without _____ those on the other side of the fence.

    ☐ bespeaking
    ☐ eulogizing
    ☐ lampooning
    ☐ vilifying
    ☐ caricaturing
    ☐ maligning

10. Though occasionally used in practice, very few forms of corporal punishment have been _____ by the military, due less to the Geneva Conventions than to the overwhelmingly negative popular response to reports of abuse.

    ☐ upbraided
    ☐ sanctioned
    ☐ endorsed
    ☐ considered
    ☐ rejected
    ☐ polarized

11. The budget debate progressed well for the first few months, in spite of all the ardent and sometimes bitter squabbling, but slowly descended into a _____ of competing interests and claims.

    ☐ quagmire
    ☐ covenant
    ☐ feud
    ☐ morass
    ☐ quarrel
    ☐ accord

12. The difference between similes and metaphors is subtle, but for the poet who takes his or her work seriously, absolutely _____ .

    ☐ synoptic
    ☐ null
    ☐ optional
    ☐ crucial
    ☐ nominal
    ☐ requisite

13. It is _____ reasoning to characterize Keynesian economics as recommending that the limit on how much debt the government can incur should be perpetually raised, when Keynes states clearly that deficit spending must be done responsibly.

   ☐ indigenous
   ☐ corrupt
   ☐ venial
   ☐ fallacious
   ☐ specious
   ☐ axiomatic

14. In many ways, teenage rebellion can be seen as the effect of a communication gap between an older generation's calcified language and the protean _____ of the new generation.

   ☐ patois
   ☐ defiance
   ☐ prolixity
   ☐ insubordination
   ☐ verbosity
   ☐ jargon

15. His cantankerous reputation was cemented by years of _____ at every conceivable opportunity.

   ☐ Imputing
   ☐ grousing
   ☐ assaulting
   ☐ protesting
   ☐ convulsing
   ☐ imbibing

16. Last St. Patrick's Day, the police were called when people in the neighborhood witnessed a small _____ in progress outside of a bar.

   ☐ fracas
   ☐ discourse
   ☐ altercation
   ☐ battle
   ☐ colloquy
   ☐ mutiny

17. Given her sheltered upbringing and the limited breadth of experience imposed on her by economic circumstance, her work reflected a surprisingly _____ sensibility.

- ☐ shallow
- ☐ eclectic
- ☐ profound
- ☐ multifarious
- ☐ callow
- ☐ facile

3

18. Many people expect documentary filmmakers to be dispassionate and objective, but Michael Moore has a reputation for never missing a chance to _____ against those with whom he disagrees.

- ☐ rail
- ☐ advertise
- ☐ fulminate
- ☐ inveigle
- ☐ strain
- ☐ aspirate

19. The movie critic was best remembered for the way he used the language of food to describe films, for example, how he praised Iñarritu's action sequences by comparing them to a _____ empanada.

- ☐ insipid
- ☐ spectacular
- ☐ brilliant
- ☐ piquant
- ☐ zesty
- ☐ stupefying

20. Every few years, someone manages to survive a skydive with a parachute that doesn't open, often with only a few broken bones, some _____, and a gash or two.

- ☐ torpor
- ☐ trauma
- ☐ bruises
- ☐ finesse
- ☐ lesions
- ☐ contusions

Drill: 20 Hard Questions

1. As official _____ from Japan to this country, he was called upon to answer questions about the Japanese government's position on various issues.

    - ☐ envoy
    - ☐ tyro
    - ☐ emissary
    - ☐ neophyte
    - ☐ ascetic
    - ☐ libertine

2. While the group's street protests had had an aggressive, uncompromising tenor, once admitted to the halls of power to begin formal lobbying, its leaders wisely chose to _____ the stridency of their rhetoric.

    - ☐ metamorphose
    - ☐ gild
    - ☐ wane
    - ☐ palliate
    - ☐ succor
    - ☐ damp

3. The women's rights movement has been mostly _____ in the Middle East, but it is likely that activists will be newly galvanized by the political upheavals currently sweeping the region.

    - ☐ dogged
    - ☐ quiescent
    - ☐ interminable
    - ☐ lissome
    - ☐ abeyant
    - ☐ feckless

4. Debate rages on between proponents and detractors of corporal punishment and the death penalty, though even the most ardent supporter agrees that punishments must be _____ and the justice system evenhanded and thorough.

    - ☐ equitable
    - ☐ clement
    - ☐ delimited
    - ☐ apposite
    - ☐ tantamount
    - ☐ merciful

5. Peer-reviewed journals are a sacred cow of most scientific rationalists, but studies have shown that the premise of impartiality is _____ , as results tend to be colored by the personal proclivities and suppositions of the experimenters.

☐ inane
☐ prejudicial
☐ fatuous
☐ chimerical
☐ fallible
☐ vexing

6. The description of the restaurant as a garden of _____ delights is fair enough, as Chef Marcel conjures up a menu of texture and taste that calls into question one's preconceived notions of what constitutes a meal.

☐ salubrious
☐ epicurean
☐ carnal
☐ voluptuous
☐ terrestrial
☐ gustatory

7. Most of his books drone on and on for chapter after chapter, each one providing yet another example of his thesis, the _____ of which can be found in précis form in the tome's first few pages, and which is recapitulated from that point on.

☐ gist
☐ adage
☐ pith
☐ stub
☐ nimbus
☐ nut

8. In order to ascertain the efficacy of the new GRE vis-à-vis the old one, it will be necessary not only to collect, but also to _____ detailed score reports from test-takers from both groups, as only by studying the differences and similarities in results can proper inferences be drawn.

☐ aggregate
☐ ratiocinate
☐ collate
☐ juxtapose
☐ agglomerate
☐ glean

9. In World War I, trenches were dug so that the soldiers could avoid the near constant
    _____ from the other side of the line of battle, but not even a trench could
    protect a battalion from grenades or aerial bombardment.

    ☐ volleys
    ☐ provocations
    ☐ fervency
    ☐ imprecations
    ☐ goadings
    ☐ salvos

10. Cary Grant's reputation as a suave and _____ ladies man extended beyond
    the silver screen to his real life, where he was known to never let a woman pull out
    her own chair, in keeping with the custom of gentlemen at that time.

    ☐ consummate
    ☐ genteel
    ☐ debonair
    ☐ waggish
    ☐ courtly
    ☐ cosmopolitan

11. Focusing primarily on self-awareness, empathy, and honest self-expression, the
    communication process known as "nonviolent communication" states that the
    attempt to find parity in a relationship is a fallacious principle, as any notion of
    fairness is entirely _____ .

    ☐ subjective
    ☐ introverted
    ☐ pragmatic
    ☐ utilitarian
    ☐ illicit
    ☐ personal

12. Education has become a kind of albatross in American politics, in that a speech with
    any hint of _____ is actually more pernicious to a politician's reputation
    than one with numerous signs of ignorance, or even outright stupidity.

    ☐ bromide
    ☐ erudition
    ☐ patrimony
    ☐ condescension
    ☐ cerebrality
    ☐ bloviation

13. Laurent Cantet's *Time Out* tells the true story of a man so obsessed with retaining the _____ of plenitude even after he is discharged from his employment that he doesn't even tell his wife and his kids about his termination.

- ☐ corollaries
- ☐ paradigms
- ☐ semblance
- ☐ prepossessions
- ☐ veneer
- ☐ consequences

14. What people fail to remember about Don Juan is that his astronomical number of amatory adventures were due more to his _____ approach to seduction than any surfeit of charisma or skillfulness.

- ☐ sumptuous
- ☐ lurid
- ☐ covert
- ☐ indiscriminate
- ☐ blanket
- ☐ sybaritic

15. Even the most far-reaching campaign finance reform proposals will fail to_____ the influence of money, which doesn't just buy speedboats and golf weekends in the Bahamas, but directly relates to a politician's capacity to run for office.

- ☐ attenuate
- ☐ graft
- ☐ pander
- ☐ abate
- ☐ importune
- ☐ indemnify

16. In their landmark study of Victorian literature's relationship to feminism, Gilbert and Gubar _____ the many ways in which 19th-century women writers created characters that fit into archetypes of "angel" and "monster."

- ☐ interrogate
- ☐ interpolate
- ☐ debunk
- ☐ limn
- ☐ explode
- ☐ castigate

17. While it's inarguably prejudiced to imply that there is some kind of innate
_____ in certain countries, it's more reasonable to say that certain cultures
are more willing to prioritize relaxation and a sense of moderation between work and
play.

    ☐ obtundity
    ☐ enfeeblement
    ☐ enervation
    ☐ languor
    ☐ seemliness
    ☐ lethargy

18. Autodidacts may argue that the enforced lucubration of a standard education is
_____ , but while some people are able to learn without outside guidance
and strictures, most people learn better when accountable to others.

    ☐ slack
    ☐ prudent
    ☐ lax
    ☐ extraneous
    ☐ unnecessary
    ☐ sagacious

19. The best of Sigur Ros's music evokes _____ landscape, as if the music had
transported one to some twilit avenue in a long since abandoned city.

    ☐ a dusky
    ☐ an urban
    ☐ a crepuscular
    ☐ a precipitous
    ☐ an avuncular
    ☐ a civic

20. Some historians argue that at least in so far as the broad strokes are concerned,
cataclysmic events such as the Great Depression are _____ , due to what
some have termed "the inertia of history."

    ☐ ineluctable
    ☐ incontrovertible
    ☐ interminable
    ☐ infallible
    ☐ inexorable
    ☐ unspeakable

Solutions: 20 Easy Questions

1. **Didactic, Moralistic.** The children's story was "seemingly" simple—which means it was not actually simple. Instead, the story took some kind of "turn"—meaning that it changed in some way—and "admonished readers to always be honest." That is, it took a turn by talking about morals or prescribing correct behavior.

    Magnanimous (generous) and *beneficent* (good, or doing good) are an incorrect pair. *Garrulous* (overly talkative, wordy) and *futile* (ineffective, useless) have no relationship.

2. **Mitigate, Forestall.** That "floodwaters had already breached the library's walls" sounds very bad—the water is already inside. The pivot "but" tells you that the sentence is going to change direction, and indeed, the volunteers are "hopeful," so you're looking for something good in the blank—although it doesn't seem like they're going to cure the problem entirely. A good fill-in would be something like "limit" or "hold back."

    Exacerbate (make more severe, aggravate), *abase* (reduce in prestige, humiliate), *bolster* (support, boost), and *flummox* (confuse) do not contain any pairs.

3. **Divisive, Combative.** The most important words here are the pivots "nevertheless surprised" and "indeed," which tell you that the candidate actually stayed true to his campaign promise. That means he acted cooperatively, which is contrasted with the actions of his predecessor. A good fill-in would be "uncooperative."

    Irate and *infuriated*, both of which mean "angry," are an incorrect pair. *Impulsive* (moved or swayed by emotional or involuntary urges) and *wily* (crafty or cunning) have no relationship.

4. **Pacify, Mollify.** This sentence provides the clues that when Steve "got angry," returning him "to his normal demeanor" was "almost impossible." His normal demeanor must be something like "not angry," so you're looking for something like the verb "calm" in the blank.

    Condemn (censure; sentence), *judge* (form an opinion about), *incense* (infuriate), and *influence* (determine or guide) do not contain any pairs, though *condemn* and *judge* are close.

5. **Undergird, Buttress.** The target is both the data and the findings—the blank contains what the data will do to the findings. You have the clue that the results were promising (but surprising, indicating some uncertainty about the apparent conclusion), and you have a same-direction pivot (the semicolon). Thus, her next step would likely be to "verify" or "corroborate" the findings.

    Gainsay (deny or prove false) and *undermine* (weaken or subvert secretly) are a pair. *Eschew* (shun, avoid, or abstain from) and *lecture* (speak at length) are unrelated.

6. **Espouses, Professes.** This sentence originally posits that there is "no fundamental difference" between two things, but the overall point is that the two things do look different on the surface. That means you want someone who does the opposite of "spews chauvinist vitriol on television," such as someone who quietly "expresses" it. A good fill-in would be "communicates."

Denies and *reneges* (renounces or denies) are an incorrect pair. *Eschews* is also pretty close to that pair. *Substantiates* goes beyond "communicates," meaning to support or verify, and is too positive to go with "a bigoted viewpoint."

7. **Stimulus, Impetus.** Prior to 1957, Rachel Carson was already concerned about aerial pesticide spraying, but the lawsuit caused her to begin work on the book. A good fill-in would be "inspiration."

Atrocity (extremely wicked or cruel act) and *catastrophe* (disaster) have similar spins, but they are not really a pair. *Climate* (the general weather conditions in an area over a long period), which presents a theme trap, and *conspiracy* (a secret plan by two or more people to do something unlawful) have no relationship.

8. **Subtle, Nuanced.** In this sentence, the commentator is described as finding it easy to split people into "good ... and bad" categories. This is a very simplistic way of looking at the world. Someone with a more complex worldview would be unlikely to break things down so simplistically.

Belligerent (inclined to aggressive hostility), *philosophical* (devoted to the study of knowledge; calm about difficulties or disappointments), *aberrant* (deviating from the normal or proper course, especially in behavior, or atypical), and *peaceful* (tranquil) have no relationship.

9. **Opacity, Inscrutability.** Joyce's book is described as "stream of consciousness," with "convoluted puns and obscure allusions." The adjectives "convoluted" and "obscure" are the most important part of this sentence. They tell you that the novel is likely hard to understand. A good fill-in would be "difficulty" (specifically, of understanding).

Elaborateness (marked by complex detail; intricacy), *meaninglessness* (nonsense), *informality* (relaxed style), and *uniqueness* (the quality of being one of a kind) have no relationship. While *meaninglessness* might seem tempting, it's too extreme to be correct.

10. **Unstable, Precarious.** The situation in Europe is described as bad enough that even a small incident might lead to a catastrophe. This means that everything is on the brink of disaster. You could fill in the blank with something like "shaky."

Drab (dull, colorless, or cheerless), *illegitimate* (not authorized by the law), *unsafe* (not safe; dangerous), and *churlish* (uncivil, boorish, or vulgar) have no relationship, though all are negative.

11. **Bolstered, Fortified.** The second half of this sentence is not relevant to the blank. All you need to notice is the contrast between "warming" and "record low temperatures" as well as the pivot "while." Clearly, record low temperatures would not help an argument about global warming. A good fill-in would be "helped."

Subverted (undermined, in terms of power or authority) and *subordinated* (made inferior or subservient) are an incorrect pair. *Defined* (described exactly) and *supplanted* (replaced, substituted for) have no relationship.

12. **Serious, Substantive**. The debate coach values "gravitas" (seriousness) and argues that "quips" (witty remarks) and "gibes" (taunts) don't belong in a certain kind of argument. "Serious" and "substantive" is the only set that works.

Polite could work, but it has no pair. *Shallow, competitive,* and *cantankerous* (disagreeable or difficult to deal with) have no relationship.

13. **Filched, Poached**. The most important word here is the adjective "similar." If both *South Park* and *College Humor* created a similar spoof, then one of them must have "stolen" the sketch from the other.

Amalgamated and *combined* are an incorrect pair. *Indulged* (allowed oneself to enjoy) and *assumed* (supposed without proof) have no relationship. *Assumed* can mean "took or began to have (power or responsibility)" or even "took on or adopt (an appearance, manner, or identity)," but you wouldn't use *assume* to mean the taking any other kind of item, such as a comedy spoof.

14. **Rejection, Renunciation**. Abstract Expressionism is described as "characterized by geometric shapes and swathes of color." Clearly this is very different from "realist painting." A good fill-in would thus be something like "repudiation," which means a rejection or a refusal to deal with something.

Memento (an object serving as a reminder; souvenir) and *commemoration* (a service, celebration, etc. serving to remember a person or event) are an incorrect (and imperfect) pair. *Manifestation* (the action or fact of showing an abstract idea; symptom or sign) and *vindication* (exoneration, acquittal) have no relationship.

15. **Penetrate, Infiltrate**. You are told that Nathan Hale was a spy working for the nascent (coming into being) United States, and that he was captured by the British. That means he must have been involved in some kind of espionage in "British-controlled" New York. A good fill-in would be "break into."

Thwart (prevent [someone] from accomplishing something) and *conquer* (take control of by military force) are vaguely related, but are not quite a pair. *Permeate* (spread throughout; pervade) and *research* have no relationship.)

16. **Insinuation, Innuendo**. The pivot "more by X than Y" implies some kind of contrast between the two elements. The second element here is "straightforward vulgarity." You want to contrast that with something. The adjective "sexual" may seem to confuse things; you need a word that will undercut it, such as "allusion."

Conversation (an informal verbal exchange) and *rapport* (a harmonious relationship) are not quite a pair. *Blatancy* (obviousness) and *illusion* (something that looks or seems different from what it is) are almost opposites.

17. **Dormant, Inactive**. The blank is there to describe "inflation" (in a way that contrasts with being entirely "dead"). You're told that in the future, the purchasing power of the dollar may fall, which means there will be inflation. So inflation may come back at any time. A good fill-in would be something like "dormant" (there aren't a lot of simple words that get across this meaning).

Paralyzed (unable to move or act), *indigent* (impoverished or needy), *itinerant* (traveling from place to place), and *problematic* (presenting a difficulty) have no relationship.

18. **Barbaric, Primitive.** Boxers are described as having to punch each other in the face, which isn't "civilized." In order to do this, they would need to access a part of themselves that was "not so civilized" (which will work well enough as a fill-in here).

Seething and *irate* are an incorrect pair, both meaning "angry." *Insidious* (seductive but harmful; treacherous, deceitful) and *dynamic* (characterized by constant change) have no relationship.

19. **Arduous, Taxing.** This sentence describes creative work as having a particular difficulty, namely that one must be "self-motivated." Some might contrast this with manual labor, but the author of the sentence wants to render them equivalent. Thus, a good fill-in would be "difficult."

Serious and *grave* are an incorrect pair. Never in the sentence is it discussed whether or not creative work is more serious than manual labor. *Inventive* (able to create, design, or think originally) and *collaborative* (made or done by two or more parties working together) have no relationship.

20. **Vehement, Heated.** If politicians "demonize" teachers unions and other jump into the "fray," the debate will get more and more "passionately angry," a good fill-in here.

Overt and *unavoidable* are not quite a pair (*overt* means "done openly," and *unavoidable* means "impossible to ignore"). *Problematic* and *tired* have no relationship.

Solutions: 20 Medium Questions

1. **Marriage, Commingling.** This sentence begins with the pivot "while," before describing religions that "insist on the primacy of their particular deity." "Syncretism" is then introduced as relating in some way to "multiple religious beliefs." Because of the opening pivot, you know syncretism should be in favor of multiple religious beliefs. The fill-in is something like "inclusion" or "mixture."

Division and *schism,* which often refers to a division within or from a religious organization, are an incorrect pair. *Exclusion* (deliberate act of omission) and *transgression* (act that violates a rule or duty; an offense) have no relationship.

2. **Consummate, Complete.** The target is the ambassador's power. You have a same-direction pivot ("hence"), and the clue is that, due to this power, he "was able to draft and finalize the agreement unilaterally" (seems like a lot of power for a diplomat). A good fill-in would be something like "a lot of" or "total."

Tyrannical and *dictatorial* are a pair that goes too far, introducing a meaning (exercising total power, in a cruel way) that isn't supported by any clues in the sentence. *Tertiary* (third) and *enigmatic* (mysterious) have no relationship.

3. **Declaim, Trumpet.** The portion of this sentence after the comma is not actually relevant to the blank. All you need to determine is what most politicians do in regards to "their views." Clearly, they like to "proclaim" or "announce" those views.

Invoke and *adduce* are an incorrect pair. *Disparage* (belittle or discredit) and *parrot* (repeat mindlessly) have no relationship.

4. **Colloquium, Symposium.** The sentence tells you that the organization has somehow acquired a "haphazard and often chaotic set of bylaws and regulations." Thus, it is likely that they will want to get everyone together in order to reconcile all these rules. A good fill-in would be "meeting."

Intervention and *mediation* are an incorrect pair. *Introduction* and *acclamation* (loud demonstration of approval or welcome) have no relationship.

5. **Cloistered, Sheltered.** The pivot word "though" tells you that you are going to contradict the first portion of this sentence, which says that writers ought to have "some experience of life." Your blank should go against that notion, and because you already have "solitary," a good fill-in word would be "protected."

Enigmatic and *cryptic* (having hidden meaning; mysterious) are an incorrect near-pair. *Idiosyncratic* (unique to an individual; eccentric, quirky) and *susceptible* (likely to be influenced or harmed by something specific) have no relationship.

6. **Nonchalance, Indifference.** In this sentence, the key is the word "belie," which functions as a kind of pivot. "Belie" means "to misrepresent or contradict," suggesting a contrast to "his deep sense of responsibility." A good fill-in for the blank would be "not caring."

Mirth and *felicity* are an incorrect pair, both meaning something like "happiness," though *mirth* additionally often implies laughter. *Concern* and *sagacity* (keen judgment) have no relationship.

7. **Xenophobic, Bigoted.** The blank here is defined by the second half of the sentence. Patriotism represents the "elevation of one country to the rank of quintessential on earth," that is, saying or believing that one country is the epitome or purest example among all countries on earth. So your blank should be something that involves the "demonization of other people." A good fill-in would be "prejudiced."

Minatory and *truculent* are not quite a pair (the former means "threatening," while the latter means "aggressively defiant"), and *unethical* and *nationalistic* have no relationship to each other. It is certainly true that excessive patriotism is *nationalistic,* but this word does not match the clue in the sentence.

8. **Forbearance, Temperance.** It's important to know the word "debauchery" (meaning "excessive indulgence in sensual pleasures") to solve this question. The sentence describes a husband-to-be who will *not* be engaging in debauchery at the bachelor party, so you need a word that describes someone who exhibits "self-control" or "moderation."

MANHATTAN
PREP

Fiat (authoritative decree) and *autonomy* (the right to self-government; independence) are not quite a pair, and are incorrect anyway. *Gentility* (the state of belonging to polite society; refinement of manner) and *tenacity* (the quality of being persistent or stubborn) have no relationship.

9.   **Vilifying, Maligning.** The rally here is described as discussing politics "humorously but civilly, without" doing the thing in the blank. A good fill-in for the blank would be "abusing" or "badmouthing."

Lampooning and *caricaturing* make an incorrect pair, both meaning "mocking or ridiculing," though *caricaturing* specifically means to do so by exaggerating particular features or traits. Though they are close to the correct meaning for your blank, the sentence mentions that the rally was "humorous." This means that *lampooning* and *caricaturing*, both of which imply a kind of humorous teasing, would be welcome at the rally, so not plausible for the blank. *Bespeaking* (suggesting; ordering or reserving something in advance) and *eulogizing* (to praise highly, especially at a memorial service) have no relationship (and the latter is the opposite of what you want here).

10. **Sanctioned, Endorsed.** The second half of this sentence tells you that reports of corporal punishment receive an "overwhelmingly negative popular response." This means that the military would be unlikely to "authorize" these forms of abuse.

Upbraided (criticized), *considered, rejected,* and *polarized* (broken up into separate groups) have no relationship.

11. **Quagmire, Morass.** The first part of the sentence, which describes how the budget debate "progressed well … in spite of … squabbling," is very important. If you didn't see that, you might be tempted to choose the wrong words here. However, because of the pivot "but," you want something that contrasts with something that progresses well. A good fill-in would be "mess" or "muddle."

Feud and *quarrel* are an incorrect pair. While they correctly get across the negative spin you want for our blank, they don't address the idea of progressing badly, and the "but" indicates a need to contrast with a situation that was always prone to "squabbling." *Covenant* and *accord* are an incorrect pair, both indicating an agreement.

12. **Crucial, Requisite.** This is a tough question, because the sentence gives you only "subtle" as a clue. Your blank should oppose it, but you don't want the opposite of "subtle" (which would be something like "obvious," which clearly doesn't make any sense here). Instead, you need to think about the overall meaning of the sentence. Most likely, the point is that the difference between similes and metaphors is "important."

Null and *nominal* are an incorrect pair, both meaning "insignificant." *Synoptic* (presenting a summary of the whole) and *optional* have no relationship.

13. **Fallacious, Specious.** This sentence is thick with content, and it's important that you understand all of it. You are given two statements about economics. First, that Keynesian economics may or may not recommend that "the limit (on government debt) should be perpetually raised." Then you are told definitively that Keynes says "deficit spending must be done responsibly." If the latter is true, then it is

likely that he would *not* have made the former recommendation. So your blank should say something like "incorrect."

Indigenous (native to or naturally occurring in a region), *corrupt, venial* (forgivable or pardonable), and *axiomatic* (self-evident or unquestionable) have no relationship. In addition, *axiomatic* is the opposite of what is needed for the blank.

14. **Patois, Jargon.** This sentence is describing rebellion as the effect of a communication gap, which you will need to make concrete with the blank. Something "protean" (meaning "tending to change frequently or easily") is being compared to the "older generation's calcified language." Actually, the best fill-in for your blank is simply "language."

Defiance and *insubordination* are an incorrect pair, both meaning something like "disobedience." *Prolixity* and *verbosity* are another incorrect pair, which introduces a theme trap, as both words mean "wordiness."

15. **Grousing, Protesting.** "Cantankerous" means "bad-tempered and argumentative." Because there is no pivot here, you simply need a word that means those things. A good fill-in for the blank would be "arguing" or "complaining."

Imputing (attributing or blaming), *assaulting* (physically attacking), *convulsing* (suffering violent involuntary contraction of the muscles), and *imbibing* (drinking) have no relationship.

16. **Fracas, Altercation.** In this sentence, you need to figure out what kind of thing would result in the police being called—likely, some kind of "crime" or "fight."

Discourse and *colloquy* are an incorrect pair, both meaning "conversation." *Battle* may be close to what you want, but relates to a larger event than a bar fight. *Mutiny* (open rebellion against authorities) is not related to the others.

17. **Eclectic, Multifarious.** In this sentence, the word "surprisingly" is functioning as a pivot, disagreeing with the portion before the comma. There, you learn that the woman in question had a "sheltered upbringing" and a "limited breadth of experience." Your blank should be the opposite of that. A good fill-in would be "varied" or "not limited."

Shallow and *facile* are an incorrect pair, in that both can mean "superficial." *Profound* has the right spin, but it isn't the opposite of "limited" or "sheltered." *Callow* (immature or inexperienced) has no relationship with the other choices, and it incorrectly agrees with "limited breadth of experience."

18. **Rail, Fulminate.** The word "but" acts as a pivot here, taking you in the opposite direction of the adjectives initially used to define documentary filmmakers: "dispassionate" and "objective." A good fill-in would be "speak out."

Advertise (draw attention to publicly in order to promote sales), *inveigle* (win, or win over, by flattery), *strain* (make a strenuous effort), and *aspirate* (pronounce a sound in the exhalation of breath) have no relationship. Note that *inveigle* is *not* the same as *inveigh* (which does not appear as a choice but would have been a suitable correct answer, as it means "express angry disapproval"—the GRE sometimes plays on commonly confused words).

19. **Piquant, Zesty.** There are two important portions of this sentence to focus on. First, the word "praised," implying that the critic's review will be positive. The second part is the way he's described as using "the language of food to describe films." So you want two words that are positive and that could also be used to describe food.

Spectacular and *stupefying* are an incorrect pair. They are both positive, but they aren't generally used to describe food. *Insipid* (bland, tasteless, or flavorless) and *brilliant* have no relationship, and *insipid* is the opposite of what is needed in the blank.

20. **Bruises, Contusions.** In this sentence, a short list of possible injuries after a skydiving accident is described. Two of the items are "broken bones" and "a gash," which means your blank should be a physical injury different from those two. A good fill-in would be "bruises."

Torpor (a state of physical inactivity; apathy, lethargy), *trauma* (physical injury; shock following a disturbing event or injury), *finesse* (skillful or adroit handling), and *lesions* (wounds, ulcers, tumors, etc.) include no synonym pairs. In addition, *finesse* is not a physical symptom, as are the other two clues given in the sentence, while *torpor* is a physical condition but not an injury.

Solutions: 20 Hard Questions

1. **Envoy, Emissary.** The person in question is serving as "official" something for Japan to another country, and is "called upon to answer questions about the Japanese government's position." A good fill-in would be something like "representative" or "ambassador."

Tyro and *neophyte* are an incorrect pair, both meaning "beginner." *Ascetic* (self-denying; austere) and *libertine* (one who is debauched or without moral restraint) are not synonyms, though both have something to do with self-control, in opposite ways.

2. **Palliate, Damp.** The target is both the leadership and the "stridency of their rhetoric"—you need the relationship between those two things. "While" is an opposite-side pivot. In the first part of the sentence, the protests are "uncompromising." Thus, in the second part, they should be softer, more on the side of compromising. Since "stridency" means harshness and is on the same side as "uncompromising," the group thus chose to "reduce" or "tone down" the stridency.

Metamorphose, gild, wane, and *succor* do not contain any pairs. *Wane* means "decrease" and is an attractive trap answer. However, *wane* is an intransitive verb—that is, something (such as the moon) *wanes* on its own; you can't *wane* an object. Therefore, the word does not fit in this sentence. *Metamorphose* (change) could work, but it doesn't indicate the direction of the change (increase or decrease), which the blank needs to do in order to show that the leaders "wisely" chose to do something. *Gild* (cover in gold; give a deceitfully pleasing appearance to) and *succor* (aid, assist, or relieve) have no relationship.

3. **Quiescent, Abeyant.** The clue here is that "activists will be newly galvanized." Because of the pivot "but," this means you need a blank that means the opposite of "galvanized." A good fill-in word would be "dormant" (implying that the movement is quiet but could rise again).

Dogged (persistent, tenacious, or stubbornly determined), *interminable* (endless), *lissome* (flexible or easily bent), and *feckless* (ineffective, lacking in vitality) have no relationship.

4. **Equitable, Apposite.** The first half of this sentence sets up the topic, but the important information is in the second half. There, you're told about the "most ardent supporter [of corporal punishment]." This supporter agrees with detractors on at least one thing, for which "evenhanded and thorough" is a clue. A good fill-in for your blank would be "deserved" or "fair."

Clement and *merciful* are an incorrect synonym pair. They both go against the spin that the blank calls for. *Delimited* (having limits established; bounded) and *tantamount* (equivalent; virtually the same as) are not related.

5. **Chimerical, Fallible.** The portion of this sentence after the blank tells you that "results tend to be colored by ... personal proclivities and suppositions." This provides an explanation of the blank, which in turn is trying to tell you something about "impartiality." That last portion describes something the exact opposite of "impartial," so a good fill-in for your blank would be "wrong" or "nonexistent."

Inane and *fatuous* are an incorrect pair, both meaning "silly." While the "premise of impartiality" may not in fact exist, that doesn't make it silly. *Prejudicial* (harmful; detrimental) and *vexing* (irksome; irritating) have no relationship.

6. **Epicurean, Gustatory.** Everything in this sentence relates to food, whether it's the "texture and taste" or the "notion of what constitutes a meal." This means you need a word that relates to food. A good fill-in would be "culinary."

Carnal (relating to physical, esp. sexual, activities) and *voluptuous* (characterized by luxury or sensual pleasure) are an incorrect pair, relating to sensual delights rather than those merely relating to food. *Salubrious* (promoting health or well being) and *terrestrial* (of, on, or relating to the earth) have no relationship.

7. **Gist, Pith.** The verb "drone" has a very specific meaning, implying that someone is going on at length in a dull or boring way. The implication is that the point could be made more efficiently. This sentence then tells you that a précis (summary) can be found in the tome's first few pages. This précis is really the book's "essence" or "thrust," which is the kind of word you want for the blank.

Adage (a traditional expression of a common observation), *stub* (a short part left after a larger part was broken off), *nimbus* (a circle of light), and *nut*, which among its many definitions can mean "a hard problem or task," have no relationship.

8. **Collate, Juxtapose.** The final portion of this sentence describes "studying the differences and similarities" between two different things. This implies you'll be doing some sort of comparison, so a good fill-in word would be "compare."

Aggregate, agglomerate, and *glean* are an incorrect triple, all meaning "gather." While gathering the data together is required in order to make a comparison, the sentence already said "not only to collect." All of these words are just fancy versions of "collect," which you don't need to repeat. *Ratiocinate,* which means "to reason logically," doesn't match any other choice. In addition, it doesn't quite fit the context: you can reason logically *about* the score reports, but you wouldn't reason the score reports themselves.

9. **Volleys, Salvos.** The second half of this sentence doesn't tell you anything interesting. In fact, everything you need to know comes from the few words before the blank: "trenches were dug so that soldiers could avoid" something. What would you avoid in a trench? "Bullets," more or less, or "barrages," if you wanted to get a little fancier.

Provocations and *goadings* are an incorrect pair, though *goad* specifically means "to provoke by prodding." *Fervency* (fervor; strong feeling of excitement) and *imprecations* (offensive words or phrases said in anger) have no relationship.

10. **Genteel, Courtly.** Near the beginning of the sentence, Cary Grant is described as suave, meaning "confident and elegant." Your blank should not mean the exact same thing, or it would be redundant. Instead, you want a word that is best exemplified by someone who always pulls out a woman's chair, such as "well-mannered."

Debonair and *cosmopolitan* are an incorrect pair. These words mean "sophisticated," but they don't necessarily imply good manners. *Consummate* (complete or perfect) and *waggish* (humorous in a playful way) have no relationship.

11. **Subjective, Personal.** The sentence states that the attempt to find "parity," or fairness, is "fallacious," or logically incorrect. How could fairness be illogical? Only if it isn't real or objectively determinable. A good fill-in would be "prejudiced" or "based on feelings."

Pragmatic and *utilitarian* are a near-pair, meaning "practical." *Introverted* (introspective) and *illicit* (unlawful) are not related.

12. **Erudition, Cerebrality.** This sentence compares the blank with speeches that feature "ignorance" and "stupidity." You also want something that relates to "education." A good fill-in would be "knowledge," which is the result of education.

Bromide (commonplace or trite saying) and *bloviation* (talking at length in a pompous or boastful way) both have some relationship to speech, but they aren't a pair and neither relates to "education" or "ignorance." *Condescension* (patronizing attitude; disdain) is similar to *bloviation,* but both disagree with the clue "actually" (it is not surprising that condescension would be resented by voters!), and neither contrasts properly with "ignorance." *Patrimony* (inheritance from father or other male ancestor) is unrelated to everything else.

13. **Semblance, Veneer.** In this sentence, you're told about a man who has been fired and doesn't tell his wife and kids. This somehow relates to "plenitude," which is "the condition of being full or complete." Clearly, if you get fired and don't tell your family, it's because you want to pretend that you're still okay. A good fill-in word would be "appearance."

Corollaries and *consequences* are an incorrect pair. *Paradigms* (things serving as an example or model) and *prepossessions* (attitudes or beliefs formed beforehand) have no relationship.

14. **Indiscriminate, Blanket.** The sentence tells you that Don Juan had "an astronomical number of amatory adventures," but that it was not because he had a "surfeit of charisma or skillfulness." What might explain this discrepancy? Perhaps if Don Juan weren't particularly choosy. A good fill-in for the blank would be "not choosy."

Sumptuous and *sybaritic* are an incorrect pair, meaning "luxurious" and "devoted to luxury or pleasure," respectively. While they both describe someone like Don Juan, they don't explain how he had so many lovers. *Lurid* (gruesome, shocking) and *covert* (not openly done; veiled) have no relationship.

15. **Attenuate, Abate.** The sentence indicates that "even" major campaign finance reform will "fail" to do something to "the influence of money." This money "directly relates" to a politician being able to become a politician, so the influence of money must be pretty strong. Thus, the reform proposals will fail to "lessen" or "reduce" the influence.

Graft (join or unite), *pander* (cater to the lowest or most base desires), *importune* (harass with constant demands; annoy, irritate), and *indemnify* (protect against loss or damage) have no relationship. On the GRE, the choices for a given blank will always be of the same form of speech; here, they are verbs. Don't confuse the verb *graft* with the noun *graft*, which means "acquisition of money (or other valuable) in dishonest or questionable ways" and represents a theme trap here.

16. **Interrogate, Limn.** There are no pivots in this sentence, so you simply need a word that fits the description of a book that explores the "many ways in which 19th-century women writers…." In other words, you can just fill in the blank with "explore." Note that "interrogate" is being used in a figurative sense here (i.e., it's not referring to a literal interrogation, as of a criminal), though the goal of both types of interrogation is to pry deeply into an issue.

Debunk and *explode* are an incorrect pair, meaning "disprove." *Interpolate* (insert between parts, pieces, or things) and *castigate* (criticize or punish severely) have no relationship. *Castigate* almost fits into a triple with the incorrect pair, but it's more of a criticism than an attempt to disprove something.

17. **Languor, Lethargy.** This sentence creates a contrast with the pivot "while" between a positive and negative view of the same fact. The positive view is that certain cultures prioritize "relaxation" and "moderation between work and play." The negative view of this would be something akin to "laziness."

Enfeeblement and *enervation* are an incorrect pair, meaning "weakening" or "weakness." Though they are close to what you want, they imply a forceful taking away of energy, which is not the same as simply being lazy or tired. *Obtundity* (lessening of intensity; dulling or deadening) and *seemliness* (the state or condition of conforming to standards of proper conduct) have no relationship.

18. **Extraneous, Unnecessary**. Autodidacts ("those who teach themselves") would argue against "enforced" lucubration (study) and "standard" education. A good fill-in might simply be "unnecessary."

Slack and *lax* are an incorrect pair, meaning "loose." *Prudent* and *sagacious* are an incorrect pair, meaning "wise; having good judgment."

19. **Dusky, Crepuscular.** The only clue in this sentence comes in the second half, a "twilit avenue in a long since abandoned city." So you want a word that implies "twilit" and "abandoned," such as "dark."

Urban and *civic* are something of a pair here. Though they both reflect the sentence's reference to a "city," they fail to correctly reference either "twilit" or "abandoned," which are really the most descriptive terms in the original sentence. *Precipitous* (extremely steep) and *avuncular* (relating to an uncle; kind to younger people) have no relationship.

20. **Ineluctable, Inexorable**. The key phrase here is "the inertia of history." Inertia is "resistance to change," so this phrase must mean that history is on track and can't deviate from that track. So your blank here should be something like "unchangeable."

Incontrovertible (not able to be denied or disputed), *interminable* (endless), *infallible* (incapable of making mistakes or being wrong), and *unspeakable* (not able to be expressed in words; too horrible to express in words) have no relationship.

Chapter 4

of

Text Completion & Sentence Equivalence

Learning Vocabulary

In This Chapter...

Practical Strategies & Games for Learning Vocabulary

Flash Card Games and Activities

Use Roots Ahead of Time

Using Social Media to Buttress Your Vocabulary Studies

Chapter 4:
Learning Vocabulary

Many students want to know how many words they have to learn in order to get a high score on the GRE, but this is actually a more complicated issue than it might at first appear.

Imagine this: You tell us you know everyone in your university graduating class! All 2,000 people! Well, how can we test this astounding assertion? One good way would be to start by picking 10 reasonably well-known students and see if you know them. If you do, then we'll pick 10 very shy students, rarely seen around campus, and see if you know them, too. If you know all 20 students that we randomly select, then we would tend to believe your assertion that you know all 2,000 people, or some number very close.

That's what the GRE is doing. They're not testing you on a couple hundred words because they want you to know those couple hundred words. They're testing you on 100+ easier words in the first Verbal section, and then if you do well, they're testing you on 100+ harder words in the second Verbal section. If you do well at all the words they hit you with, the GRE is assuming (and rewarding you for) presumably having a much larger vocabulary than was actually tested.

It would be a truly pointless process if you could simply memorize the dictionary definitions of 1,000 vocabulary words, then the GRE tested you on those words using the definitions you memorized, and then you could get a good GRE score and forget about those words. That's not going to happen. Students who try it end up disappointed. (We suspect that these are the same students who spent all of school asking, "Is this going to be on the test?")

Quite frankly, when you learn words for the GRE, you are trying to trick the test into thinking that, for the past 10+ years of your life, you have been the model English student who looked up all the words you didn't know in *The Scarlet Letter* and *The Great Gatsby,* and then spent 4 years in university reading university-level material, going back to look things up or ask questions every time you got stumped. And then, if you've been out of school, that you've continued reading college-level material ever since.

Simulating that level of verbal knowledge (when you haven't actually been doing the things listed above) takes some work. It can be done! But it's very important to *learn*—not just memorize—vocabulary words.

Many students make the mistake of memorizing dictionary definitions of words without really understanding those definitions or being able to comfortably use those words in sentences. Memorizing by itself is not learning. It is not flexible. If you've learned *torpid*, you shouldn't be thrown off by *torpor*. If you've learned *anthropology* and *engender*, you should be able to make some reasonable assumptions about *anthropogenesis*.

You want to learn words like *traduce* and *bonhomie* in the same way you know words like *study* and *mistake*—that is, you can barely even remember a time when you didn't know those words.

For sources of difficult material, try *The Economist* (economist.com), *Scientific American* (scientificamerican.com), *Smithsonian* (smithsonianmag.com), *Foreign* (foreignaffairs.com), *MIT Technology Review* (technologyreview.com), or any of the articles posted on aldaily.com (that's "Arts and Letters Daily"). Of course, these are precisely the same resources recommended for improving your reading comprehension; certainly, it is possible to do both at the same time!

If you've ever learned a foreign language, think about the words that were easiest to learn. When you're in class, most of the words you learn (stove, tire, classroom, grandmother) seem equally important. But when you are actually in a foreign country, trying to speak that language, it is *very, very easy* to learn and remember words and phrases like "bathroom" and "How much?" and "No pigs' feet, please." That is, the easiest things to learn are things that you *really wanted to know* at the time that you looked them up. It's easier to retain a new word when there's a "hole" in your knowledge that you just cannot wait to fill.

Similarly, if you are reading something interesting and come across a word you don't know, and then you look up the word and consider its usage in the sentence you were just puzzling over—well, that's almost as good as learning the word "bathroom" when you really needed to use one.

Finally, don't hesitate to look up or ask someone about words you *thought* you knew, but seem that to be used in novel ways. (Did you notice what just happened there? As a noun, a *novel* is a book-length work of fiction, but as an adjective, *novel* means "new, original.") How about the use of *informed by* in the sentence, "Her historical analysis of family dynamics in the antebellum South is informed by an academic background in feminist theory"? Clearly, an "academic background in feminist theory" can't talk—*informed by* means "influenced by" in this context. Or the use of *qualified* in the sentence, "Dr. Wong could give only qualified approval to the theory, as the available data was limited in scope." (*Qualified* here means "limited, conditional, holding back.")

If you read a definition of a word—on a flash card, in a test prep book, or anywhere else—and it doesn't make sense to you, look up the word in several online dictionaries (Dictionary.com, TheFreeDictionary.com, and m-w.com), ask someone, and/or simply Google the word to see how other people are using it.

Once you've studied the definition, read the word in context, and worked the word into conversation a few times (this may cause your friends to look at you funny, but it'll be worth it!), that word is probably yours for life.

Finally, in embarking on your vocabulary-learning journey, it is crucial to cultivate a productive attitude.

Learning 500–1,500 new words certainly seems daunting (although an assiduous approach will indubitably be conducive to a virtuosic lexical performance!). Some students say, "I'm already a college graduate. Why do I have to spend months studying for this exam? That's just too much time."

Here's one way to look at it: if you do physical exercise for only one hour a week, you've almost thrown that time away, because that's not enough time to get results. But if you exercise for five hours a week, you'll end up in much better shape! That is, it's exercising *insufficiently* that is a waste of time. Learning words *shallowly* is also a waste of time.

Similarly, if you spend three weeks cramming for the GRE—memorizing words just for the GRE score, without really becoming a more verbally educated person—you probably won't improve your score that much, and it really will seem like you wasted your time, because what you're doing is really about the GRE and nothing else. But if you spend months developing a more erudite vocabulary, improving your comprehension of graduate-level articles, and becoming significantly more articulate, then you have remodeled your brain for the better. That time is not lost! Those skills will benefit you forever (i.e., in graduate school!).

Here's something to think about—the GRE test writers aren't evil. They don't want to hold you back. They want to test real skills. Sure, you might be able to game the test a little bit with tricks and quick fixes, but probably not enough to achieve your goal score.

A serious, academic approach to GRE study isn't about tricks and quick fixes. It's about the actual material and skills that the GRE is designed to test. And no amount of time is too much to spend on becoming a more knowledgeable person, equipped with hundreds of new words that can be assembled in infinite combinations to express your ideas for decades to come.

Practical Strategies and Games for Learning Vocabulary

How to Make and Use Flash Cards

Flash cards are a time-tested way to learn vocabulary, and we like them a lot. You can make your own, or you can use Manhattan Prep's *500 Essential Words* and *500 Advanced Words* GRE Flash Card sets. While we're big fans of our own flash cards (we made them after all!), evidence has shown that you're more likely to retain the information if you make the cards yourself.

If you decide to make your own flash cards, try to write sentences for each word, and add synonyms or extra information where appropriate. Here is a sample of one of our flash cards that you might wish to use as a model for making your own:

torpid
(adj)

Also *torpor* (noun)

Definition: Slow, sluggish, lazy

Usage: After a massive Thanksgiving dinner, Jane felt too **torpid** to even get up off the couch. "My **torpor** is overwhelming," she said.

You can find a word's synonyms by using the "Thesaurus" tab on **Dictionary.com**, although make sure you click on a synonym and verify that it really is similar in meaning—many thesauruses will give more than 20 synonyms for a single word, but most of them won't be that closely related (and some will be quite obscure). Make sure to look at the etymologies of any words you don't know. This is how you learn the roots of words; such knowledge will occasionally allow you to work out the definitions of words you've never seen before!

So, flash cards are pretty important, but here's what a lot of people actually *do* with flash cards:

Okay, here's my enormous stack of flash cards. How many is this? 500? Okay, let's start. Synoptic. Hmmn, I don't know. Okay, I guess I'll just look at the answer, then. Oh, okay. Next. Turpitide. Hmmn, I don't know. Okay, I guess I'll just look at the answer, then. Oh, okay. Next. Platitude. Hmmn, I don't know. Okay, I guess I'll just look at the answer, then. Oh, okay. Next...

You see how this is getting you nowhere?

One problem with this approach is that your brain has no motivation to actually remember much, because, deep down, it knows that the information is already written on the flash card, and you'll be seeing that flash card again next time it comes up in the rotation. (You forget way more than you remember—imagine if you remembered everything you saw, did, ate, etc., in just a single day! Your brain dumps well over 99% of the information it is presented with. You need to give it a very good reason to do otherwise!)

The other problem with this approach is that you have no idea when you're "done," and it rarely feels like you're making any progress. Instead, use this method:

1. Pull out a small stack of cards, perhaps 20.

2. Go through the stack one word at a time. When you get one right, *take it out of the stack* and lay it aside.

3. As you continue, the stack will get smaller and smaller. It will become easier and easier to remember the words that are left.

Now you're done. You did a set. Move on to another set if you like.

Because this exercise has an ending (as opposed to just cycling through your flash cards over and over again), you get to feel a sense of accomplishment when you're finished.

Depending on your timeline and goal score, you might decide to do this once or twice per day. In fact, if you are working a full-time job and have a hard time studying on weeknights, make a vow that you can do this one thing *every* day, no matter what (if you're really tired, you can make it a 12–15 card set rather than 20, but you should do at least a little vocab every single day).

Flash Card Games and Activities

One benefit of physical flash cards (as opposed to various electronic study tools) is that you can physically spread out and group your flash cards in a way that is not possible when you can only see one card at a time on a screen.

Here are some strategies that take advantage of the old-school properties of flash cards:

Whack-a-Word: Whack-a-Mole is an arcade game in which you have to hit a bunch of mechanical creatures with a mallet before the time runs out. Play Whack-a Word by spreading out a huge pile of flash cards on a table, bed, or floor, and then trying to remove words from the pile by defining them without looking at the card. If you get a word wrong, put it aside in a "to review" pile. If you end up with words you don't know anything about, make a stack and try the technique mentioned on the previous page. Once you've learned those words better, spread them all back out and play Whack-a-Word one more time. Whack-a-Word is also fun with a friend. Take turns defining words and removing them from the spread, working together to clear the space as quickly as possible.

4

Storytelling: Take a stack of about 20 cards. Shuffle, and don't look at the first card. Think of a topic for your story—something funny and interesting. It's very important that every sentence in your story *defines* the word in question. For example, if you decide to tell a story about robots and monkeys, and your first card says *captious* ("tending to find fault or raise petty objections"), you wouldn't want to write, "Monkeys are captious," because that doesn't really help you define the word. Instead, write something like: "The monkeys were captious creatures, always arguing about some little thing or another." Now you turn to the next card, *itinerary*…

> The Robot/Monkey war began when a monkey went on vacation and misread an item on his itinerary, causing him to accidentally invade Robot Headquarters when he really just meant to visit the Monkey Art Museum. The robots were jingoists, so patriotic towards their robot kingdom that the accidental monkey invasion was interpreted as a declaration of war. The robots considered waging a war of espionage, secretly assassinating the monkey king, but decided that they'd have better luck with direct warfare. Providentially, the monkeys discovered oil in Monkeyland and were able to sell it to buy weapons to defend themselves. One taciturn monkey finally got the courage to speak up and suggest that the monkeys engage in ninja training. A meal of sushi helped whet their appetites for the training.

You can see where this is going, and it's ridiculous—but a fun way to learn! The brain retains information much better when it *does something* with that information (such as using words in sentences) rather than merely *looks at* information.

More on Storytelling and Using Words in Sentences

You can also use storytelling as a vocabulary learning technique without involving flash cards. Use any GRE vocabulary list or source and write a story using 20 or more words—either one per sentence or as many as you can incorporate.

If you're not so big on telling stories, try writing a daily journal entry using some number of words per day.

You could even vow to work a certain number of words per day into your regular emails to unsuspecting colleagues and family members. (Use caution when dropping bombastic language on your boss, but why not try out your new lexicon on your parents? They'll probably be glad to hear from you no matter how grandiloquent you become!)

MANHATTAN
PREP

Chat with a Study Buddy

Another fun technique is to find a study partner and agree to email or text each other every day using a certain number of GRE words in your emails (three seems about right—if you make the task too daunting, it might be too hard to stick with the plan).

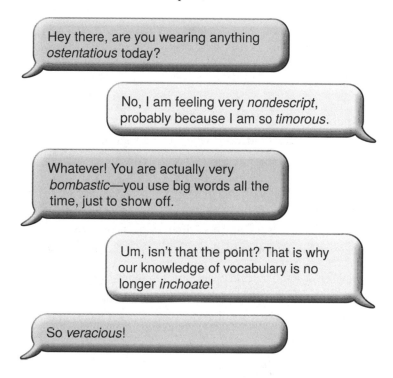

Use Roots Ahead of Time

The Appendix of this book includes a targeted Root List. Take a good look through it.

Take judicious advantage of roots. There is no doubt that you need to know a good number of Latin and Greek roots to understand modern English academic vocabulary. Many words are easily decomposed into roots and can be understood clearly in terms of those roots.

Because the meaning of words may have changed quite a bit since the time of the Roman Empire, though, some words now have misleading roots or derivations. During the exam itself, you have to be very careful when you resort to root analysis to guess an unknown word's meaning. The GRE loves to use words with surprising meanings. For instance, *baleful* does not mean "full of hay bales"—it means threatening or menacing. Although a *scribe* is a person whose job is to copy by hand, *proscribe* isn't really about writing—it means prohibit or condemn.

Still, if you learn that a word *doesn't* relate very logically to its roots, that can be helpful in itself. Many words have strange and memorable relationships with their etymological roots. For instance, the word *desultory* means "lacking in method or purpose; disappointing." That's not so interesting, but if you know that the word comes from a Latin word describing circus riders who *jumped from* horse to horse (*de* = from, *sult* = jump), then you might remember the word *desultory* better. *Proscribe*, meaning "to forbid by law or denounce," contains the root *scribe* (as in *script, scribble, scripture,* etc.) because, in ancient times, to *proscribe* was to publish a record of someone's punishment—to condemn or sentence that person publicly.

Here are a few more favorites (more information like this appears in *500 Essential Words* & *500 Advanced Words* GRE Flash Card sets from Manhattan Prep):

4

> **Amortize** (gradually pay off a debt, or gradually write off an asset) contains the root "mort," meaning death. **Amortization** is when a financial obligation dies a long, slow death.
>
> **Anachronism** (something that is not in its correct historical time; a mistake in chronology, such as by assigning a person or event to the wrong time period)—the prefix "ana" means "against," and "chron" means "time." This is one word you can work out entirely with a knowledge of roots: **anachronistic** means "against time."
>
> **Legerdemain** (sleight-of-hand, trickery, deception) comes from Middle French, meaning "light of hand". The modern French word for hand is *main,* which is related to the root in the English *manual* (relating to hands, as in *manual labor*) and *manumit* (free from slavery, untie the hands).
>
> **Malediction** (a curse) has the prefix *mal* (meaning "bad," of course). The root "dict" comes from "dicere" (to say) and also appears in *dictator, dictionary,* and *indict* (connect to a crime), as well as in **malediction**'s antonym, *benediction* (blessing).

Not all words have a cool story or a helpful derivation. For instance, *pulchritude* means beauty. The reason that seems so weird (*You're so pulchritudinous* really doesn't sound like a compliment) is that the Latin root "pulcher," meaning "beautiful," doesn't occur in any other English words.

So recognize that roots are just one of many helpful tools. One good way to proceed is to go through the Root List in the Appendix and just focus on roots that actually look familiar to you (and like something you'd be able to spot in the future); for instance, *circum* (meaning "around") appears in *circumference,* and it's pretty hard to miss the root in *circumnavigate, circumcise, circumambulate,* and *circumlocution.* So you might make a flash card for this and other roots that seem most useful to you.

Using Social Media to Buttress Your Vocabulary Studies

Do you spend all day on Facebook or Twitter? Developing a social network around your word network is an incredible way to make vocabulary fun, and to get other people's perspective on words that are new to you. In fact, scientific studies show that a having a social group related to your studies can substantially improve learning.

Supposedly, your Facebook friends are your, well… friends, right? So they should be supportive of your GRE efforts. Try announcing on Facebook that you're studying for the GRE and will be posting vocabulary words for the next few months.

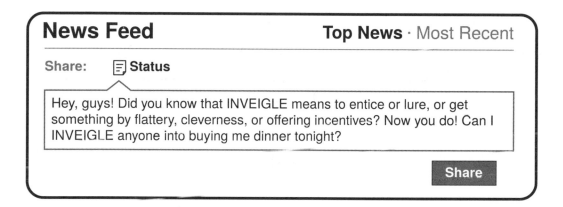

If you post a word and its definition as your status update, it only takes one hilarious comment from a friend (some people have way too much time on their hands) to help you remember the word forever.

Manhattan Prep maintains a Facebook presence (we're "Word Beast"), and we were pleased to see that someone posted the word *deleterious* (meaning "harmful or damaging") in a status update ("Does anyone actually use that word?").

A friend wrote back:

> "Deleterious" is used quite a bit in genetics. For example, "Epigenetic silencing of transposable elements may reduce 'deleterious' effects on neighboring gene expression in the genome.'"

The original poster replied, "I looked for examples of this word's use in a sentence. It seems that 'deleterious effects' is indeed the way it is most often used."

Now that's how to learn *deleterious*!

You can also use Twitter as a tool for learning vocabulary. You can follow Manhattan Prep at:

http://twitter.com/manhattanprep

But don't just be a follower. Start up a Twitter account (if you haven't already) and Tweet each word you study. You can simply post words and definitions, or try using the words in sentences (or both!).

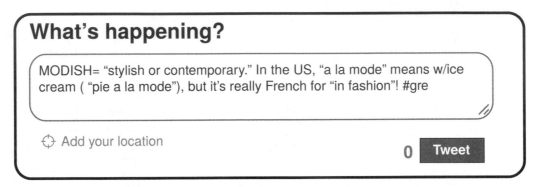

Try tagging your Tweets with #gre or #grevocab, and you'll find a lot of new friends who are also studying for the GRE. It's a word party!

Chapter 5

of

Text Completion & Sentence Equivalence

Idioms & Metaphorical Language

In This Chapter...

List of Idioms & Metaphorical Language

Chapter 5
Idioms & Metaphorical Language

The following section contains expressions that are appropriate for use in the type of writing excerpted on the GRE, and that often appear in writing about culture, literature, business, science, and history.

It also contains words used metaphorically; for instance, an *albatross* is large web-footed bird, but it is also a burden or obstacle, as in the expression *an albatross around one's neck* (from "The Rime of the Ancient Mariner," in which a sailor had to wear an albatross around his neck as punishment for his sins).

This section will be extremely helpful for many non-native speakers of English. Others may simply want to look over it and see if there are any "surprises."

Idioms are not the same as vocabulary words and are not likely to appear in GRE answer choices; rather, they are likely to appear in complex Text Completion sentences and especially in Reading Comprehension passages. This content is important for both areas of the GRE.

To increase retention of this material, try to use these expressions in your own sentences.

The idioms are followed by a 20-question drill allowing you to test your understanding of these expressions when used in complex sentences.

List of Idioms & Metaphorical Language

"…" – Quote marks can indicate 1) that the word or phrase is not to be taken literally; 2) the introduction of a new, made-up word or phrase. So, some context is needed to understand the meaning. For example:

> The factory employs several people who add defects and rough edges to its popular line of **"antique"** furniture. (The furniture is not really antique).

> The company has sent its top people to ethics training and courses on Aristotle in an attempt to build a **"philosophically correct"** business. (The quotes tell you that the concept of *philosophical correctness* is something new—likely invented by the company itself—rather than a well-established concept or institution.)

Account for – 1) Take into consideration or make adjustments based on; 2) cause. This is not the same as *give an account of*, which just means *explain*.

> I **accounted for** the fact that Joe is always late by telling him to meet us at 1:30 when the event is really at 2. (Here, *accounted for* means *made adjustments to compensate for*.)

> I did get us the meeting, but Ellen's hard work **accounted for** the rest of our success. (Here, *accounted for* means *caused*.)

"A given" – The use of *a given* as a noun is different from the use of *given* alone. For instance, a person's *given name* is the one *given* by his or her parents (a "first name" in the United States), and we might also say, "The truth differs from the *given* explanation." Here, *given explanation* just means *the explanation that someone gave*. Simple. However, *a given* means something taken for granted, something assumed or that does not require proof. For instance:

> When planning my wedding, it was **a given** that my parents would invite anyone they wanted, since they were paying for everything.

> It's **a given** that everyone here is against human trafficking—what we disagree about is the best way to fight it.

Albatross – A constant burden or worry; an obstacle. Literally, an albatross is a bird. The expression *an albatross around one's neck* creates the silly image of a person wearing a (dead?) bird—but that certainly sounds like a constant burden or worry!

> The city has done an admirable job of rebuilding its infrastructure and marketing itself, but the crime rate continues to be an **albatross** around the city's neck in trying to attract tourists.

All but – Almost definitely. *The bill's passage is all but assured* means that the bill will almost certainly pass.

> Your objections have arrived too late; the matter is **all but** decided.

And yet – A stronger way of saying *yet*. The expression *and yet* seems ungrammatical (two conjunctions right next to each other is very strange—we don't say *and but*), but it is an idiom used for emphasis. It indicates a surprising twist, an ironic realization, etc. It is often used at the beginning of a sentence for emphasis, and can even be used on its own, although this usage is casual.

> The company was lauded for its commitment to the environment. **And yet** its employees regularly fly in private jets, creating carbon footprints that would embarrass any true environmentalist.

MANHATTAN
PREP

Arms race – Competition between two countries to build up the best and largest supply of weapons. This term is often associated with the Cold War between the United States and the Soviet Union. Metaphorically, an arms race is a competition that implies a competitive and perhaps not entirely rational series of escalations.

> Analysts carefully watched stock prices as the two Internet giants competed in an **arms race**, expanding rapidly by buying up smaller companies with little due diligence.

Aside from – In addition to.

> **Aside from** the obvious financial benefits of investing in a socially responsible fund, you can rest assured that your money is used to maximize social good.

(Adjective) as it is, ... – This pattern is used to contrast the part after the comma with the part before. For instance, *Charming as she is, I just don't want to be friends with her anymore.*

> **As pleased as we are** to see more minorities on the board than ever before, discrimination in hiring and promotion is still a serious problem.

As well as – Sometimes, *as well as* just means *and,* as in *I had ramen for lunch, as well as a hot dog.* But *as well as* can also be used to mention one thing as a way to contrast with or emphasize another. For instance:

At best – At the most, interpreted in the most favorable way. *The seminar drew 20 people at best* means that 20 or fewer people attended.

> My college algebra teacher can barely factor a polynomial! He is qualified to teach elementary school math, **at best**.

At fault – Guilty.

> The insurance company is investigating who is **at fault** for the collision.

At loggerheads – In conflict, at a standstill.

> The strike is not likely to end soon—the transit authority and the union representatives have been **at loggerheads** for weeks.

At odds – In conflict.

> The teachers union and the state government are always at odds.

At once – 1) Immediately; 2) at the same time.

> If the hurricane comes near the coast, the governor will order us to evacuate **at once**.

> The question is whether we can pursue all three plans **at once**, or if we only have the resources to try them one at a time.

Beside the point – Irrelevant, off-topic.

The better part – The largest or longest part. *The better part* does *not* have to be good! The word *better* is a bit confusing here.

> For **the better part** of human history, slavery has been a reality. (The speaker is *not* saying that slavery is good. The speaker is saying that, for most of human history, slavery has existed.)

> When the oil magnate died, he left **the better part** of his fortune to his third wife, and only a small sliver to his children.

Bite the hand the feeds you – This expression means exactly what it sounds like (think of a mean and not-very-smart dog). Although informal sounding, this expression has appeared in business writing.

> The music industry **bites the hand that feeds it** when it penalizes consumers who share (and therefore publicize) their favorite songs with friends.

Brook – Tolerate, allow. Often used with the word *no*. You could say *The dictator will not brook dissent*, but a more common usage would be *The dictator will brook no dissent*.

(Verb) by so (verb)ing – The second verb is equivalent to or causes the first verb. He *defaults by so refusing* means *when he refuses, he is defaulting* (that is, neglecting to fulfill the duties of a contract). *By so agreeing* also occurs on its own, meaning *by agreeing to do the thing that was just mentioned*.

> He agreed to run as the Green Party candidate though he already holds a Democratic Party chairmanship, which he effectively **abandoned by so agreeing**.

The case at issue – The matter at hand, the thing we are discussing.

> Usually, raising prices results in a drop in demand, but in **the case at issue**, the price jump convinced consumers that the product was a luxury good, thus spurring demand from those who wished to be perceived as wealthy.

Caught red-handed – Caught in the act of doing something wrong, so that the person cannot deny guilt. The expression refers to having blood on one's hands.

> The company could no longer claim that the fish in the river were all dying from natural causes once it was **caught red-handed** dumping waste at the river's mouth.

Colored by – Influenced or prejudiced by.

> Her skeptical opinions regarding unbridled capitalism were **colored by** her upbringing in a factory town devastated by outsourcing.

Couldn't have come at a better time – The same as *could hardly have come at a better time,* this expression means that something happened at the best possible time, such as at a very convenient moment or just in time to prevent disaster.

Curry favor – To try to gain favor (such as preferential treatment from a boss) through flattery or servile behavior. The expression is derived from French and is not related to *curry,* the food.

Cut bait – Give up, abandon an activity. Often part of the expression *fish or cut bait,* to *cut bait* is to stop fishing.

> As much as he wanted to be an entrepreneur, after a year of struggling, he **cut bait** and asked his former boss for his old job back.

Due diligence – Research or analysis done before taking action (such as investing); care that a reasonable person would take to prevent harm to others.

> The company was expanding so rapidly that it didn't have time to do its **due diligence**; a number of unexceptional employees were hired as a result.

En masse – All together, in a group. This expression is from French and is related to the word *mass.* Like many foreign expressions, *en masse* is often written in italics.

> The protesters marched **en masse** to the palace.

Entree – Admittance, permission to enter. Most people in the United States think of an entree as the main dish of a meal, but it originally was an appetizer—a dish that leads into the main course (the word is related to "enter"). A person who wants to rise in society might seek an *entree* into a certain social group.

> For disadvantaged young people, good public schools can provide an **entree** into the middle class.

Fishy – Suspicious, unlikely, questionable, as in a *fishy* story. This expression probably arose because fish smell very bad when they start to spoil.

For all X, Y – This sentence pattern means, "Despite X, actually Y"; that is, X and Y will be opposites, or one will be good and one will be bad. The word "actually" (or a similar word) often appears in this pattern, but doesn't have to.

> **For all** of its well-publicized "green" innovations, the company is one of the worst polluters in the state.

Former and latter – When two things are mentioned, the first one is the *former* and the second one is the *latter*.

> Your grades are slipping, and you've been very secretive about your behavior—it's **the latter** of these things that worries your father and me the most.

> I intend to choose a business school based on reputation and cost, the **former** more so than the **latter**.

For show – For appearances only.

> The politician's speechifying in regards to eradicating poverty is all **for show**; when he actually had the chance to improve the lot of the poor, he voted against expanding the social safety net.

For years to come – Until much later. *The consequences won't affect us for years to come* means that they *will* affect us, but not for the next several years.

> My parents are only in their sixties and are healthy and active, so I am hopeful that my children will get to enjoy their grandparents **for years to come**.

Full throttle – With much speed and energy. On a related note, sometimes *juice* is used to mean *energy*.

> The plan is to go ahead **full throttle** as soon as the money for implementation comes through.

Garden-variety – Ordinary, common.

Gloss over, paper over, whitewash – These are all expressions for covering up a problem, insult, etc. rather than addressing it or fixing it. Think of a dirty floor that you just put a pretty rug on top of instead of cleaning. Because *gloss* is slippery (think of lip gloss), *gloss over* often has the sense of trying to smoothly and quickly move on to something else.

> The government had been accused of trying to whitewash the scandal, **glossing over** any discussion of the issue in press conference after press conference. The press secretary claimed it was a question of national security, but everyone knew that the president was simply trying to protect his reputation.

Go down the tubes – Become much worse, fail. One theory is that this expression is about the plumbing attached to toilets.

Go sour – Think of milk going bad—that's the idea behind the expression *go sour*. A relationship *goes sour* before the couple breaks up. An economy *gone sour* can't be good. This is not the same as the expression *sour grapes,* which refers to pretending something you can't have wasn't any good anyway, as in, *Her hatred of the rich is just sour grapes—if she could afford luxury, she'd take all she could get.*

Hand-wringing – An excessive expression of concern, guilt, or distress.

> There has been much **hand-wringing** (or **wringing of hands**) over falling test scores, but the rising costs of a college degree are far more worrying in terms of America's continuing relevance in the global economy.

Hold the line vs. **toe the line** – *Hold the line* means *keep something the same*. It is a reference to (American) football, in which you don't want the opponent to get the ball past the line of scrimmage in the middle of the field. To *toe the line* is to conform to a policy or way of thinking, or follow the rules. One theory about the origin of the expression is that, on ships, barefoot sailors were made to line up for inspection—that is, to put their toes on an actual line on the deck of the ship.

> My boss doesn't want to hear original ideas at all—he just wants me to **toe the line**.

> If colleges cannot **hold the line** on rising tuition costs, students will have to take on even more crippling loan burdens.

However much, as much as – Even though, no matter how much.

> **However much** people may agree that saving money is a virtue, the majority of Americans don't have sufficient funds for any kind of emergency.

> **As much as** I'd like to attend your wedding, I just can't afford a trip to Taiwan.

In contrast to – This phrase is important in inference questions on Reading Comp. If a writer says *In contrast to X, Y is A*, you can draw the conclusion that *X is not A*. For instance:

> *In contrast to our competitor's product, our product is made with organic materials.* (This means that our competitor's product is *not* made with organic materials, which very well could be the answer to a question about what we can infer from the passage.)

Just cause – *Just* as an adjective means *justified, legal, fair. Just cause* means a legally sufficient reason. In some legal codes, an employer must show *just cause* for firing an employee.

Legions or **is legion** – *Legions* are large military units, generally consisting of a few thousand soldiers. Saying that a group is *legion* is saying that it is large.

> Surely, the developers could have foreseen that **legions** of Mac users would protest when news emerged that the new version of the software would not be Mac-compatible.

> The former governor has been called a demagogue by many commentators who nevertheless must grudgingly admit that her supporters **are legion**, populating rallies in every state.

5

MANHATTAN
PREP   149

"No X *or* Y" vs. "no X *and* Y" – When you are talking about having two things, saying "salt *and* pepper" is very different from saying "salt *or* pepper." However, when you are talking about a lack of two things, *and* and *or* can often be used to express the same idea. The following two sentences have the same meaning:

> Pioneer towns were characterized by little access to the outside world **and** few public institutions.

> Pioneer towns had almost no access to the outside world **or** public institutions.

Not (adjective) – Of course, putting *not* before an adjective indicates the opposite. However, sometimes it indicates a softer or more polite way to say something. If someone asks if you like the meal he cooked or the outfit he is wearing, and you know him well enough to be honest, you might say, *It's not my favorite*. Sometimes we say something like *not irrelevant* instead of simply *relevant* in order to indicate that we are correcting someone else's misconception:

> Concern about foreign debt is **not misplaced**. (Here, we mean that we should be concerned! We also may be implying that others incorrectly think we should *not* be concerned.)

Not only X, but also Y (also appears as **Not only X, but Y**) – This is a two-part expression, introducing the first part before adding on the second, more extreme or surprising part. For instance:

> The executive was **not only** fired, **but also** indicted for fraud.

> He **not only** bought his girlfriend an iPhone for her birthday, **but also** took her entire family on a vacation to the Catskills.

Not X, let alone Y – The meaning is *Not X and definitely not this even more extreme thing, Y*. For instance:

> Our remaining funds are **not** enough to get us through the week, **let alone** pay next month's payroll. (Here, getting through the week is less expensive than next month's payroll, so if we can't afford the cheaper thing, we *definitely* can't afford the more expensive thing.)

No worse than – Equal to or better than.

> Although exotic, this illness is really **no worse than** the common flu.

On its face – At first appearance, superficially. If someone says *on its face*, you can expect that later on, the person will give the "real story." In a Reading Comprehension passage, seeing *on its face* is a good clue that the author's main idea will probably be the opposite of what *seems* true at first glance.

> **On its face,** the donation seems like a selfless act of philanthropy. However, the wealthy donor mainly made the donation for the tax benefits.

Only looks (adjective) – Appears (some certain way) but isn't really.

> She **only looks** homeless—she is actually a famous and wealthy artist who lives eccentrically.

On par with – Sometimes *on a par with*, this expression comes from golf and means *about equal to* or *equivalent to*.

Opening salvo – A *salvo* is a simultaneous discharge of gunfire or release of bombs. Metaphorically, an *opening salvo* is something that starts a fight.

> The introduction of Bill H.R. 2, given the inflammatory name "Repealing the Job-Killing Health Care Law Act," was seen by some as an **opening salvo** by the Republicans.

Outside of the home – Working *outside of the home* means having a regular job, such as in an office. However, working *out of your home* is actually working at home. If that's hard to understand, think of the expression *living out of your car*, which actually means living *in* your car—the idea is that you leave the car to go "out" but return back to the car as your base, just as someone who works *out of her home* leaves the home to go to meetings, for example, but uses the home as a central point.

> The study compared incomes of women who had worked **outside of the home** to incomes of women who worked **out of their homes** as freelancers or owners of small businesses.

Per se – In itself, by itself, intrinsically. From Latin, often written in italics. *Per se* is often used to indicate that while X isn't *naturally* or *the same as* Y, it still has the same effect as Y.

> The policy isn't sexist, **per se**, but it has had a disproportionate impact on women that deserves further study.

Press for – Argue in favor of. Think of *pushing people* towards what you want them to do.

> The advocates **pressed for** greater regulation of child-care providers.

Rabid – Rabies is a disease that some animals (dogs, raccoons, etc.) contract and that causes the animal to become insane and violent. Thus, we use *rabid* (having rabies) metaphorically to mean *zealous* or *excessively* or *angrily passionate*. One symptom of rabies is *foaming at the mouth*, which is also an expression for being extremely (and violently or irrationally) angry.

> One debater called himself a "peace activist" and his opponent a "**rabid** right-wing gun nut." His opponent called himself a "champion of the American way" and his opponent a "**rabid** anti-American zealot."

5

Ranks of – The people in a group other than the leaders. Many people know the word *rank* as "a level or grade," as in *A general has a higher rank than a sergeant*. The other use of *ranks* is also originally related to the military: the *ranks* or sometimes the *rank and file* means all the regular soldiers (not the officers).

> Among the **ranks** of our alumni are two senators and many famous authors.

Reap and **sow** – These are metaphors related to farming, and specifically the idea that the seeds that you plant (or *sow*) determine what you will later harvest (or *reap*). *Sow* is pronounced the same as *so*, and the past tense is *sown*, as in *Having sown the love of knowledge in the minds of children, the teacher's influence extended well past her own lifetime*. A common expression is *You reap what you sow*.

> He worked night and day in the strange new country, never stopping to rest, for he knew he would **reap** his reward when his family greeted him as a hero for all the money he had sent back home.

Red flag – Warning sign or something alarming.

> Bernie Madoff's sustained, ultrahigh returns should have been a **red flag** for the banks with which he did business.

Red herring – Something irrelevant that distracts from the real issue. A herring is a fish. One theory for the origin of the expression is that criminals trying to escape the police would sometimes rub a smelly fish across their trail as they ran away in order to mislead the dogs used to track them down.

> When the company was robbed, police immediately suspected Johnson, who purchased a brand-new Maserati just after the crime was committed. This turned out to be a **red herring**, however, as it was Johnson's wife, who'd just come into a large inheritance, who bought the car.

Reign vs. **reins** – Reign means "rule (noun)," as in *Conditions have improved under the king's reign*. *Reins* are leather straps used by a rider to control a horse. Both words are often used metaphorically.

> People were worried when the inexperienced new CEO took the **reins** of the multinational corporation, but under her **reign**, profits soared.

(Adjective)-ridden – Dominated, burdened, or afflicted by (adjective). In a *disease-ridden slum*, it's pretty obvious that the meaning is bad, but actually, adding *-ridden* to anything makes the meaning bad. If someone said *an equality-ridden society*, that person is actually against equality! *Ridden* can also be used alone, as in *The neighborhood was ridden with crime*.

Scarcely or **Scarce** – Sometimes *scarce* is used where it sounds like the adverb *scarcely* is needed. This is an idiomatic usage:

> She lived a lavish lifestyle she could **scarce** afford. (She could not afford the lifestyle.)

Save – But or except. As a verb, of course, *save* means *keep safe, store up, set aside*. But as a preposition or conjunction, *save* can be used as follows:

> All of the divisions of the company are profitable **save** the movie-rental division.
> (This means that the movie-rental division was not profitable.)

> He would have been elected president, **save** for the scandal that derailed his campaign
> at the last minute.
> (Here, *save* means "if not.")

School of thought – A group of people with similar beliefs or perspective on things, or the beliefs themselves. If a GRE writer says *One school of thought argues X*, it is probably the case that the author is about to say the opposite (calling something a *school of thought* can emphasize that it's not the only way to think about the issue).

> One **school of thought** says that companies don't need to "give back" directly to communities, because their economic activity causes money to "trickle down" to everyone through taxes; a competing **school of thought** says that companies benefit from a nation's infrastructure and education system, which confers an ethical obligation to be philanthropic.

Sight vs. **site** vs. **cite** – To **sight** is to see, or discover by looking. A **site** is a location. To **cite** is to reference or give credit to.

> The sailors had nearly given up hope when they finally **sighted** land. When they
> reached the shore, they planted a flag on the **site** of their landing.

> A good research report **cites** relevant studies.

So much as – This phrase is used an adverbial intensifier. In *My teacher is so awful, she won't so much as answer a question*, the meaning is that, whatever the teacher will do, it is not "as much as" answering a question—it is something less than that. It can also be used as a synonym for *but rather*.

> After her husband decided to take up day trading and lost $100,000 in one day, she
> wouldn't **so much as** look at him.

> She's not an iconoclast **so much as** an attention-hound; she'd do anything for the
> spotlight.

Sound the depths – Explore, investigate, or look into something really deeply. This expression is a metaphor based on the idea of a "sounding line," which is a rope with a weight on the bottom that you drop to the ocean floor to see how deep the ocean is.

> Other books have dealt with the topic in a superficial way, but this is the first book
> to really **sound the depths** of the response of the British lower class to the American
> Revolution.

5

Steeped in – Immersed in, saturated with. A teabag **steeps** in hot water. A person **steeped in** classic literature really knows a lot about old, famous books.

> The Met's new youth-targeted campaign seeks to answer the question of whether music lovers **steeped in** hip-hop and pop can learn to love opera.

Stem from – Be caused by. This is related to the idea of a plant's *stem.*

> The psychologist believed that his neurosis **stemmed from** events in his childhood.

Hold sway over – Have great power or influence over a person, group of people, or place.

> Repressive governments are suspicious of those who **hold sway over** the people, and often imprison or execute such people.

Table – In American English, to *table* something means to postpone discussion of it until later. (In British English, to *table* a bill is the opposite—to submit it for consideration.)

Take umbrage – Become offended.

> With 15 years of experience on all kinds of campaigns, she **took umbrage** of her sexist coworker's suggestion that she was only qualified to develop advertising for "women's products."

The very idea (or *the very notion*, etc.) – This expression is used to express a strong contrast.

> The author conjures up a drifting yet haunting word picture that challenges **one's very notion** of what constitutes a story. (This means that the author's strange "word picture" story goes against the most basic things that we think must be true about stories.)

Trappings – Accessories, the characteristic items, products, etc. that come with or are associated with something. Think of the side dishes or condiments that come with a meal. The *trappings* of fame include invites to fancy parties and free items from companies.

Vanguard and **avant-garde** – The *avant-garde* (French for *in front of the guard*) were the leading soldiers at the front of an army. *Vanguard* is derived from *avant-garde* and means the same thing. Metaphorically, the *avant-garde* (noun or adjective) or vanguard (noun) are innovators, those at the forefront of any movement or those "ahead of their time." Sometimes, the *avant-garde* seems a little crazy or scary at first.

> While Google has won the search engine wars, in 1994 Yahoo was on the **vanguard** of search technology.

> She arrived at the mixer in a dress that was a little **avant-garde** for the otherwise conservative Yale Club—she would have looked more appropriate at an art gallery or Lady Gaga concert.

Wanting – *Wanting* means lacking, insufficient, or not good enough (as in, *I read the book and found it wanting*). This makes sense when you think about a person who is *left wanting*—that is, the person is *left wanting* something good. Conversely, a person who *wants for nothing* is someone who already has everything.

With a grain of salt – To take something (a statement, claim, etc.) *with a grain of salt* is to maintain a small amount of skepticism. The origin of this expression is related to an old belief that a small amount of salt could help protect against poison.

> Take the consultant's advice **with a grain of salt**—the software he's recommending is produced by a company that is also a client of his.

With respect to, in some respects – These expressions are not really about giving respect. *With respect to* (or *in respect to*) just means *about*. The expression *in some respects* just means *in some ways*.

> **With respect to** your request for a raise, I'm afraid no one is getting one this year.

Wreak havoc – Cause destruction. The past tense of *wreak* is *wrought*.

> Unsurprisingly, a combination of heroin abuse and living on the streets can really **wreak havoc** on a person's health.

5

Drill: Decoding Idioms

Each sentence below is written in American English that is idiomatic, but still appropriate for academic writing. Pick the multiple-choice answer that best expresses the meaning of the original sentence.

Complete this quiz "open book"—feel free to go back and look up anything you want in this book, and to use any online dictionary (such as dictionary.com). You will gain much more from the process of looking things up and decoding the statements than you would by merely testing yourself in the usual manner.

1. In contrast to the Swedish social welfare system, Ireland's does not provide paid paternity leave.

    A. Ireland's social welfare system does not provide paid paternity leave and Sweden's does.

    B. The Swedish and Irish social welfare systems are different in many ways, and Ireland's does not provide paid paternity leave.

    C. Both the Swedish and Irish social welfare systems provide paid paternity leave.

2. He can hardly be called a liberal, for his voting record belies the beliefs he professes to hold.

    A. He is not really a liberal because he votes in a way that goes against liberalism.

    B. He is a very strong liberal and always supports liberal beliefs with his vote.

    C. He is slightly liberal, and his voting record goes along with his beliefs.

3. However much the committee may be deadlocked now, the progress made to this point has been nontrivial.

    A. The committee is now committed to one course of action and is making progress.

    B. The committee members are fighting with one another, but have made progress on one point they were discussing.

    C. Although it is true that the committee is stuck and not moving forward, it has already made significant progress.

4. Although the book has addressed the issue of educational equity head on, it has sidestepped the thorny question of school vouchers.

    A. The book talked about owning stock in education, but it has talked in an indirect way about the painful issue of school vouchers.

    B. The book talked directly about equality in education, but it avoided talking about the controversial issue of school vouchers.

C. The book talked in a smart way about fairness in education, but it only gave an overview of the controversial issue of school vouchers.

5. Her appointment to the office is all but assured.

   A. She has a meeting at the office, but the time is not set.

   B. She will almost certainly be given a new job or leadership role.

   C. She may be promoted, but it is not likely.

6. You discount the consultant's prescription at your peril.

   A. You put yourself in danger by dismissing the consultant's recommendations.

   B. Paying less for the consultant's advice is not a wise idea.

   C. You have gotten a good deal on a dangerous medicine.

7. Davis seemingly spearheaded the project and has taken credit for its success. Nonetheless, those in the know are aware of his patent appropriation of the ideas of others.

   A. Davis seems to have led the project, and he took credit for it. However, those who know the real situation know that he openly stole other people's ideas.

   B. Davis was the leader of the project and got the credit, and those who know about what happened know that he used the intellectual property of other people in an appropriate way.

   C. Davis seems to have damaged the project, though he took credit for its success. However, those who know the real situation know that he used other people's ideas.

8. The experiment only looks like a success.

   A. It is not possible to see the experiment as anything but a success.

   B. The experiment seems successful, but we don't know for sure.

   C. The experiment has the appearance of a success, but really is a failure.

9. On its face, the dispute is over how the groundbreaking study should be attributed when published. But in actuality, the scientists are arguing because their leader will brook no opposition to his own perspective on their findings.

   A. The dispute is directly about who should get credit for the study. But really, the lead scientist will not "go with the flow" of opposition to his own theories.

   B. The dispute at first seems to be about the study's attribution. But really, the lead scientist will not tolerate opposition to his own theories.

   C. The dispute is directly about who sould get credit for the study. But really, the lead scientist will not encourage opposition to his own theories.

10. We will not likely reconcile the apparent discrepancy for years to come.

    A. It will probably take us many years to show that what looks like a contradiction really isn't.

    B. We do not want to work out a difference of opinion in the coming years.

    C. Over the next several years, we will probably not attempt to work out what seems like an error.

11. The dictator had tyranized his people for too long. As dissident thinkers began to sway public opinion, the country's increasingly marginalized leader reaped the bitter fruits of his cruel reign.

    A. The dictator was disabused of his tyranny, and as rebellious thinkers began to have political power, their tyrannical leader was pushed to the margins.

    B. The dictator had been cruel to his people, and as thinkers who disagreed with the government began to influence regular people, the regime lost influence and power.

    C. The dictator had abused his people, and as thinkers whose ideas went against the government began to influence people, agricultural exports became bitter and expensive.

12. A variable-rate mortgage is no worse in this respect than a fixed-rate one.

    A. There is something bad about a fixed-rate mortgage, and that same quality is better or equally bad in a variable-rate mortgage.

    B. A variable-rate mortgage does not indicate less respect than a fixed-rate mortgage.

    C. If you look at it a certain way, a variable-rate mortgage is the same or better than a fixed-rate one.

13. As to whether Dr. Stuttgart is a token academic on a board of otherwise mercenary executives, you need look only at the board's response to the latest crisis, when Dr. Stuttgart was at once turned to for counsel and granted discretionary power over the board's funds.

    A. If there is a question about whether the main reason Dr. Stuttgart is on the board is so the executives who only care about money can look good, then the only way to answer that question is to look at the board's response to the latest crisis, when Dr. Stuttgart was put in charge and given power over the board's money.

    B. If you want to know whether Dr. Stuttgart is really an academic even though he is on a board of executives who will do anything to win, then the best place to look for an answer is at the board's response to the latest crisis, when Dr. Stuttgart was asked for his advice and allowed to secretly control the board's money.

5

C. If you are questioning whether the main reason Dr. Stuttgart is on the board is so the executives who only care about money can look good, then you can easily answer that question by looking at the board's response to the latest crisis, when the board asked for Dr. Stuttgart's advice while at the same time giving him power to spend the board's money on whatever he thought was best.

14. The author is seemingly a garden-variety Marxist.

A. The author seems to be a Marxist who has a lot of diversity in his or her opinions.

B. The author is a Marxist who is concerned with many different Marxist issues.

C. It seems as though the author is a typical Marxist, but that may not really be true.

15. The windfall could hardly have come at a better time: by agreeing to a company restructuring he didn't really understand, he had just inadvertently reduced his holdings in the family business.

A. The disaster happened at a very bad time, because he had also just agreed to a company reorganization that he didn't understand and that improperly reduced his control over the family business.

B. He suddenly received some money at a very convenient time, because he had just agreed to a company reorganization that he didn't understand and thus had accidentally reduced how much of the family business he owned.

C. The good fortune could have happened at a better time, because he had also just agreed to a company reorganization that he didn't understand and that reduced his portion of the family business.

16. Which of the following, if true, best reconciles the apparent discrepancy?

A. Which of the following is true and shows that a contradiction does not really exist?

B. Which of the following, if it happened to be true, would show that what looks like a contradiction really isn't?

C. Which of the following, if it happened to be true, would help us accept a contradiction?

17. The evidence has been taken as supporting Fujimura's conclusion.

A. Other people have interpreted the evidence in a way that makes it seem to support Fujimura's conclusion.

B. The evidence definitely supports Fujimura's conclusion.

C. The evidence has been deeply understood by others in a way that allows them to effectively support Fujimura's conclusion.

18. Hardly an atypical example, this shifty, hedging, practically unreadable document is paradigmatic of corporate memos.

   A. This memo switches positions often, holds back information, and is very hard to read. It is a very poor example of corporate memos.

   B. Although this memo refuses to take a stand, tries to reduce the writer's risk, and is very hard to read, it is a poor example of corporate memos and should not be judged to be representative.

   C. This memo is evasive or tricky, avoids taking a stand so as not to risk being wrong or offensive, and is almost unreadable. However, this is pretty standard for a corporate memo.

19. Which of the following best underscores the argument that a failure to enforce the regulation is on par with publicly condoning illegal dumping?

   A. Which of the following most weakens the argument that a failure to enforce the regulation is just as bad as publicly tolerating illegal dumping?

   B. Which of the following most strengthens the argument that a failure to enforce the regulation is just as bad as publicly tolerating illegal dumping?

   C. Which of the following most emphasizes the argument that a failure to enforce the regulation is worse than publicly tolerating illegal dumping?

20. The central idea is juxtaposed with the results of a study that seemingly corroborates a long-derided school of thought.

   A. The central idea is placed next to and contrasted with evidence that seems to support the ideas of a group of people whose ideas have been looked down on or made fun of for a long time.

   B. The central idea is judged to be better than evidence that seems to support the ideas of a group of people whose ideas have been looked down on or made fun of for a long time.

   C. The central idea is placed next to and contrasted with evidence that supports the ideas of a group of people whose ideas used to be looked down on or made fun of.

Solutions: Decoding Idioms

1. (A)

2. (A)

3. (C)

4. (B)

5. (B)

6. (A)

7. (A)

8. (C)

9. (B)

10. (A)

11. (B)

12. (A)

13. (C)

14. (C)

15. (B)

16. (B)

17. (A)

18. (C)

19. (B)

20. (A)

5

Appendix A
of

Text Completion & Sentence Equivalence

Roots List

In This Chapter...

Roots List

Many words in English, especially those that come from Latin or Greek, have more than one "part." Here is the basic pattern:

Word	=	Prefix	+	Root	+	Suffix
EXCISION	=	EX	+	CIS	+	ION

The root contains the original core meaning of the word, although this meaning may have changed over time. Here, the root *cis* means "cut."

The prefix alters that meaning in some way. Here, the prefix *ex-* means "out" or "away."

Together, the prefix and the root handle most of the meaning: *ex* + *cis* = excise, or "cut away."

Finally, the suffix determines the part of speech. The suffix *–ion* means "the action of doing X," so *excision* means "the act of cutting away."

Be careful! Many words do not break down so cleanly. Also, roots can be misleading. The original meaning of a word may have only been related in a *metaphorical* sense to the meaning of its original parts. Moreover, over time, many words drift very far from their original, etymological meaning (some words transform so much that they come to mean the *opposite* of their original meaning).

Study roots, prefixes, and suffixes primarily to solidify your vocabulary. On the test, you can and should use your root knowledge to guess at the meaning of unknown words. Realize, however, that roots are most helpful *now*, while you're studying —not the day of the test. Be sure to learn the full dictionary meanings of vocabulary words.

Part I: Roots

This list includes a broad selection of roots and illustrative examples that often appear on the GRE. The examples have been chosen specifically to illustrate the root and thus to avoid meaning drift. Nearly all the roots are Latin or Greek. This list is not exhaustive; it is meant to provide a useful reference.

The definitions given for the harder words are brief. Remember to consult your dictionary for nuances.

ROOT	MEANING	EXAMPLES
ac	sharp *or*	**ac**id
acer	point *or*	**acr**id = sharp, bitter (of smell or taste)
acri	high	**acer**bity = bitterness
acro		**acri**mony = sharpness of words, behavior, or feeling
		acme = highest point, best level
		acrophobia = "high + fear" = fear of heights
		acumen = sharpness of intellect

ROOT	MEANING	EXAMPLES
ag **act**	drive *or* lead *or* do	**ag**ent, **act** dem**ag**ogue = "people + lead" = leader who appeals (falsely) to the people re**act** = do in response
alt	high	**alt**itude, **alt**imeter ex**alt**ed = "out + high" = raised high
ambul	walk	circum**ambul**ate = "around + walk" = walk around in a circle per**ambul**ator = "around + walk" = baby carriage
anim	spirit *or* breath	**anim**ate un**anim**ous = "one + spirit" = in complete agreement equ**anim**ity = "even + spirit" = calmness, balance under stress magn**anim**ity = "great + spirit" = nobility of spirit, generosity pusill**anim**ous = "tiny + spirit" = cowardly, without courage
arch	rule	an**arch**y = "not + ruler" = chaos, lack of government
aud	hear	**aud**ience, **aud**ible **aud**itory = related to hearing
bell **belli**	war	re**bell**ion **bell**icose = ready to fight, warlike **bell**igerent = "war + do" = hostile, provocative, or actually at war
cad **cid**	fall	de**cad**ent = "away + fall" = in a state of decline, often self-indulgent re**cid**ivism = "back + fall" = tendency to relapse to earlier behavior or crime
ced **cess** **ceed**	go *or* yield	pro**ceed**, suc**ceed**, ex**ceed**, re**ced**e **ced**e = yield ante**ced**ent = "before + go" = earlier event or cause pre**ced**ent = "before + go" = earlier example **cess**ation = end of an action
chron	time	**chron**ological, **chron**ic ana**chron**ism = "not + time" = something out of place in time dia**chron**ic = "through + time" = relating to change over time
cis **cide**	cut *or* kill	in**cis**ive = "into + cut" = cutting to the heart of a matter, direct ex**cis**ion = "out + cut" = act of cutting out, removing regi**cide** = "king + kill" = murder of a king
clud **clus** **claus**	close	in**clud**e, ex**clud**e, in**clus**ion, **claus**trophobia pre**clud**e = "before + close" = prevent, rule out beforehand oc**clud**e = "against + close" = block off or conceal
crat **crac**	rule	demo**crac**y auto**crat**ic = "self + ruler" = relating to an absolute ruler or tyrant
cred **creed**	believe	in**cred**ible, **creed** **cred**ence = acceptance, trust **cred**ulity = readiness to believe, gullibility in**cred**ulous = skeptical, unwilling to believe
dei	god	**dei**fy = "god + make" = make into a god, glorify

ROOT	MEANING	EXAMPLES
demo **dem**	people	**demo**cracy **demo**graphic = related to a population, or a segment of a population pan**dem**ic = "all + people" = something affecting everyone, usually a disease en**dem**ic = "in + people" = native to a population **dem**agogue = "people + lead" = leader who appeals (falsely) to the people
dict	say	pre**dict**, contra**dict**, juris**dict**ion bene**dict**ion = "good + say" = blessing vale**dict**ory = "farewell + say" = expressing a farewell (often by a speech)
duc	lead *or* pull	pro**duc**e, ab**duc**t, con**duc**t de**duc**e = "away + lead" = determine from general principles **duc**tile = able to be led easily (people) or to be drawn out into wire (metals) in**duc**t = "in + lead" = admit as a member
dur, dure	hard *or* lasting	**dur**able, en**dure**, en**dur**ance, **dur**ation, **dur**ing **dur**ess = compulsion, restraint by force ob**dur**ate = "against + hard" = hard of heart, stubborn
equi **equa**	equal *or* even	**equa**tion, **equa**tor **equi**table = dealing fairly on all sides **equa**nimity = "even + spirit" = calmness under stress, balance **equi**vocate = "equal + voice" = say something open to more than one interpretation in order to mislead or to avoid commitment **equa**ble = uniform, steady, unchanging
fac **fec** **fic** **fy**	do *or* make	terri**fy**, puri**fy**, paci**fy**, aff**ec**t, eff**ec**t, **fac**t, artifi**fic**ial rare**fy** = "rare + make" = make thin, pure, less dense veri**fy** = "true + make" = confirm as true sancti**fy** = "holy + make" = make holy dei**fy** = "god + make" = make into a god, glorify bene**fic**ent = "good + do" = doing good for others male**fic**ent = "bad + do" = doing harm or evil **fac**ile = easily done or understood, lacking depth or authenticity **fac**ilitate = to make easy, help to happen **fac**titious = artificial, made-up, fake
fer	carry *or* bring	trans**fer**, of**fer**, **fer**tile, **fer**ry proli**fer**ate = "offspring + carry" = multiply in number voci**fer**ous = "voice + carry" = shouting loudly and angrily
ferv	boil	**ferv**ent = zealous, intense in feeling ef**ferv**escent = "away + boil" = being bubbly, showing exhilaration per**ferv**id = "through + boil" = overexcited, overwrought
fid	trust *or* faith	**fid**elity, con**fid**ence dif**fid**ence = "not + faith" = hesitant, lacking in self-confidence per**fid**ious = "detrimental + faith" = disloyal, treacherous

ROOT	MEANING	EXAMPLES
flect **flex**	bend	**flex**ible, re**flect**, de**flect**
flu **flux** **fluct**	flow *or* wave	**flu**id, **fluct**uate, in**flux** con**flu**ence = "together + flow" = a flowing together super**flu**ous = "over + flow" = unnecessary, wasteful melli**flu**ous = "honey + flow" = having a smooth flow like honey ef**flu**vium = "out + flow" = by-product, (bad) exhalation
gen	kin *or* kind *or* birth	**gen**try = upper class **gen**tility = high social status, or conduct becoming of that status hetero**gen**eous = "different + kind" = consisting of diverse parts homo**gen**eous = "same + kind" = consisting of one substance
gno	know	a**gno**stic = "not + know" = someone who isn't sure (often about God's existence) dia**gno**sis = "through + know" = identification of (medical) causes & issues pro**gno**sticate = "before + know" = predict, foretell co**gno**scente (pl. cognoscenti) = "with + know" = expert in a subject
graph **gram**	write	auto**graph**, dia**gram**, **gram**mar, **graph**ic, tele**gram** mono**graph** = "one + write" = a written report or paper on a narrow subject
grade **gress**	step *or* go	pro**gress**, re**gress**, ag**gress**ive, con**gress** retro**grade** = "backward + go" = moving backward trans**gress**ion = "across + step" = violation of a law or rule di**gress** = "away + go" = deviate from a subject
greg	flock *or* herd	ag**greg**ate = "toward + flock" = collect or add up con**greg**ate = "together + flock" = gather together e**greg**ious = "outside + flock" = conspicuously bad, flagrant **greg**arious = sociable, companionable
her **hes**	stick	ad**her**e = "to + stick" = stick to co**hes**ive = "together + stick" = sticking or fitting together
jac **ject**	throw	e**ject**, tra**ject**ory, inter**ject**, ob**ject**ion, re**ject** ab**ject** = "away + thrown" = extremely bad
jur	law *or* swear	**jur**y, **jur**isdiction ab**jur**e = "away + swear" = renounce or reject ad**jur**e = "toward + swear" = command, urge
leg **lex** **lect** **log**	word *or* speak *or* read *or* study	**lect**ure, mono**log**ue, chrono**log**ical, **lex**icon neo**log**ism = "new + word" = new word or expression eu**log**y = speech of praise (often after death)
locu **loqu**	speak	circum**locu**tion = "around + speak" = wordiness or evasion in speech e**locu**tion = "out + speak" = art of speaking well in public **loqu**acious = very talkative

ROOT	MEANING	EXAMPLES
luc **lus**	light *or* shine *or* clear	**luc**id = clear, sane, full of light e**luc**idate = "out + shine" = make clear, explain trans**luc**ent = "through + shine" = permitting (some) passage of light pel**luc**id = "through + clear" = absolutely clear lack**lus**ter = dull, lacking brilliance
meter **metr**	measure	**metr**ic, alti**meter**, peri**meter**
mit **miss**	send	dis**miss**, e**mit**, trans**mit** **miss**ive = letter, written message re**miss** = "back + sent" = negligent, careless, lax
morph	shape	a**morph**ous = "without + shape" = shapeless meta**morph**ose = "change + shape" = transform
nom	name	**nom**inate = appoint to a position pseudo**nym** = "false + name" = a fake name used by an author
path	feeling	anti**path**y = "against + feeling" = strong dislike **path**etic = arousing pity
pel **puls**	drive *or* push	ex**pel**, pro**pel** dis**pel** = "away + drive" = scatter, make vanish com**pel**ling = "together + drive" = convincing, forceful, attention-grabbing
phob	fear	acro**phob**ia = "high + fear" = fear of heights
phon	sound	mega**phon**e, tele**phon**e, **phon**ics homo**phon**e = "same + sound" = a word pronounced like another word caco**phon**ous = "bad + sound" = unpleasant sounding eu**phon**y = "good + sound" = pleasing sound (usually of words)
port	carry	**port**er, trans**port**ation, im**port**, ex**port**, de**port**
pos **pon**	put	im**pos**e, ex**pos**e, op**pos**e, op**pon**ent, **pro**ponent de**pos**e = "down + put" = remove a leader, or take testimony superim**pos**e = "over + on + put" = place over
prob **prov**	prove *or* test	**prob**e, **prov**e, im**prov**e, ap**prov**e **prob**ity = honesty, integrity re**prov**e = "back + prove" = scold, admonish, express disapproval
rog	ask	inter**rog**ation, inter**rog**atory pre**rog**ative = "before + ask" = special right ar**rog**ate = "toward + ask" = claim or take (without the right) ab**rog**ate = "away + ask" = abolish, nullify (a law or rule)
sanct	holy	**sanct**uary = holy place **sanct**ify = "holy + make" = make holy sacro**sanct** = holy, untouchable **sanct**imonious = hypocritically or falsely holy
sci	know	**sci**ence pre**sci**ent = "before + know" = knowing ahead of time, able to predict events omni**sci**ence = "all + know" = state of knowing everything

MANHATTAN
PREP   169

ROOT	MEANING	EXAMPLES
scrib script	write	**scrib**ble, **scrib**e, **script**, pre**scrib**e
sec sect	cut	**sect**ion, **sect**or, inter**sect** bi**sect** = "two + cut" = cut in half **sect** = a subdivision or segment of a group, often of a religion
sed	sit	super**sed**e = "above + sit" = replace, transcend by being better
sequ secu sic	follow	**sequ**ence, con**sequ**ence, con**secu**tive extrin**sic** = "outside + follow" = external to something's nature intrin**sic** = "inside + follow" = internal to something's nature ob**sequ**ious = "toward + follow" = overly obedient, submissive, flattering
simil simul	similar	as**simil**ate = "toward + similar" = make or become a similar part of something **simil**itude = likeness, correspondence between two things **simul**acrum = image, semblance
son	sound	**son**ar, **son**ic **son**orous = full of rich sound dis**son**ance = "apart + sound" = discord, clash of sounds
spec spect spic	look	**spect**acle, in**spect**, retro**spect** circum**spect** = "around + look" = cautious, prudent per**spic**acious = "through + look" = able to perceive hidden truth
ten tain tend	hold *or* have *or* stretch *or* thin	re**tain**, con**tain**, ob**tain**, ex**tend** **ten**able = able to be held or maintained **ten**acity = courage, persistence, ability to hold fast abs**tain** = "away + hold" = refrain from dis**tend** = "away + stretch" = bloat, swell, expand **ten**uous = thin, weak at**ten**uate = "toward + thin" = make or become thinner or weaker
theo the	god	a**the**ist = "not + god" = someone who doesn't believe in God poly**the**ist = "many + god" = someone who believes in many gods apo**theo**sis = "from + god" = elevation to godlike status, or something that has that status
tract	drag *or* draw *or* pull	**tract**or, at**tract**, con**tract**, de**tract**, ex**tract**, re**tract** **tract**able = able to be led, obedient, easily managed abs**tract**ed = "away + drawn" = withdrawn into one's mind
trud trus	push *or* thrust	in**trud**e, ex**trud**e unob**trus**ive = "not + against + push" = not noticeable or attention-drawing abs**trus**e = "away + push" = hard to comprehend
veh vect	carry	**veh**icle, con**vect**ion, **vect**or in**vect**ive = "in + carry" = bitter criticism, denunciation **veh**ement = "carried (away) + mind" = passionate, nearly violent

ROOT	MEANING	EXAMPLES
ven **vent**	come	inter**ven**e, pre**vent**, in**vent**, e**vent**, ad**vent**ure, **vent**ure pro**ven**ance = "forward + come" = source, or history of ownership contra**ven**e = "against + come" = oppose, violate, or contradict
ver	true	**ver**ify = "true + make" = confirm as true **ver**acity = truthfulness or truth a**ver** = "toward + true" = assert, declare
vert **vers**	turn	re**vert**, extro**vert**, intro**vert**, ad**vers**e, inad**vert**ent, a**vers**ion, a**vert**, in**vert** **vers**atile = able to adapt easily, ready for many uses di**vert** = "away + turn" = turn aside or distract contro**vert** = "against + turn" = dispute in argument, engage in contro**vers**y
voc	voice *or* call	**voc**al, in**voc**ation equi**voc**ate = "equal + voice" = say something open to more than one interpretation in order to mislead or to avoid commitment **voc**iferous = "voice + carry" = shouting loudly and angrily
vol	will	bene**vol**ence = "good + will" = kindness, readiness to do good for others male**vol**ent = "bad + will" = wishing harm, ready to do evil **vol**untary – done of one's own free will

Part II: Prefixes

You must be even more careful with prefixes than with roots. Certain prefixes have relatively stable meanings (e.g., *bene-* pretty much always means "good"), but other prefixes, especially short ones that correspond to prepositions, can take on a variety of different meanings. The sense of the whole word is often unpredictable. Take a simple word: *describe* = "from + write." It is not obvious how the particular meaning of *describe* originates from the combination of the prefix *de-* and the root *scrib*.

Even if the meanings of the prefix and the root remain stable, the word itself may still take an unpredictable turn. For instance, *polygraph* = "many + write". How we would work out from the roots that a *polygraph* is a "lie-detector test" (which writes down lots of physiological data at once) is anyone's guess. Do not simply rely on knowing the prefix and the root separately—always learn the modern English meaning of the word itself.

Most of the examples in the following list can also be found in the roots list, so that you can see both the root and the prefix in action and reinforce the word in your memory.

PREFIX	MEANING	EXAMPLES
a- **an-** **ana-**	not *or* without	**a**theist = "not + god" = someone who doesn't believe in God **a**gnostic = "not + know" = someone who isn't sure (often about God's existence) **an**archy = "not + ruler" = chaos, lack of government **ana**chronism = "not + time" = something out of place in time **a**morphous = "without + shape" = shapeless
ab- **abs-**	away from	**ab**normal, **ab**sent, **ab**duct **abs**tain = "away + hold" = refrain from **abs**tracted = "away + drawn" = withdrawn into one's mind **ab**jure = "away + swear" = renounce or reject **ab**ject = "away + thrown" = in a low, hopeless, depressed condition **ab**rogate = "away + propose law" = abolish, nullify (a law or rule) **abs**truse = "away + push" = hard to comprehend **abs**temious = "away + liquor" = moderate in appetite or drinking
ad- **can drop d** **and double** **next letter** **ac-, ag-, as-** **at- etc.**	to *or* toward	**ad**here = "to + stick" = stick to **ad**jure = "toward + swear" = command, urge **ac**crete = "toward + grow" = grow or pile up bit by bit **ag**gregate = "toward + flock" = collect together **as**similate = "toward + similar" = make or become a similar part of something **ar**rogate = "toward + ask" = claim or take (without the right) **at**tenuate = "toward + thin" = make or become thinner or weaker
ante-	before	**ante**cedent = "before + go" = earlier event or cause **ante**diluvian = "before + flood" = ancient, primitive
anti- **ant-**	against *or* opposite	**anti**biotic = "against + life" = chemical that kills bacteria **anti**pathy = "against + feeling" = strong dislike **ant**agonism = "against + struggle" = opposition, active hostility

PREFIX	MEANING	EXAMPLES
auto-	self	**auto**graph = "self + write" = sign one's own name
		autocratic = "self + ruler" = like an absolute ruler or tyrant
		autonomous = "self + law" = independent, self-contained
be-	Thoroughly *or* affect with	**be**grudge = "thoroughly + complain" = give unwillingly
		beguile = "affect with + trick" = deceive, divert in an attractive way
		benighted = "thoroughly + night" = unenlightened, in figurative darkness
		beseech = "thoroughly + seek" = beg, implore
		besiege = "thoroughly + blockade" = surround, press upon
		besmirch = "affect with + dirt" = make dirty
bene- **ben-**	good	**bene**diction = "good + say" = blessing
		beneficent = "good + do" = doing good for others
		benevolence = "good + will" = kindness, readiness to do good for others
		benign = "good + birth" = favorable, gentle, harmless
bi-	two	**bi**sect = "two + cut" = cut in half
		bifurcate = "two + fork" = split into two branches
caco-	bad	**caco**phonous = "bad + sound" = unpleasant sounding
circum-	around	**circum**ambulate = "around + walk" = walk around in a circle
		circumlocution = "around + speak" = wordiness or evasion in speech
		circumspect = "around + look" = cautious, prudent
con- **com-** **co-**	with *or* together	**con**tract, **con**tain, **con**duct
		con**greg**ate = "together + flock" = gather together
		cohesive = "together + stick" = sticking or fitting together
		compelling = "together + drive" = convincing, forceful, attention-grabbing
		confluence = "together + flow" = a flowing together
		cognoscente (pl. cognoscenti) = "with + know" = expert in a subject
contra- **contro-** **counter-**	against	**contra**dict
		contraband = "against + command" = illegal goods
		countervail = "against + worth" = compensate for, counteract, oppose
		contravene = "against + come" = oppose, violate, contradict
		controvert = "against + turn" = dispute in argument, engage in controversy
de-	from *or* away *or* down	**de**fame, **de**odorize, **de**flect, detract
		deduce = "away + lead" = determine from general principles
		decadent = "away + fall" = in a state of decline, often self-indulgent
		derivative = "away + stream" = originating from something else, lacking originality
		depose = "down + put" = remove a leader, or take testimony
di- **dia-**	two *or* through *or* across *or* between	**dia**meter, **dia**gonal
		dichotomy = division into two opposing parts
		diagnosis = "through + know" = identification of (medical) causes & issues
		diachronic = "through + time" = relating to change over time

PREFIX	MEANING	EXAMPLES
dis- **dys-** **di-**	away *or* not *or* bad	**dis**allow, **dis**respect, **dis**miss, **dis**illusion, **di**vide **dis**pel = "away + drive" = scatter, make vanish **di**vert = "away + turn" = turn aside or distract **dis**sonance = "bad + sound" = discord, clash of sounds **dis**tend = "away + stretch" = bloat, swell, expand **dif**fidence = "not + faith" = hesitant, lacking in self-confidence **di**gress = "away + go" = deviate from subject **dys**topia = "bad" + utopia (future/imaginary world)
duo-	two	**duo**poly = "two + sell" = condition in which there are only two sellers
en-	in	**en**demic = "in + people" = native to a population
eu-	good	**eu**logize = "good + speak" = praise highly (often after death) **eu**phony = "good + sound" = pleasing sound (usually of words)
ex- **e-** **ef-**	out *or* away *or* from	**e**mit, **ex**pel, **ex**ceed, **ex**it, **e**ject, **ex**port **ex**alted = "out + high" = raised high **ex**cision = "out + cut" = act of cutting out, removing **e**locution = "out + speak" = art of speaking well in public **e**gregious = "outside + flock" = conspicuously bad, flagrant **e**lucidate = "out + shine" = make clear, explain **ef**fluvium = "out + flow" = by-product, exhalation (often bad)
exter- **extra-** **extr-**	outside of	**exter**ior, **extr**eme **extra**curricular = "outside + course" = an activity pursued at school outside of normal course studies **extr**insic = "outside + follow" = external to something's nature
hetero-	other *or* different	**hetero**geneous = "different + kind" = consisting of diverse parts
homo-	same	**homo**phone = "same + sound" = a word pronounced like another word **homo**geneous = "same + kind" = consisting of one substance
hyper-	above *or* over	**hyper**sensitive, **hyper**active **hyper**bole = "above + throw" = exaggeration
hypo-	below *or* under	**hypo**allergenic **hypo**thesis = "under" + thesis = tentative assumption to explore **hypo**dermic = "under + skin" = injected beneath the skin
in- **im-**	in *or* into *or* on	**in**spect, **im**port, **in**ject **in**cisive = "into + cut" = cutting to the heart of a matter, direct **in**duct = "in + lead" = admit as a member
in- **im-**	not	**in**credible, **im**possible, **im**penetrable, **in**evitable
infra-	below	**infra**red, **infra**structure
inter- **intro-**	between	**inter**national, **inter**vene, **inter**ject **inter**polate = "inside + polish" = fill in missing pieces, words, or data **intro**spect, **intro**vert, **intro**duce

PREFIX	MEANING	EXAMPLES
intra- intr-	within or into	**intra**muscular, **intra**mural **intr**insic = "inside + follow" = internal to something's nature
magn-	big or great	**magn**ificent **magn**animity = "great + spirit" = nobility of spirit
mal- male-	bad	**mal**adjusted **male**volent = "bad + will" = wishing harm, ready to do evil **male**ficent = "bad + do" = doing harm or evil **mal**adroit = "bad" + adroit (skillful) = lacking skill
mega- megalo-	big or great or million	**mega**phone **megalo**mania = "great + mad" = insane belief that one is all-powerful
meta-	beyond or change	**meta**morphose = "change + shape" = transform
micro-	small	**micro**scope, **micro**processor
mis-	bad or hate	**mis**apply, **mis**take, **mis**interpret **mis**anthropy = "hate + human" = hatred of humankind **mis**ogyny = "hate + women" = hatred of women
mono-	one	**mono**culture **mono**graph = "one + write" = a written report or paper on a narrow subject **mono**poly = "one + sell" = condition in which there is only one seller
multi-	many	**multi**ple, **multi**national **multi**farious = "many + places" = diverse, varied
neo-	new	**neo**logism = "new + word" = new word or expression **neo**phyte = "new + planted" = beginner, novice
non-	not	**non**sensical, **non**profit **non**descript = "not + described" = lacking distinctive qualities **non**pareil = "not + equal" = without equal
ob- can drop b and double next letter oc-, etc.	in front of or against or toward	**ob**jection **ob**durate = "against + hard" = hard of heart, stubborn **oc**clude = "against + close" = block off or conceal **ob**sequious = "toward + follow" = overly obedient, submissive, flattering
omni-	all	**omni**present, **omni**potent **omni**science = "all + know" = state of knowing everything
pan-	all	**pan**demic = "all + people" = something affecting everyone, usually a disease
para-	beside	**para**llel, **para**phrase
per-	through or detrimental to	**per**mit **per**spicacious = "through + look" = able to perceive hidden truth **per**ambulate = "through + walk" = walk through, inspect **pel**lucid = "through + clear" = absolutely clear **per**fervid = "through + boil" = overexcited, overwrought **per**fidious = "detrimental + faith" = disloyal, treacherous

PREFIX	MEANING	EXAMPLES
peri-	around	**peri**meter **peri**pheral = "around + carry" = on the outskirts, not central **peri**patetic = "around + walk" = moving or walking from place to place
poly-	many	**poly**technical, **poly**gon **poly**theist = "many + god" = someone who believes in many gods **poly**glot = "many + tongue" = someone who speaks many languages
pre-	before	**pre**cede **pre**cedent = "before + go" = earlier example **pre**rogative = "before + ask" = special right **pre**clude = "before + close" = prevent, rule out beforehand **pre**scient = "before + know" = knowing ahead of time, able to predict events
pro-	forward *or* before *or* for	**pro**ponent **pro**gnosticate = "before + know" = predict, foretell **pro**venance = "before + come" = source, or history of ownership
re-	back *or* again	**re**do, **re**state, **re**flect, **re**tract, **re**ject, **re**cede **re**miss = "back + sent" = negligent, careless, lax **re**cidivism = "back + fall" = tendency to relapse to earlier behavior or crime
retro-	backward	**retro**active, **retro**spect **retro**grade = "backward + go" = moving backward
sub-	below *or* under	**sub**standard, **sub**marine **sub**ordinate = "below + order" = in a lower rank, controlled by higher ranks **sub**liminal = "below + threshold" = below the level of consciousness
super-	above *or* over	**super**natural, **super**ior **super**fluous = "over + flow" = unnecessary, wasteful **super**ficial = on the surface **super**impose = "over + on + put" = place over **super**sede = "above + sit" = replace, transcend by being better
syn-	together *or* with	**syn**thesis = "together + thesis" = combination of ideas **syn**cretism = "together + Cretan cities" = fusion of ideas and practices **syn**optic = "together + eye" = taking a comprehensive view
trans- **tra-**	across *or* beyond *or* through	**trans**fer, **tra**jectory, **tran**smit, **trans**portation **trans**gression = "across + step" = violation of a law or rule **trans**lucent = "through + shine" = permitting (some) passage of light
un-	not	**un**happy **un**obtrusive = "not + against + push" = not noticeable or attention-drawing
uni- **un-**	one	**uni**form, **uni**cycle **un**animous = "one + spirit" = in complete agreement

MANHATTAN
PREP

Part III: Suffixes

Fortunately, suffixes are much more stable in meaning than roots or prefixes, meaning you know most of them already—just by speaking and reading in English! However, it is still worth looking over this list, in particular to examine how suffixes often change one part of speech into another.

SUFFIX	DESCRIPTION	PART OF SPEECH	MADE FROM	EXAMPLES
-able **-ible**	able to be X-ed	adjective	verb	think**able**, desir**able**, inconceiv**able**, frang**ible**, feas**ible**
-al **-ial** **-ile**	relating to X	adjective	noun *or* verb	triv**ial**, critic**al**, lab**ile**, duct**ile**, versat**ile**
-ance **-ancy** **-ence** **-ency**	state *or* process of doing X *or* being X	noun (abstract)	verb *or* adjective	intellig**ence**, flipp**ancy**, decad**ence**, exorbit**ance**, despond**ency**
-ant **-ent**	doing X	adjective *or* noun	verb	accord**ant**, account**ant**, cogniz**ant**, differ**ent**, intransig**ent**, ferv**ent**
-ar **-ary**	related to X	adjective	noun	sol**ar**, stell**ar**, pol**ar**
-ate (usually pronounced like ate) **-ite**	do X	verb	root	interrog**ate**, prevaric**ate**, mut**ate**, ign**ite**, exped**ite**
-ate (usually pronounced like it) **-ite**	formed by doing X *or* related to doing X	noun *or* adjective	verb	aggreg**ate**, insubordin**ate**, perquis**ite**, requis**ite**
-dom	state of being X *or* condition related to X	noun (abstract)	noun *or* adjective	free**dom**, fief**dom**, wis**dom**
-er **-or**	doer of X	noun (person)	verb	speak**er**, runn**er**, wander**er**
-fic	making into X *or* causing X	adjective	noun *or* adjective	horri**fic**, beati**fic**, proli**fic**, sopori**fic**
-fy **-ify**	make into X cause X	verb	noun *or* adjective	magni**fy**, dei**fy**, indemni**fy**, ossi**fy**, rei**fy**
-ful	filled with X	adjective	noun	bounti**ful**, beauti**ful**, plenti**ful**, fret**ful**, art**ful**

SUFFIX	DESCRIPTION	PART OF SPEECH	MADE FROM	EXAMPLES
-ic -iac	relating to X	adjective or noun	noun or verb	man**ic**, man**iac**, asept**ic**, bombast**ic**
-ification	process of making into X	noun (action)	noun or adjective	desert**ification**, ram**ification**, beaut**ification**, ed**ification**
-ine	relating to X	adjective	noun or verb	saturn**ine**, mar**ine**, sal**ine**, clandest**ine**
-ish	similar to X	adjective	noun or adjective	redd**ish**, mul**ish**, fiend**ish**, lout**ish**
-ism	system or characteristic of X	noun (abstract)	noun or adjective or verb	capital**ism**, social**ism**, commun**ism**, stoic**ism**, anachron**ism**, euphem**ism**
-ist -istic	characteristic of X or a person who espous- es X	adjective or noun	noun or adjective	capital**ist**, social**ist**, commun**ist**, anachron**istic**, euphem**istic**
-ite	native or adherent of X	noun	noun or adjective	anchor**ite**, Ludd**ite**, sybar**ite**
-ity -ty	state or quality of be- ing X or doing X	noun (abstract)	adjective or verb	polar**ity**, certain**ty**, convex**ity**, perplex**ity**
-ive -ative	tending toward the action of X	adjective	verb or noun	exclus**ive**, act**ive**, cohes**ive**, author**ative**, evas**ive**
-ize -ise	make into X	verb	adjective or noun	eulog**ize**, polar**ize**, scrutin**ize**, lion**ize**, advert**ise**, improv**ise**
-ization -isation	process of making into X	noun (action)	adjective	character**ization**, polar**ization**, lion**ization**, improv**isation**
-less	without X	adjective	noun	harm**less**, guile**less**, feck**less**
-ment	state or result of doing X	noun	verb	develop**ment**, judg**ment**, punish**ment**
-ory	characteristic of doing X or a place for doing X	adjective or noun	verb	refract**ory**, sav**ory**, deposit**ory**, compuls**ory**, mandat**ory**
-ous -ious -ose	characteristic of being X or doing X	adjective	verb or noun	carnivor**ous**, dev**ious**, numer**ous**, melliflu**ous**, mendac**ious**, verb**ose**
-tion -ation -ion	process or result of doing X	noun (action)	verb	pollu**tion**, crea**tion**, destruc**tion**
-tude	state or quality of being X	noun (abstract)	adjective	soli**tude**, vicissi**tude**, pulchri**tude**, desue**tude**

Appendix *of* B

Text Completion &
Sentence Equivalence

1,000 Words for the GRE

In This Chapter...

500 Essential Words for the GRE

500 Advanced Words for the GRE

500 Essential Words for the GRE

The list below contains 500 *essential* words that you should learn for the GRE. Do not move ahead to the *advanced* word list until you have learned these (advanced words can be found later in this appendix).

This list contains all of the words in the Manhattan Prep 500 Essential Words for the GRE flash card set (available for purchase on our website, on Amazon.com, and at major bookstores). However, the flash cards contain *much* more information about each word, including synonyms, etymologies, and idiomatic usages. If you already have the flash cards, we suggest using those as your primary study tool, and using this list as an alphabetic reference.

WORD	P.O.S	DEFINITION	USAGE
abate	(verb)	Reduce, diminish	Her stress over spending so much money on a house abated when the real estate broker told her about the property's 15-year tax abatement.
abdicate	(verb)	Formally give up the throne (or some other power or responsibility)	King Edward VIII of England famously abdicated the throne in order to marry an American divorcée. / Parents can be charged with neglect for abdicating their responsibilities towards their children.
aberrant	(adj)	Abnormal, deviant	The teen's aberrant behavior made his family suspect that he was using drugs. / Losing rather than gaining weight over the holidays is certainly an aberration.
abhor	(verb)	Detest, regard with disgust	"Go out with you?" she replied. "I abhor you! I would rather stab myself with a rusty bread knife than be your girlfriend!"
abjure	(verb)	Give up, renounce; repudiate, recant, or shun (especially formally or under oath)	To become a citizen of the United States, you must abjure loyalty to the nation of your birth. / Since enrolling in that nutrition class, she has abjured sugar and saturated fats.
abrasive	(adj)	Rough, suitable for grinding or polishing (such as sandpaper); causing irritation or annoyance	Could the inside of this mascot costume be any more abrasive? It's rubbing my skin raw! I have some seriously abrasive remarks for whomever designed this thing.
abridge	(verb)	Condense or curtail; shorten by omitting parts throughout while retaining the main idea	Our romantic vacation was abridged when the babysitter called to say that the kids were sick and we should come home. / Audio books are almost always abridged, since few people want to listen to a 200-hour book.
abstain	(verb)	Hold back, refrain (especially from something bad or unhealthy); decline to vote	The church board voted on whether to hold an abstinence rally to encourage young people not to become sexually active; while most members voted in favor, one voted against and two abstained, with one abstainer commenting that, as far as she knew, the church's teens were pretty abstemious already.

WORD	P.O.S	DEFINITION	USAGE
acme	(noun)	Summit, peak, highest point	The acme of my vacation was when I finally climbed to the acme of the mountain and enjoyed the gorgeous vista.
activism	(noun)	The practice of pursuing political or other goals through vigorous action, often including protests and demonstrations	Lindsay's parents had a hard time accepting that, after incurring $100,000 in student loans, their daughter had decided to enter the low-paying field of environmental activism.
adhere	(verb)	Stick (to), such as with glue, or to a plan or belief	I have a message board that adheres to my refrigerator with magnets; on it, I've written some affirmations to help me adhere to my diet plan.
admonish	(verb)	Mildly scold; caution, advise, or remind to do something	She was an exacting boss who castigated an employee for jamming the copier, yet she merely admonished her five-year-old for the same offense.
adverse	(adj)	Opposing, harmful	Pioneer women persevered despite adverse circumstances, even when fording a river—baby in one arm, leading a horse with the other—against an adverse current.
advocate	(verb, noun)	Speak or argue in favor of (verb); a person who pleads for a cause or on behalf of another person (noun)	I cannot possibly vote for a candidate who advocates oil drilling in federally protected nature preserves. / Children often have advocates appointed to represent them in court.
aesthetic	(adj, noun)	Concerning the appreciation of beauty or good taste, pertaining to the science of what is beautiful (adj); a set of principles or tastes guiding an artistic practice (noun)	The twins were so different. One possessed a truly baroque aesthetic, preferring golden, gilded decor. The other lived in a world of pure logic, untouched by any aesthetic sense whatsoever; art did not move him, his house was bare, and he married his wife solely because she was a master of calculus.
affable	(adj)	Warm and friendly, pleasant, approachable	The professional wrestler played at belligerence in the ring, but in real life, he was quite an affable fellow: sociable, easy-going, and always ready to lend a hand.
affectation	(noun)	Fake behavior (such as in speech or dress) adopted to give a certain impression	I'm annoyed whenever Americans move to England and suddenly start speaking with an affected British accent; such affectations, when practiced by celebrities, are only likely to alienate their fans.
aggrandize	(verb)	Make greater; exaggerate	I can't stand when my coworker aggrandizes her role in our group projects. / Stop it with your constant self-aggrandizing—we don't care how many automobiles you own!

MANHATTAN
PREP

WORD	P.O.S	DEFINITION	USAGE
aggregate	(verb, adj)	Gather together, amount to (verb); constituting a whole made up of constituent parts (adj)	While some of the company's divisions did better than others, in aggregate, we made a profit. / Concrete is created when crushed rock or glass is aggregated with cement; in aggregate, concrete is stronger than cement alone.
alacrity	(noun)	Cheerful or speedy willingness	Any boss wants an employee to respond with alacrity to his or her requests, handling them promptly and with enthusiasm.
alienate	(verb)	Cause to become unfriendly, hostile, or distant	The talk-show host was trying to help, but only alienated her viewers when she suggested that they cope with a tough economy by checking themselves into a spa.
alleviate	(verb)	Lessen, make easier to endure	The stimulus package has alleviated the pangs of the Great Recession, but times are still tough.
ambiguous	(adj)	Not clear, hard to understand, open to having several meanings or interpretations	The meaning of this ancient text is ambiguous—either we are missing some cultural context, or else the writer actually wanted to be mysterious.
ambivalent	(adj)	Uncertain; unable to decide, or wanting to do two contradictory things at once	I've been accepted to two amazing graduate programs, one inexpensive and close to home, and one in a big, exciting city. I'm ambivalent—I don't know how I'm going to decide. / When I asked you if you thought we'd get married some day, your ambivalence hurt my feelings.
analogous	(adj)	Comparable, corresponding in some particular way (making a good analogy)	In the U.S., whenever opponents of a war want to suggest that the war is unwinnable, they point out all the ways in which the war is analogous to the Vietnam War.
anarchy	(noun)	Absence of law or government; chaos, disorder	Once the dictator was assassinated, the country fell into total anarchy, as none of the opposition groups were strong enough to seize power.
anoint	(verb)	Rub or sprinkle oil on; make sacred, such as by a ceremony that includes applying oil to someone	After Principal Smitters raised test scores over 60% at her school, it was only a matter of time before she was anointed superintendent by a fawning school board.
anomaly	(noun)	Deviation from what is common; inconsistency	While the cosmetics division of this company has many female executives, it is an anomaly; in the rest of the company, sadly, only 4% of management positions are filled by women.
antagonize	(verb)	Make hostile or unfriendly	"Josie! Stop antagonizing your little brother! Give him back that firetruck and tell him you're sorry for pulling his hair!"

MANHATTAN
PREP   183

WORD	P.O.S	DEFINITION	USAGE
antipathy	(noun)	Deep dislike, aversion, or repugnance, sometimes without reason	As an environmentalist, Mr. Subramanian had nothing but antipathy for the mining company drilling in and polluting his hometown.
apathy	(noun)	Not caring; absence of feeling; lack of interest or concern	Many parents of teenagers are concerned by their indolent teens' apathy about the future. Few teens are totally apathetic, however, many get quite excited about video games, flirting, or trips to the mall.
apocryphal	(adj)	Of questionable authenticity; false	I'm sorry, but this putative letter from George Washington that you found at a garage sale is clearly apocryphal—it is riddled with anachronisms (for instance, Washington was long dead by the time silent films were invented), and also, Washington most certainly didn't refer to Martha Washington as "baby."
appease	(verb)	Pacify, satisfy, relieve; concede to belligerent demands, sometimes at the expense of principles	My mother is so angry she wasn't the first person we called when the baby was born—I'm hoping to appease her by spending Christmas at her house this year.
appreciable	(adj)	Enough to be perceived, considerable	She ruefully concluded that the "Pot Pie Diet" was a scam and had made no appreciable difference in her appearance—after four weeks, she had lost three-quarters of a pound.
arbitrary	(adj)	Based entirely on one's discretion; capricious, unreasonable, or having no basis	The judge's rulings were truly arbitrary: one defendant got community service for stealing a television, and another got three years for the same crime. / It doesn't really matter which brand of baking soda you buy, just arbitrarily pick one so we can get out of this grocery store before dinnertime.
arcane	(adj)	Known or understood by only a few; obscure, secret	To win at *Jeopardy*, you must be full of arcane knowledge. / The wizard's shop was full of arcana, from Latin-to-Ancient Greek dictionaries to entire books on magic spells relating only to elephants.
archaic	(adj)	Characteristic of an earlier period, ancient, primitive	The school's archaic computer system predated even floppy disks—it stored records on tape drives! / Sometimes, when you look up a word in the dictionary, certain definitions are marked "archaic"—unless you are a Shakespeare scholar, you can safely ignore those archaisms.
arduous	(adj)	Very difficult, strenuous; severe, hard to endure	The arduous hike up rocky terrain was all worth it once the hikers reached the summit. / It was an arduous winter on the prairie; the family barely survived.

MANHATTAN
PREP

WORD	P.O.S	DEFINITION	USAGE
articulate	(adj, verb)	Using language in a clear, fluent way (adj); speak distinctly or give clarity to an idea (verb)	She's so articulate that I'm sure she'll make a good lawyer. / The group voted on who would be the best spokesperson, able to articulate their needs to the panel.
artifact	(noun)	Any object made by humans, especially those from an earlier time, such as those excavated by archaeologists	The archaeologists dug up countless artifacts, from simple pottery shards and coins to complex written tablets. / The girl's room was full of the artifacts of modern teenage life: Justin Bieber posters, *Twilight* books, and a laptop open to Facebook.
artless	(adj)	Free of deceit or craftiness, natural, genuine; lacking skill or knowledge, crude, uncultured	Children can be so artless that, when you try to explain war to them, they say things like, "But isn't that mean?"/ His artless attempt at negotiating a raise began with "I need more money, please" and ended with "Okay, sorry I asked."
ascertain	(verb)	Find out with certainty	Hopefully, the investigation will allow us to ascertain who is at fault here.
ascetic	(adj, noun)	abstinent or austere in lifestyle (adj); a person who leads an austere and simple life without material pleasures, esp. someone who does this for religious reasons (noun)	Ascetics such as monks actually take vows of poverty. / The graduate student lived an ascetic existence, her apartment containing only a futon couch and a single bowl and set of chopsticks, which she used to eat ramen noodles every night.
assuage	(verb)	Make milder, relieve; soothe, pacify, or calm	After losing a million-dollar account, he tried to assuage his furious boss by pointing out that he was close to winning a new account worth at least as much.
audacious	(adj)	Very bold or brave, often in a rude or reckless way; extremely original	He audaciously asked for a raise after working at the company for less than two months!
augment	(verb)	Make larger	If you memorize the definitions on all of these flash cards, you will have notably augmented your vocabulary!
austere	(adj)	Severe in manner or appearance; very self-disciplined, ascetic; without luxury or ease; sober or serious	Her design sense was so minimalist as to be austere; all-white walls, hard, wooden furniture, not a single picture, throw pillow, or cozy comfort anywhere. / The graduation speaker delivered an austere message: the economy is bad, and academic success alone isn't enough to succeed in the job market.

WORD	P.O.S	DEFINITION	USAGE
autonomous	(adj)	Self-governing, independent	As leader of an autonomous region, the newly elected president was received as a peer by some world leaders, although he was not entitled to send a representative to the United Nations. / It is normal for young people to desire greater autonomy as they grow up.
aver	(verb)	Declare or affirm with confidence, say	"Despite your insistence that ethics are completely situational," said the philosophy professor, "I aver that the existence of natural rights inevitably leads to certain immutable ethical boundaries."
avid	(adj)	Enthusiastic, dedicated, passionate; excessively desirous	An avid cyclist, she was on her bike every weekend, and even bought the same bike that Lance Armstrong last used in the Tour de France. / Avid of power, the young Senator compromised every principle to gain the support—and money—of large corporations.
balk	(verb)	Refuse to proceed or to do something	At the company retreat, he reluctantly agreed to participate in the ropes course, but balked at walking over hot coals as a "trust exercise."
base	(adj)	Morally low, mean, dishonorable; of little or no value; crude and unrefined; counterfeit	His philanthropy was underlied by truly base motives—he not only craved the fawning publicity his donations brought, but he was actually funneling drug money through the Children's Defense Fund! / The supposed "gold bricks" were really base metals covered in a very thin layer of real gold.
belie	(verb)	Contradict or misrepresent	The actress's public persona as a perky "girl next door" belied her private penchant for abusing her assistants and demanding that her trailer be filled with ridiculous luxury goods. / The data belie the accepted theory—either we've made a mistake or we have an amazing new discovery on our hands!
benign	(adj)	Harmless; favorable; kindly, gentle, or beneficial; not cancerous	He was relieved when the biopsy results came back, informing him that the growth was benign. / He's a benign fellow. I'm sure having him assigned to your team at work will be perfectly pleasant.
bogus	(adj)	Fake, fraudulent	The back of this bodybuilding magazine is full of ads for bogus products—this one promises 22-inch biceps just from wearing magnetic armbands!
bolster	(verb)	Strengthen or support	The general requested reinforcements to bolster the defensive line set up at the border. / Some people believe that self-affirmation exercises are an effective way to bolster self-esteem and even performance.

WORD	P.O.S	DEFINITION	USAGE
boor	(noun)	Rude, ill-mannered, or insensitive person; a peasant or country bumpkin	Milton was such a boor that, when Jane brought him home to meet her parents, he laughed at their garden gnome and made fun of everyone's hairstyles in old family photos. "Don't be so boorish!" said his mortified girlfriend.
buffer	(noun)	Something that shields, protects, absorbs shock, or cushions	During the colonial era, England wanted Georgia as a buffer between its original colonies and Spanish Florida. / A railroad car has a buffer (similar to a bumper on a car) to absorb shock in case of contact with other cars. / When Joel came out to his family, he used his mother as a buffer. He knew she would be supportive, so he allowed her to relay the news to everyone else, and to relay their responses back to him.
bureaucracy	(noun)	Government characterized by many bureaus and petty administrators or by excessive, seemingly meaningless requirements	Some nations have a worse reputation for bureaucracy than others; in order to get a visa, he had to file papers with four different agencies, wait for hours in three different waiting rooms, and, weeks later, follow up with some petty bureaucrat who complained that the original application should've been filed in triplicate.
burgeon	(verb)	Grow or flourish rapidly; put forth buds or shoots (of a plant)	The dictator was concerned about the people's burgeoning discontent and redoubled his personal security. / Spending an hour a day on vocabulary studies will soon cause your lexicon to burgeon.
buttress	(verb, noun)	Support or encourage (verb); a support or prop, esp. projecting from and supporting the wall of a building (noun)	A self-defense class really helped to buttress Elaine's confidence. / David used his Ph.D. as a buttress against criticism. "I have a doctorate," he would say. "I just don't think you can understand."
bygone	(adj, noun)	Past, former (adj); that which is in the past (usually plural noun)	At the nursing home, the time to reminisce about bygone days was pretty much all the time. / It's tempting to spend our whole high school reunion talking about bygones, but instead, let's toast to the future!
cacophony	(noun)	Harsh, discordant, or meaningless mixture of sounds	The first day of elementary school marching band practice was nothing but cacophony, as students who hadn't learned to play their instruments at all nevertheless banged on or puffed air into them.
candid	(adj)	Open, sincere, honest	Allow me to be candid: you do look rather portly in those pants, and I think you should wear something else. / You have been really secretive about where you've been going after work; we could use a little more candor in this relationship.

WORD	P.O.S	DEFINITION	USAGE
canonical	(adj)	Authorized, recognized; pertaining to the canon, or body of accepted rules, standards, or artistic works	School boards often start controversies when replacing canonical books in the curriculum with modern literature; while many people think students should read works more relevant to their lives, others point out that *Moby Dick* is part of the canon for a reason.
capricious	(adj)	Acting on impulse, erratic	The headmaster's punishments were capricious—break the rules one day, you get a warning; break them another day, you get expelled. / Who needs a plan? A date is more fun with a little caprice—-let's just start driving and see what we find!
cartography	(noun)	Mapmaking	The invention of better navigation tools had major effects on cartography—the more ships knew precisely where they were sailing, the better the world could be mapped.
castigate	(verb)	Criticize severely; punish in order to correct	At the grocery store, the mother attracted stares when she castigated—rather than merely admonished—her child for throwing a box of instant oatmeal.
catalyst	(noun)	Causer of change	The young manager was a catalyst at the stodgy old company—once he introduced employee laptops, telecommuting, and mobile workstations, even the most conventional of employees totally changed the way they worked.
caustic	(adj)	Capable of corroding metal or burning the skin; very critical or sarcastic	Wait, those chemicals are caustic! You need safety gloves and goggles before performing this experiment, or else you risk not only getting your skin burned off, but also some seriously caustic remarks from our chemistry teacher.
censure	(noun, verb)	Strong disapproval or official reprimand (noun); to issue such disapproval or reprimand (verb)	The senator was censured by the Senate for campaign fund improprieties; in fact, he narrowly avoided being expelled from office.
chauvinism	(noun)	Fanatical patriotism or blind enthusiasm for military glory; undue or biased devotion to any group, cause, etc.	He's such a chauvinist that he denies that any other nation could be better than ours at anything—he insists our wine is better than France's, our ski slopes are better than Norway's, and even that we grow more rice than China!
chronological	(adj)	Arranged in or relating to time order	Joey, I'm afraid you've done the assignment wrong—the point of making a timeline is to put the information in chronological order. You've put it in alphabetical order instead!

WORD	P.O.S	DEFINITION	USAGE
clamor	(verb)	Noisy uproar or protest, as from a crowd; a loud, continuous noise	As soon as a scent of scandal emerged, the press was clamoring for details. / The mayor couldn't even make herself heard over the clamor of the protestors.
clinch	(verb)	Make final or settle conclusively; to fasten or hold together	When their best player was benched, the team fell behind, but once he was allowed back in the game, the team was able to clinch the win. / These two pieces have been clinched together with a clamp while the glue dries.
coalesce	(verb)	Come together, unite; fuse together	While at first everyone on the team was jockeying for power and recognition, eventually, the group coalesced and everyone was happy to share credit for a job well-done. / East and West Germany coalesced into a single country in 1990.
cogent	(adj)	Very convincing, logical	Studying logic is an excellent way to improve at formulating cogent arguments. / Nurses who work in the Alzheimer's ward must develop skills for communicating with people who are often not cogent.
commensurate	(adj)	The same in size, extent, etc., equivalent; proportional	According to the course catalog, you may take Advanced Japanese following Japanese III or with commensurate experience with the language.
complacent	(adj)	Self-satisfied, smug; overly content (and therefore lazy, neglectful, or some other bad quality)	The coach gave a pep talk: "I know we've never won a championship before, but we do have an advantage over the six-time state champions we're about to play—they have grown complacent with their success, and now they just assume they'll win without having to sweat."
complementary	(adj)	Completing; fitting together well; filling mutual needs	"That scarf really complements your outfit," said Elle. "Thanks for the compliment," said Danica. / The couple had complementary personalities—when Omar got overwhelmed with the details, Lee took care of everything, and when Lee got too introspective, Omar cheered him up with an insatiable zest for life.
compliant	(adj)	Obeying, submissive; following the requirements	Those who are not compliant with the regulations will be put on probation and possibly expelled. / A compliant child, he never gave his parents any trouble.
concede	(verb)	Give in, admit, yield; acknowledge reluctantly; grant or give up (such as giving up land after losing a war)	The negotiations were pointless, with each side's representatives instructed by their home countries to make no concessions whatsoever. / Quebec was a French concession to Britain in the Treaty of Paris in 1763. / I suppose I will have to concede the argument now that you've looked up evidence on Wikipedia.

WORD	P.O.S	DEFINITION	USAGE
conciliatory	(adj)	Reconciling, appeasing, attempting to make the peace	The hotel manager was horrified at how the guest had been treated, and approached him in a conciliatory manner, offering him numerous freebies and apologizing repeatedly.
concur	(verb)	Approve, agree	John Locke wrote that justice is based on the social contract, and I concur—in fact, my latest book is all about contractual justice.
condone	(verb)	Overlook, tolerate, regard as harmless	While underage drinking is illegal, at many universities, it is tacitly condoned by administrations that neglect to enforce antidrinking policies.
confer	(verb)	Consult, compare views; bestow or give	A Ph.D. confers upon a person the right to be addressed as "Doctor" as well as eligibility to pursue a tenure-track professorship. / Excuse me for a moment to make a call—I can't buy this car until I confer with my spouse.
connoisseur	(noun)	Expert, especially in the fine arts; person of educated, refined tastes	A chocolate connoisseur, Mom eschews grocery store brands and will only eat 80% cocoa-or-higher artisanal chocolate that is less than a week old.
console	(verb, noun)	Lessen the suffering or grief of (verb); a control panel, or small table or cabinet (noun)	I was unable to console Tina after she fell asleep at the console of her airplane and thereby failed her pilot's exam.
consolidate	(verb)	Unite, combine, solidify, make coherent	She consolidated her student loans so she would only have to make one payment per month. / As group leader, Muriel will consolidate all of our research into a single report.
constrict	(verb)	Squeeze, compress; restrict the freedom of	The children strongly disliked being gussied up in constrictive clothing for a formal wedding. / Tourism is now allowed in North Korea, but tourists must stay with official tour groups, and their movements are heavily constricted.
construe	(verb)	Interpret or translate	I don't know how you construed my comment as an insult. All I said was, "Wow, I never knew you could sing."
contentious	(adj)	Controversial; prone to causing arguments, especially gratuitous or petty ones	The death penalty is a contentious issue. / My uncle is so contentious that every attempt I made to introduce an uncontroversial topic met with failure; he ranted and raved about the weather, trees, math, and my daughter's enjoyment of oatmeal.

WORD	P.O.S	DEFINITION	USAGE
contextualize	(verb)	Place in context, such as by giving the background or circumstances	Virginia Woolf's feminism is hard to truly understand unless contextualized within the mores of the highly restrained, upper-class English society of her time.
conundrum	(noun)	A riddle; any mystery	Sherlock Holmes is famous for his ability to solve the most complex conundrums with simple observation. / The new mystery novel presents an interesting spin on the classic locked-room conundrum—how did the perpetrator get in and out of the White House without being detected?
converge	(verb)	Move towards one another or towards a point; unite	I know we're driving to the wedding from different states, but our routes ought to converge when each of us hits I-95—maybe we could converge at a Cracker Barrel for lunch!
conversant	(adj)	Knowledgeable about or experienced with	For an opera singer, she is unusually conversant in physics—she just explained the purpose of the Large Hadron Collider.
conversely	(adverb)	In an opposite way; on the other hand	I am not here to argue that lack of education causes poverty. Conversely, I am here to argue that poverty causes lack of education.
convoluted	(adj)	Twisted; very complicated	Your argument is so convoluted that I'm not even able to understand it enough to start critiquing it. / To get from the hotel room to the pool requires following a convoluted path up two staircases and down two others—to get to someplace on the same floor we started on!
copious	(adj)	Plentiful, bountiful	Although she took copious notes in class, she found that she was missing a big picture that would have tied all the information together. / The fertile, copious land yielded a rich harvest.
corroborate	(verb)	Support, add evidence to	You're telling me you were 30 miles away riding a roller coaster when the school was vandalized? I have a hard time believing that. Is there anyone who can corroborate your story?
cosmopolitan	(adj)	Belonging to the entire world, at home globally; free from local or national prejudices or attachments	Trapped in a small town, he dreamed of a more cosmopolitan existence filled with world travel, exotic cuisine, and scintillating parties where he would meet famous authors and other cosmopolites.
countenance	(noun, verb)	Facial expression or face (noun); approve or tolerate (verb)	Her countenance said it all—the look on her face was pure terror. / I saw you cheating off my paper, and I can't countenance cheating—either you turn yourself in or I'll report you.

WORD	P.O.S	DEFINITION	USAGE
counterintuitive	(adj)	Against what one would intuitively expect	Although it seems counterintuitive, for some extreme dieters, eating more can actually help them to lose weight, since the body is reassured that it is not facing a period of prolonged starvation.
counterpoint	(noun)	Contrasting item, opposite; a complement; the use of contrast or interplay in a work of art	The play's lighthearted, witty narrator provides a welcome counterpoint to the seriousness and grief expressed by the other characters. / The hot peppers work in counterpoint to an otherwise sweet dish.
counterproductive	(adj)	Defeating the purpose; preventing the intended goal	The candidate's attempt to win swing votes in Ohio was actually counterproductive—following his speech in Toledo, his poll numbers actually went down 5%.
covert	(adj)	Secret, veiled, undercover	The soldier trained to be part of covert operations, moving silently and remaining out of the enemy's sight.
crafty	(adj)	Cunning, skillful in deception or underhanded schemes	A crafty play in basketball is the "head-fake"—moving the head in one direction slightly prior to running in the other direction, to try to get a tiny head start on a disoriented pursuer.
craven	(adj)	Very cowardly, lacking courage	The nervous soldier feared he would turn craven in his first firefight, but he actually acted quite bravely.
credibility	(noun)	Believability, trustworthiness	Many famous "experts" with "Dr." before their names are not medical doctors at all. Any television "doctor" who turns out to have a Ph.D. in botany, for instance, ought to suffer a serious drop in credibility.
credulous	(adj)	Gullible; prone to believing or trusting too easily or without enough evidence	"Did you know you can wash your ears by turning your head on its side in the shower and letting the water run straight through your head?" said the father to his five-year-old daughter. "I'll try that!" said the credulous little girl.
crescendo	(noun; verb)	Steady increase in force, intensity, or the loudness of a musical passage; a climactic moment or peak (noun); to rise in volume or intensity (verb)	Mrs. Higgins did love the symphony, but she was also coming down with a migraine—by the time the music reached its towering crescendo, her head was pounding. / The administration tried to ignore the protest, but finally had to address the issue when the demonstration reached a crescendo.
culminate	(verb)	Reach the highest point or final stage	A Ph.D. program generally culminates in a written dissertation and its defense to a committee.

MANHATTAN
PREP

WORD	P.O.S	DEFINITION	USAGE
cynical	(adj)	Thinking the worst of others' motivations; bitterly pessimistic	Shilpa was so cynical that even when her friends threw her a surprise party, she figured that they only did it so they wouldn't feel so guilty about all the mean things they must be saying behind her back.
daunt	(verb)	Discourage, dishearten, lessen the courage of	Amazingly undaunted after his accident, Devon vowed to complete a marathon in his wheelchair. Not even a dented rim on mile 19 could daunt him—he dauntlessly completed the race anyway.
debase	(verb)	Degrade; lower in quality, value, rank, etc.; lower in moral quality	You have debased yourself by accepting bribes. / Members of the mainstream church argued that the fringe sect was practicing a debased version of the religion, twisting around its precepts and missing the point. / I can tell from the weight that this isn't pure gold, but rather some debased mixed metal.
debunk	(verb)	Expose, ridicule, or disprove false or exaggerated claims	Galileo spent his last years under house arrest for debunking the widely held idea that the Sun revolved around the Earth. / The show *MythBusters* debunks pseudoscientific claims.
decorous	(adj)	Behaving with propriety and good taste; polite	Miss Etiquette writes an advice column about decorum. One writer asked, "What's the most decorous way to tell guests exactly what I want for my wedding?" Miss Etiquette replied, "Young lady, there is no decorous way to solicit gifts, and even asking that question is entirely indecorous of you."
deem	(verb)	Judge; consider	"You can take the black belt exam when I deem you ready, and not a moment before," said the karate instructor.
deface	(verb)	Vandalize, mar the appearance of	Ernest was charged with three counts of vandalism after being caught defacing a row of townhouses with spray paint.
defamatory	(adj)	Slanderous, injurious to someone's reputation	One interesting issue in free speech law is defamation. / The political blogs are filled with defamatory language; it seems anyone with a computer and an opinion can destroy a politician's reputation these days.
default	(noun, verb)	Failure to act, neglect (noun); fail to fulfill an obligation, especially a financial one (verb)	The government is cracking down on for-profit colleges where a large percentage of the graduates cannot use their degrees to gain employment and end up defaulting on their student loans. / You must elect a new health plan by December 31st or by default you will be re-enrolled in the plan you selected last year.

WORD	P.O.S	DEFINITION	USAGE
deference	(noun)	Respectful submission; yielding to the authority or opinion of another	In many cultures, young people are expected to show deference to older people at all times. / I'm not an expert in databases—I'll defer to our programmers on that decision. / Ingrid deferred her college admissions for a year so she could travel the world.
deflect	(verb)	Cause to curve; turn aside, esp. from a straight course; avoid	The purpose of a shield is to deflect arrows or bullets from an enemy. / Every time he was asked a difficult question, Senator Warrington deflected by changing the topic, saying he'd answer later, or even—insincerely, it seemed—calling for a moment of prayer.
deleterious	(adj)	Harmful, unhealthful	The Resident Assistant told the first-year students, "I think you will find not only that drugs are illegal and will result in expulsion, but also that drug abuse will have a deleterious effect on anyone's grades."
delineate	(verb)	Mark the outline of; sketch; describe in detail	I do need the cash, but I'm not signing up for this psychological experiment unless you delineate what's going to happen.
denigrate	(verb)	Belittle, attack the reputation of	Many jokes in the *Meet the Parents* trilogy come from Robert De Niro's character denigrating Ben Stiller's character for being a male nurse.
denote	(verb)	Stand as a name or symbol for; indicate (This word contrasts with "connote," which describes what something implies or suggests beyond its literal meaning.)	The company's brand denotes quality; the marketing team has done a fantastic job of associating the company's image with fine service. / There's nothing in the denotation of "crotchety" [grumpy, having strong and irrational preferences] that indicates any particular group of people, but due to the expression "crotchety old man," the word connotes, for many people, an image of an especially unpleasant male senior citizen.
deride	(verb)	Mock, scoff at, laugh at contemptuously	The manager really thought that deriding his employees as "stupid" or "lazy" would motivate them to work harder; instead, it motivated them to constantly hide his office supplies as an act of revenge.
derivative	(adj)	Derived from something else; not original	The singer's first album was a disappointment, derivative of several hit albums from the previous year, as though a management team had simply picked out the elements from other popular songs that they thought would make the most money.
desiccate	(verb)	Thoroughly dried up, dehydrated	The key to maintaining odor-free shoes is to desiccate the insole by placing a drying agent, such as a small pouch of baking soda, inside the shoe between wears. / Beef jerky is a desiccated meat product.

WORD	P.O.S	DEFINITION	USAGE
detached	(adj)	Impartial, disinterested; unconcerned, distant, aloof	He found her detached demeanor inappropriate for a funeral. It's fine to politely ask how someone died, but it's not appropriate to coldly question a relative on the medical history of the deceased. / The divorce proceeding was full of anger and recriminations, but the judge was able to make a detached decision.
deterrent	(noun)	Something that restrains or discourages	Some argue that the death penalty is a deterrent to crime; that is, the point is not just to punish the guilty, but to frighten other prospective criminals.
diatribe	(noun)	Bitter, abusive attack or criticism; rant	I'd stay out of the living room for a while—Grandpa's on another one of his diatribes about how it's un-American to call a large coffee a "venti." You can hear him ranting from here!
didactic	(adj)	Intended to instruct; teaching, or teaching a moral lesson	She might have been Teacher of the Year at work, but at home, her husband wished she would turn off her didactic personality. "Honey," he said, "I really don't need you to use everything as a learning opportunity." / The child was disappointed when the storybook turned didactic in the end, with the teddy bears—and the reader—being admonished never to lie.
digress	(verb)	Go off-topic when speaking or writing	Grandpa digressed quite a bit while you were in the kitchen—he was telling us an old war story, but somehow now he's ranting about how nobody celebrates Arbor Day anymore. That digression could take awhile.
din	(noun)	Loud, confused noise, esp. for a long period of time	This hotel was described as "near all the hot spots," but I didn't realize that I wouldn't be able to sleep due to the all-night din from partygoers.
disabuse	(verb)	Free someone from a mistake in thinking	Do you really believe that toilets flush one way in the Northern hemisphere and another way in the Southern? Any physicist would be happy to disabuse you of that silly notion.
discerning	(adj)	Having good judgment or insight; able to distinguish mentally	In an age in which we are bombarded with advertising, it's important to be a discerning consumer. For instance, the term "all natural" is not federally regulated and doesn't have to mean anything at all, so a smart shopper still reads ingredients.
discredit	(adj)	Injure the reputation of, destroy credibility of or confidence in	Congresswoman Huffman's opponent tried to use her friendship with a certain radical extremist to discredit her, even though the congresswoman hadn't seen this so-called extremist since sixth grade summer camp.

WORD	P.O.S	DEFINITION	USAGE
discrepancy	(noun)	Difference or inconsistency	When there is a discrepancy between a store's receipts and the amount of money in the register, the cashier is suspected of pocketing the difference.
discriminating	(adj)	Judicious, discerning, having good judgment or insight (as an adj, positive spin; as a verb, negative spin!)	He is a man of discriminating tastes—all his suits are handmade in Italy, and I once saw him send back an entrée when he complained that black truffle oil had been substituted for white. The chef was astounded. / You can tell a real Prada bag by the discriminating mark on the inside.
disingenuous	(adj)	Insincere, not genuine	Steven's offer of help turned out to be disingenuous; when it was finally time for me to move, he was nowhere to be found! / My dog's wide-eyed expression of remorse for playing with the children's toys must be disingenuous, because she continues to snatch a toy every chance she gets.
disinterested	(adj)	Unbiased, impartial; not interested	Let's settle this argument once and for all! We'll get a disinterested observer to judge who can sing the highest note.
disjointed	(adj)	Disconnected, not coherent, jerky	The novel seemed disjointed, as though whole chunks of it were missing, or as though the author had tried to stitch together drafts of several different stories.
dismiss	(verb)	Allow to disperse or leave; fire from a job; put aside or reject, especially after only a brief consideration	"Before I dismiss class," said the teacher, "I want to remind you of the importance of dismissing biases in your research by ruling out or adjusting for factors other than the variable you are testing that may have led to your results."
dispassionate	(adj)	Unbiased, not having a selfish or personal motivation; calm, lacking emotion	The defendant tearfully described how much her young child needed her at home, but the judge, who dispassionately sentenced her to 10 years for selling drugs, was unmoved.
dispatch	(noun, verb)	Speed, promptness; send off or deal with in a speedy way	So, you want to be a bike messenger? I need messengers who approach every delivery with alacrity, care, and dispatch—if the customers wanted their packages to arrive slowly, they'd use the post office. / Acting with all possible dispatch, emergency services dispatched a rescue squad to the scene.
disperse	(verb)	Scatter, spread widely, cause to vanish	Because the demonstrators didn't have a permit, the police showed up with megaphones, demanding loudly that the crowd disperse. / Get the hose so I can disperse the dirt on our driveway.

WORD	P.O.S	DEFINITION	USAGE
disposition	(noun)	A person's general or natural mood; tendency	She was possessed of a kind and helpful disposition—she wouldn't just help you move, she'd bring home-baked muffins to the affair. / I could really use some help in the kitchen, if you are so disposed.
disquieting	(adj)	Disturbing, causing anxiety	Mr. Ramirez's lack of emotion at his wife's death was disquieting—so much so, in fact, that even his own family began to suspect he'd had something to do with it. / He was deeply disquieted by the racism he encountered in his new neighborhood.
disseminate	(verb)	Scatter, spread about, broadcast	Many plants use attractive fruits to disseminate their seeds—animals eat the fruit and excrete the seeds, allowing new plants to grow. / In the 1760s, revolutionary ideas were disseminated via pamphlets such as Thomas Paine's "Common Sense."
dissent	(verb, noun)	Disagree or take an opposing view, esp. in relation to a formal body such as a government, political party, or church; such a view	Judge Antonin Scalia cast the only dissenting vote, explaining in his written decision why he thought all the other justices had it wrong. / Not every country has a right to free speech (and thus to dissent), although nations that throw dissenters in jail are condemned by the international community.
dissonance	(noun)	Harsh, inharmonious sound; cacophony; disagreement	After allowing her sixth-grader's "heavy metal" band to practice in her living room, Mrs. Rosen decided she'd better get used to dissonance.
distill	(verb)	Purify; extract the essential elements of	While traveling in certain countries, it is important to only drink distilled water so you don't get sick. / Jules, it's not necessary to read your entire PowerPoint presentation to us. Can you just distill it down to the main point?
diverge	(verb)	Differ, deviate; branch off or turn aside, as from a path	Go five miles until the old post office, then the road diverges—you want the branch that winds off to the left. / The high school sweethearts found that their paths diverged when they were accepted to different colleges.
divest	(verb)	Deprive or strip of a rank, title, etc., or of clothing or gear; to sell off holdings (opposite of invest)	When she found out that the most profitable stock in her portfolio was that of a company that tested products on animals, she immediately divested by telling her broker to sell the stock. / Once his deception was exposed, he was divested of his position on the Board.
divine	(verb)	Discover through divination or supernatural means; perceive by insight	I've been poring over these quarterly reports all day, trying to divine whether I should buy or sell this stock.

WORD	P.O.S	DEFINITION	USAGE
document	(verb)	Support with evidence, cite sources in a detailed way, create documentary evidence of	Journalists embedded with military units are able to document a war as it happens. / It's hard to deny her conclusion when her book is so well documented—she cites a relevant scientific study on practically every page.
dogma	(noun)	A system of principles laid down by an authority; established belief	It is part of the dogma of modern education that there are multiple intelligences that are equally valuable; try to suggest that some people just aren't that smart, and you'll find yourself a pariah. / Dogmatic people will never change their minds, even in the face of evidence.
dormant	(adj)	Asleep, inactive, on a break	Some famous writers' skills have lain dormant until quite late in life; Laura Ingalls Wilder didn't publish *Little House on the Prairie* until she was 65.
dubious	(adj)	Doubtful, questionable, suspect	This applicant's résumé is filled with dubious qualifications—somehow I doubt he both invented peanut butter and was a member of the first moon mission.
e.g.	(abbreviation for Latin "exempli gratia")	For example, such as	He was positively traumatized by the romantic comedies his girlfriend made him watch (e.g., *He's Just Not That into You*).
eccentric	(adj)	Peculiar, odd, deviating from the norm, esp. in a whimsical way	The old woman was eccentric but harmless—not many senior citizens wear a train conductor's uniform and carry a boom box. / The eccentricity of a planet's orbit is the amount by which it deviates from a perfect circle; in general, comets are far more eccentric than known planets.
eclectic	(adj)	Selecting the best of everything or from many diverse sources	Eclectic taste is helpful in being a DJ—crowds love to hear the latest hip-hop mixed with '80s classics and other unexpected genres of music. / The restaurant features an eclectic menu—if you don't like artisanal pasta or steak frites, try the chow mein!
eclipse	(noun, verb)	The obscuring of one thing by another, such as the sun by the moon or a person by a more famous or talented person (noun); to obscure, darken, make less important (verb)	During a solar eclipse, the moon eclipses the Sun. / Billy Ray Cyrus, who had a hit song, "Achy Breaky Heart," in the '90s, has long since found his fame eclipsed by that of his daughter, Miley.

WORD	P.O.S	DEFINITION	USAGE
efficacy	(noun)	The quality of being able to produce the intended effect	Extensive trials will be necessary to determine whether the drug's efficacy outweighs the side effects. / I am having trouble cutting my steak with this butter knife; I'm going to ask the waiter for a more efficacious implement.
egalitarian	(adj)	Related to belief in the equality of all people, esp. in political, economic, or social spheres	After moving to a more liberal part of the country, the couple was pleased to have neighbors who shared their views of egalitarian marriage—for instance, men and women could be found in equal proportions downshifting to part-time work to make time for childcare.
egregious	(adj)	Extraordinarily or conspicuously bad; glaring	Your conduct is an egregious violation of our Honor Code—not only did you steal your roommate's paper off his computer and turn it in as your own, you also sold his work to a plagiarism website so other cheaters could purchase it!
elated	(adj)	Very happy, in high spirits	I am elated that you flew my twin brother in from Australia to surprise me at my birthday party!
elevate	(verb)	Raise, lift up; lift the spirits of; move up to a higher rank or status or raise up to a higher spiritual or intellectual plane	After a year getting coffee and making copies, he hoped to be promoted to a more elevated position suitable for a law school graduate. / Our goal here at Morality Publishing is not just to sell books, but to elevate our readers social consciences.
elicit	(verb)	Call forth, bring out, evoke	The touchdown elicited wild cheers from the crowd. / While the death of Ellen's elderly cat was indeed sad, Ellen's constant, mournful looks whenever anyone mentioned any animal at all were nothing but a play to elicit sympathy.
eloquent	(adj)	Marked by forceful, fluid, apt speech; expressive, emotionally moving	Wow, he's such an eloquent speaker, he could sell snow to Antarcticans! / When Mom suggested that everyone might enjoy a museum instead of the beach, she was met with the children's eloquent looks of disgust.
embellish	(verb)	Decorate, add ornamentation; enhance (a story) with fictional or fanciful details	Every time she tells that story, she embellishes it quite a bit—at first, she was lost in the woods, and then she was found. The part with the grizzly bear was added later. / The Christmas sweater was embellished with festive jingle bells!

WORD	P.O.S	DEFINITION	USAGE
eminent	(adj)	Prominent, distinguished, of high rank	The undergraduate shocked everyone by asking the eminent old professor, "Really? What makes you such an expert?" / "Your Eminence," said the bishop to the Pope, "Don't forget this copy of your speech!"
empirical	(adj)	Coming from, based on, or able to be verified by experience or experimentation; not purely based on theory	The Ancient Greeks philosophized about the nature of matter (concluding, for instance, that everything was made of earth, water, air, and fire) without any empirical evidence; that is, the very idea of conducting experiments hadn't been invented yet. / People always knew empirically that when something is dropped, it falls to the ground; the theory of gravity later explained why.
emulate	(verb)	Copy in an attempt to equal or be better than	The ardent *Star Trek* fan emulated Captain Kirk in every way possible—right down to the uniform.
enervate	(verb)	Tire out; weaken (this definition can function both with and without an object)	After taking the SAT in the morning and playing in a soccer game in the afternoon, Trina was truly enervated before the prom even began. "You dance like a grandmother with osteoporosis," said her date.
enhance	(verb)	Raise to a higher value, desirability, etc.	The cosmetics industry stays in business because so many people want to enhance their appearances.
enigma	(noun)	Puzzle, mystery, riddle; mysterious or contradictory person	The enormous rock sculptures in Stonehenge are truly an enigma—were they created as part of a religious observance, or in deference to a great ruler? We may never know.
entitlement	(noun)	Having the right to certain privileges; believing, sometimes without cause, that one deserves or has a right to certain privileges	Many bosses complain about young people's sense of entitlement—raised on a steady diet of praise from parents and teachers, these young people are shocked to be expected to "pay their dues" at a new job.
enumerate	(verb)	Count or list; specify one-by-one	The Bill of Rights enumerates the basic rights held by every citizen of the United States. / I don't have time to enumerate all the steps involved in baking a cake—just find a recipe on the internet!
ephemeral	(adj)	Lasting only a short time, fleeting	"Thank you for this jacket that says 'Eugene's Girl,'" said Marie, "but I fear that your love will prove to be ephemeral—over the last two years, I've seen four other girls in school with the same jacket. Do you buy them in six-packs?"

WORD	P.O.S	DEFINITION	USAGE
equitable	(adj)	Fair, equal, just	As the university president was heavily biased towards the sciences, faculty in the liberal arts felt they had to fight to get an equitable share of funding for their departments.
erratic	(adj)	Inconsistent, wandering, having no fixed course	When someone engages in erratic behavior, family members often suspect drug use or mental illness. However, sometimes the person is just building a top-secret invention in the garage!
erroneous	(adj)	Mistaken, in error; improper, morally incorrect	Hilda was completely unable to assemble her new desk chair after the instructions erroneously instructed her to screw the left armrest onto a small lever on the bottom of the seat.
erudite	(adj)	Scholarly, knowledgeable; possessing deep, often systematic, knowledge	Some have said that Americans dislike erudite leaders; while German leaders frequently have Ph.D.'s, even speaking a foreign language is considered pretentious by many American voters.
eschew	(verb)	Shun, avoid, abstain from	As a vegan, he eschewed not only meat and dairy but also anything made of leather.
esoteric	(adj)	Understood by or intended for only a few; secret	In his first year of university-level physics, he felt he was merely memorizing information found in every textbook on the subject; by his fourth year, he spent his days poring over esoteric journal articles that few people had ever read or understood.
estimable	(adj)	Worthy of esteem, admirable; able to be estimated	As the first black president of the *Harvard Law Review*, Barack Obama presented an estimable résumé when he ran for president in 2008. / Riding a roller coaster is safer than driving on the highway, but there is still an estimable risk.
eulogy	(noun)	Speech of praise or written work of praise, esp. a speech given at a funeral	While it was hard for Xing to write a eulogy for his friend, he was pleased to be able to tell others at the funeral some wonderful things about him that they hadn't known. / The review of the book was pure eulogy—usually, this publication runs more balanced articles.
exacerbate	(verb)	Make worse (more violent, severe, etc.), inflame; irritate or embitter (a person)	Allowing your band to practice in our garage has greatly exacerbated my headache.
exacting	(adj)	Very severe in making demands; requiring precise attention	The boxing coach was exacting, analyzing Joey's footwork down to the millimeter and forcing him to repeat movements hundreds of times until they were correct.

WORD	P.O.S	DEFINITION	USAGE
exculpate	(verb)	Clear from guilt or blame	The security camera footage showing Mr. Murphy to have been in a casino the entire night turned out to be just the evidence needed to exculpate him of robbing a bank 50 miles away.
exhaustive	(adj)	Comprehensive, thorough, exhausting a topic or subject, accounting for all possibilities; draining, tending to exhaust	The *Standard Book of British Birds* provides an exhaustive treatment of the subject—you will find that not a single British bird has been omitted. / The rebels finally surrendered after an exhaustive siege that left them without ammunition or even food.
explicit	(adj)	Direct, clear, fully revealed; clearly depicting sex or nudity	The goal of my motivational talk is to make explicit the connection between staying in school and avoiding a life of crime.
exponent	(noun)	Person who expounds or explains; champion, advocate, or representative	An exponent of clean fuel, he petitioned the state government to commit to replacing conventional energy with solar and wind energy where possible.
extraneous	(adj)	Irrelevant; foreign, coming from without, not belonging	This essay would be stronger if you removed extraneous information; this paragraph about the author's life doesn't happen to be relevant to your thesis. / Maize, which originated in the New World, is extraneous to Europe.
extrapolate	(verb)	Conjecture about an unknown by projecting information about something known; predict by projecting past experience	No, I've never been to Bryn Mawr, but I've visited several small, private women's colleges in the Northeast, so I think I can extrapolate.
facetious	(adj)	Joking, humorous, esp. inappropriately; not serious, concerned with frivolous things	When I said, "Sure, you can take anything in my house as a souvenir of this study session," I was being facetious! I would like my nightgown back now. / He's a facetious person—I doubt he will take your offer of a spiritual quest very seriously.
facilitate	(verb)	Make easier, help the progress of	A good meeting facilitator lets everyone be heard while still keeping the meeting focused. / As a midwife, my goal is simply to facilitate a natural process.
fallacious	(adj)	Containing a fallacy, or mistake in logic; logically unsound; deceptive	The formal study of logic can enable a student to more easily identify fallacious reasoning and, furthermore, to point out its fallacies.
fanatical	(adj)	Excessively devoted, enthusiastic, or zealous in an uncritical way	We avoid our neighbors—they're fanatics who can't go five minutes without trying to convert you to their beliefs. / Mrs. Becker was fanatical about grammar, once deducting 15 points from a student's paper for a misused semicolon—and it was a physics class!

WORD	P.O.S	DEFINITION	USAGE
fanciful	(adj)	Whimsical, capricious; imaginary; freely imaginative rather than based on reason or reality	The play was set in a fanciful version of New York City, one where all the cab drivers spoke perfect English and the Statue of Liberty seemed to be in the middle of the island.
fathom	(verb)	Measure the depth of (usually of water) as with a sounding line; penetrate and discover the meaning of, understand	I cannot even remotely fathom how you interpreted an invitation to sleep on my couch as permission to take my car on a six-hour joyride!
feasible	(adj)	Possible; logical or likely; suitable	Your plan to promote our product launch with a parade is just not feasible—we don't have the money or enough time to get the permits.
fidelity	(noun)	Faithfulness, loyalty; strict observance of duty; accuracy in reproducing a sound or image	Wedding vows typically include a promise of fidelity—such as "forsaking all others as long as I may live."
figurative	(adj)	Metaphorical, based on figures of speech; containing many figures of speech (as fancy-sounding writing); related to portraying human or animal figures, as opposed to abstract objects	The painter was renowned for his figurative art, including many portraits—he had been known to say that abstract artists were just people who had never learned to draw. / Highly figurative language can be difficult for English language learners; for instance, to "throw the baby out with the bath water" refers to being too hasty and unwisely getting rid of the good with the bad.
finesse	(noun, verb)	Extreme delicacy, subtlety, or diplomacy in handling a sensitive situation or in a performance or skill (noun); use tact or diplomacy; employ a deceptive strategy (verb)	After the prince deeply insulted his hosts, the diplomat was able to finesse the situation, playing it off as a translation error and getting the negotiations back on track.
flag	(verb)	Get tired, lose enthusiasm; hang limply or droop	Our grandmother is so physically fit that she was ready to make the rounds of the entire amusement park again after lunch, while most of us were flagging and just wanted to sit.
fleeting	(adj)	Passing quickly, transitory	I had assumed our summer romance would be fleeting, so I was very surprised when you proposed marriage!
foment	(verb)	Incite, instigate, stir up, promote the growth of; apply medicated liquid to a body part	The revolutionary group was quietly fomenting a rebellion, galvanizing student radicals, leading unions in revolutionary songs, and anonymously pasting incendiary posters in every quarter of the city.

WORD	P.O.S	DEFINITION	USAGE
foreshadow	(verb)	Indicate or suggest beforehand, presage	You didn't know this was a horror movie? I thought it was pretty clear that the children's ghost story around the campfire was meant to foreshadow the horrible things that would happen to them years later as teenagers at a motel in the middle of the woods.
forfeit	(verb)	Surrender or lose as a result of an error, crime, or failure to fulfill an obligation	"The rules are clear," said the umpire. "This is a co-ed league, and if your team doesn't have at least three women, you forfeit. Sorry, everybody, no game today!" / If you are found guilty of defrauding this casino, the forfeiture of your winnings will be only the first of the consequences coming your way.
fortify	(verb)	Strengthen, invigorate, encourage	The white bread found in American grocery stores has been stripped of all the nutrients naturally found in wheat, and then artificially fortified with vitamins and minerals. / The general called for reinforcements to fortify the defenses around the capital.
fringe	(noun, adj)	On the margin, periphery (adj); the people in a group who hold the most extreme views (noun)	In America, reincarnation is a fringe belief, but in primarily Hindu countries, the belief is quite mainstream. / Stacey and Mark liked to say they lived on the fringe of the big city, but really they had just moved to the suburbs.
frugal	(adj)	Economical, thrifty, not wasteful with money; inexpensive	It wasn't terribly surprising when Lea—who was so frugal in restaurants that she always drank water, ate salad, and requested a separate check—said she had never tried lobster.
futile	(adj)	Producing no useful result, ineffective; trivial or unimportant	She spent months trying to coax Fluffy to fetch and sit, but it was futile—cats just can't be trained to perform tricks.
gainsay	(verb)	Declare false, deny; oppose	The professor is quite intolerant of challenges to her opinions—she's been known to lower the grade of any student who dares gainsay her.
garrulous	(adj)	Talkative, wordy, rambling	Uncle Bill is so garrulous that our dinner conversation lasted three hours—and the only person who said more than ten words was Uncle Bill.
gauche	(adj)	Tactless, lacking social grace, awkward, crude	It is terribly gauche to put ketchup on your steak and then talk with your mouth full as you eat it. That's the last time I ever bring you to a nice place.
gawky	(adj)	Physically awkward (esp. of a tall, skinny person, often used to describe teenagers)	As a teenager, she thought of herself as gawky and often slouched so as not to seem so much taller than her peers; of course, now that she's a supermodel, no one thinks of her as gawky at all.

WORD	P.O.S	DEFINITION	USAGE
germane	(adj)	Relevant and appropriate, on-topic	This is a business meeting, not a social club—let's keep our comments germane to the issue of the new campaign.
gist	(noun)	Main idea, essence	I didn't read the whole book, but I read enough to get the gist.
glib	(adj)	Fluent and easy in a way that suggests superficiality or insincerity	The used car salesman's description of the car was as glib as Luis expected. "This old girl sure is a distinguished old thing," he said. "She'll be good to you if you're good to her." Luis responded, "What the heck does that even mean?"
goosebumps	(noun)	The "bumps" created by hairs standing up on the skin in response to cold, fear, etc.	This detective novel is so compelling; I got goosebumps when Clarice started talking to Hannibal!
gradation	(noun)	A progression, a process taking place gradually, in stages; one of these stages	The hill's gradation was so gradual that even those on crutches were able to enjoy the nature trail. / The novel's language graded from the vernacular to the erudite so gradually that you practically didn't realize until the end that the speaker had become educated almost before your eyes.
gregarious	(adj)	Sociable, pertaining to a flock or crowd	"We need to be a little more productive and a little less gregarious," said the chemistry teacher when he saw that the two-person lab groups had devolved into clusters of five and six students standing around talking and laughing.
guile	(noun)	Clever deceit, cunning, craftiness	The game of poker is all about guile, manipulating your own body language, and patter to lead other players to erroneous conclusions about the cards you're holding.
hackneyed	(adj)	So commonplace as to be stale; not fresh or original	This screenplay is so hackneyed—the leading lady has a quirky, artsy job in the city and has a minor problem early in the movie from which the male lead rescues her, and they get together but then break up due to a misunderstanding, and then they end up together anyway, all while the female lead's "sassy" friend gives advice. Ugh. I'll bet they're auditioning Jennifer Aniston right now.
hardy	(adj)	Bold, brave, capable of withstanding hardship, fatigue, cold, etc.	While the entire family enjoyed the trip to South America, only the hardier members even attempted to hike to the top of Ecuador's tallest volcano.

WORD	P.O.S	DEFINITION	USAGE
haven	(noun)	Harbor or port; refuge, safe place	The relief workers set up the camp as a haven from persecution.
hearken	(verb)	Listen, pay attention to	"Hearken, students!" said the old-fashioned music teacher. "We are going to practice 'Hark, the Herald Angels Sing.'
hedonist	(noun)	Person devoted to pleasure	A vacation is a fine time to practice hedonism, letting your troubles go and indulging in every conceivable luxury and pleasure.
heterogeneous	(adj)	Different in type, incongruous; composed of different types of elements	Rather than build the wall with plain brick, we used a heterogeneous mixture of stones—they are not only different colors, but a variety of sizes as well.
hierarchy	(noun)	A ranked series; a classification of people according to rank, ability, etc.; a ruling body	The activist, accustomed to groups ruled by consensus, was quite surprised to find that the Eco-Action Coalition was led by a strict hierarchy: members followed orders from district leaders, district leaders from regional leaders, and regional leaders from the national head.
hodgepodge	(noun)	Mixture of different kinds of things, jumble	The comedian's book wasn't a proper memoir, but more a hodgepodge of old bits, personal stories that went nowhere, random political opinions, and childhood photos.
homogeneous	(adj)	Of the same kind; uniform throughout	While Sweden seems to have solved many of its social ills, critics point out that Sweden's largely homogeneous population doesn't present the challenges that exist in a more diverse nation with many cultures and languages.
hyperbole	(noun)	Deliberate exaggeration for effect	Oh, come on. Saying "That movie was so bad it made me puke" was surely hyperbole. I strongly doubt that you actually vomited during or following *The Back-Up Plan*.
idiosyncrasy	(noun)	Characteristic or habit peculiar to an individual; peculiar quality, quirk	Sometimes, the richer people get, the more idiosyncratic they become. After he made his first billion, he began traveling with a pet iguana, sleeping in an oxygen chamber, and, oddly, speaking with a slight Dutch accent.
illiberality	(noun)	Narrow-mindedness, bigotry; strictness or lack of generosity	Students protested the illiberality of an admissions policy that made no allowances for those from disadvantaged areas or backgrounds who may not have had access to advanced classes and tutors.

MANHATTAN
PREP

WORD	P.O.S	DEFINITION	USAGE
imminent	(adj)	Ready to occur, impending	In the face of imminent war, the nation looked to FDR for reassurance. / Everyone was excited and nervous; Madonna's arrival was imminent!
impair	(verb)	Make worse, weaken	Playing in a rock band without earplugs will almost certainly impair your hearing over time.
impartial	(adj)	Unbiased, fair	Judge Gonzales recused himself from the case because, having a personal connection to the school where the shooting took place, he did not think he could be appropriately impartial.
impede	(verb)	Hold back, obstruct the progress of	I didn't realize business school would be entirely group work; sadly, there's always at least one person in every group who impedes the group's progress more than helps it.
implication	(noun)	Act of implying or that which is implied; close connection, esp. in an incriminating way	When the boss said, "Times are tight around here, I just think you should know," the implication was that maybe we should start looking for new jobs. / She implicated her boyfriend in the robbery after less than 20 minutes of interrogation.
implicit	(adj)	Implied, not stated directly; involved in the very essence of something, unquestionable	He didn't have to be told to resign; it was implicit in his not getting the promotion that he had no future at the company. / I enjoy ice climbing with my father because, in such a dangerous situation, it's important to have a partner you trust implicitly.
implode	(verb)	Burst inward; fall apart	The startup struggled for years before it simply imploded—the management team broke into factions, all the clients were scared off, and employees who hadn't been paid in weeks began taking the office computers home with them in retribution.
inadvertent	(adj)	Unintentional; characterized by a lack of attention, careless	In attempting to perfect his science project, he inadvertently blew a fuse and plunged his family's home into darkness.
inasmuch	(adv)	In like manner, considering that (contraction of "in as much," generally followed by "as")	Inasmuch as you missed my birthday party to do the Walk for the Cure, I am not angry at all. Good for you for doing that! / Normally, a student would graduate in four years, but inasmuch as you failed several courses in your first two semesters, that will now be impossible for you.

WORD	P.O.S	DEFINITION	USAGE
incendiary	(adj)	Setting on fire, pertaining to arson; arousing strife, rebellion, etc.; "inflaming" the senses	The college suspended him for creating an incendiary website, encouraging sit-ins and protests, but the ACLU defended his right to freedom of speech. / It is illegal to bring incendiaries on a plane—there are many good reasons why you may not have a stick of dynamite in your carry-on.
incentive	(noun)	Something that encourages greater action or effort, such as a reward	A controversial program in a failing school system uses cash payments as an incentive for students to stay in school.
inchoate	(adj)	Just begun, undeveloped, unorganized	The first few weeks of language class went well, but her inchoate French was all but useless when she found herself at an academic conference in Quebec.
incipient	(adj)	Just beginning; in a very early stage	The movie producer was devastated when, due to legal trouble over the screenplay, the incipient project was crushed before it had even begun shooting.
incongruous	(adj)	Out of place, inappropriate, not harmonious	Among the student artwork posted in the halls, Angelina's submission was incongruous, a dark, gruesome, and even worldly work amidst the happy family portraits and other childish drawings.
inconsequential	(adj)	Insignificant, unimportant; illogical	You wrote a bestselling book and got a stellar review in the *New York Times*—whatever your cousin has to say about it is simply inconsequential.
incorporate	(verb)	Include, take in; combine, unite; form a legal corporation; embody, give physical form to	When a business incorporates, it becomes a separate legal entity; for instance, the business can declare bankruptcy without the owners doing so. / Local legend has it that ghosts can incorporate on one night of the year and walk among the living.
indeterminate	(adj)	Not fixed or determined, indefinite; vague	The results of the drug trial were indeterminate; further trials will be needed to ascertain whether the drug can be released. / The lottery can have an indeterminate number of winners—the prize is simply divided among them.
indifferent	(adj)	Not caring, having no interest; unbiased, impartial	Do whatever you want; I'm indifferent. I won't even notice.
inform	(verb)	Inspire, animate; give substance, essence, or context to; be the characteristic quality of	Her work as an art historian is informed by a background in drama; where others see a static tableau, she sees a protagonist, a conflict, a denouement.
ingenuous	(adj)	Genuine, sincere, not holding back; naïve	Multilevel marketing scams prey on the ingenuous, those who really think there's someone out there who just wants to help them get rich.

WORD	P.O.S	DEFINITION	USAGE
ingrained	(adj)	Deep-rooted, forming part of the very essence; worked into the fiber	Religious observance had been ingrained in him since birth; he could not remember a time when he didn't pray five times a day.
inherent	(adj)	Existing as a permanent, essential quality; intrinsic	New research seems to support the idea that humans have an inherent sense of justice—even babies become upset at puppet shows depicting unfairness, and are gratified at seeing the "bad" puppets punished.
innocuous	(adj)	Harmless, inoffensive	While it's quite acrid in here, the fumes that come from our factory are completely innocuous—you don't need a face mask unless you'd like one.
intelligible	(adj)	Able to be understood, clear	You are doing a disservice to all music by listening through those horrible speakers! None of the lyrics are even intelligible! I'll bet you have no idea what this song is even about!
intractable	(adj)	Difficult to control, manage, or manipulate; hard to cure; stubborn	That student is positively intractable! Last week, we talked about the importance of staying in your seat during the lesson. This week, she not only got up mid-class, but she actually scrambled on top of a bookcase and refused to come down! / Back injuries often result in intractable pain; despite treatment, patients never feel fully cured.
intrepid	(adj)	Fearless, brave, enduring in the face of adversity	Intrepid explorers Lewis and Clark led the first U.S. expedition to the West Coast, facing bitter winters and rough terrain.
intrinsic	(adj)	Belonging to the essential nature of a thing	Despite all this high-tech safety equipment, skydiving is an intrinsically dangerous proposition. / Communication is intrinsic to a healthy relationship.
jargon	(noun)	Vocabulary specific to a group or occupation; convoluted or unintelligible language	The information my doctor gave me was so full of medical jargon I couldn't understand it at all! I'm going to look on the Internet for something written for regular people.
jocular	(adj)	Joking or given to joking all the time; jolly, playful	If we were friends, I'm sure I'd find his antics amusing, but as his professor, I do wish he'd contribute some serious comments to the class discussion instead of his constant stream of jocular comments.
judicious	(adj)	Using good judgment; wise, sensible	In his will, the old titan of industry left little to his hard-partying younger son, and left the bulk of his estate to the more judicious older son, with instructions that the older son see that the rest of the family was taken care of.

WORD	P.O.S	DEFINITION	USAGE
juncture	(noun)	Critical point in time, such as a crisis or a time when a decision is necessary; a place where two things are joined together	We are at a critical juncture in the history of this organization: either we can remain a nonprofit, or we can register as a political action committee and try to expand our influence. / The little canoe started to sink when it split at the juncture between the old wood and the new material used to repair it.
keen	(adj)	Sharp, piercing; very perceptive or mentally sharp; intense (of a feeling)	Dogs have a keen sense of smell. / As homecoming queen, she had experienced the envy of others, but their jealousy only grew more keen when she was selected for a small role in a movie.
kudos	(noun)	Praise, honor, congratulations	"Kudos on your amazing GRE score!" said the teacher. / While the critics weren't impressed, the play received plentiful kudos from the audience.
lackluster	(adj)	Not shiny; dull, mediocre; lacking brilliance or vitality	Many young people today are so accustomed to being praised by parents and adults that they are shocked when a lackluster effort in the workplace receives the indifference or mild disapproval it deserves.
laconic	(adj)	Using few words, concise	The boss was famously laconic; after allowing his employees to present their new plan for an entire hour, he finally responded, "Fine."
lament	(verb, noun)	Mourn; express grief, sorrow, or regret (verb); an expression of grief, esp. as a song or poem (noun)	Silda said she couldn't make it to the party—she's still lamenting the death of her cat. In fact, she wrote a poem: "A Lament on the Topic of Buttons McFlufferton." Lamentably, Silda is a very bad poet.
lampoon	(noun, verb)	A harsh satire (noun); ridicule or satirize (verb)	"As a Democrat," said Bob, "I can't say I appreciated watching that comedian in the Obama mask lampoon the State of the Union address."
landmark	(noun, adj)	Object (such as a building) that stands out and can be used to navigate by; a very important place, event, etc.	The Civil Rights Act of 1964 was a landmark in the battle for equality. / In Lebanon, many roads are unmarked, and people navigate by landmarks; for instance, follow the "third house down from the water tower."
languid	(adj)	Drooping from exhaustion, sluggish, slow; lacking in spirit	We signed up for a fitness boot camp, but after a single hour of exercise in the heat, we all felt so overcome with languor that we refused to go on. Turns out the reason we need a fitness boot camp in the first place is that we're pretty languid people.
lassitude	(noun)	Tiredness, weariness; lazy indifference	It's so difficult to get anything done in the dead heat of August! I can't seem to shake my lassitude enough to get out of this hammock, much less study for the GRE.

MANHATTAN
PREP

WORD	P.O.S	DEFINITION	USAGE
laudable	(adj)	Worthy of praise	When a major discount mart fired several employees for subduing a gunman, most people considered the action a laudable act of heroism, but the discount chain fired the employees for "violating company policies." Nevertheless, the mayor lauded the former employees in a medal-granting ceremony.
lavish	(adj, verb)	Abundant or giving in abundance; marked by excess (adj); give very generously (verb)	Anita wanted to live as she imagined Beyoncé lived, and ran up huge credit card bills pursuing a lavish lifestyle she could scarcely afford. / Although her rich banker boyfriend lavished gifts on her, she didn't want to be with someone she didn't really love.
layperson	(noun)	A person who is not a member of the clergy or not a member of a particular profession (such as medicine, law, etc.)	The actress Jenny McCarthy has written a book about autism. While her experience as a parent is interesting to anyone in a similar situation, it's still important to remember that McCarthy is a layperson, not a doctor.
levity	(noun)	Lightness (of mind, spirit, or mood) or lack of seriousness, sometimes in an inappropriate way	My late uncle Bill loved practical jokes and absolutely would have approved of the iPod mix my aunt played at the wake, which added a little levity by segueing from "Amazing Grace" to the party anthem "Let's Get It Started."
levy	(verb, noun)	Collect tax from, wage war on, or enlist for military service (verb); act of collecting tax or amount owed, or the drafting of troops into military service (noun)	When England levied yet another tax on the colonists, the colonists were pushed one further step towards levying war. Soon, the worried British began to raise troops by levy.
liberal	(adj, noun)	Favorable to progress or reform; believing in maximum possible individual freedom; tolerant, open-minded; generous (adj); a person with such beliefs or practices (noun)	Split pea soup benefits from a liberal application of pepper. / Liberal reformers in Egypt pushed for freedom of speech, freedom of the press, and freedom of assembly.
libertine	(noun)	Morally or sexually unrestrained person; freethinker (regarding religion)	A famed libertine, the sitcom star was constantly in the news for cavorting with women of dubious occupations and overdosing on drugs often enough to regularly hold up production of his popular television show.
likewise	(adverb)	Also, in addition to; similarly, in the same way	Chip was baffled by all the silverware set before him, so when his host began eating salad with the smallest, leftmost fork, Chip did likewise.

MANHATTAN
PREP   211

WORD	P.O.S	DEFINITION	USAGE
log	(verb, noun)	Keep a record of, write down; travel for or at a certain distance or speed (verb); a written record (noun)	Lawyers who bill by the hour have to be sure to log all the time they spend on every client's case. / You cannot get your pilot's license until you have logged 40 hours of flight time.
loquacious	(adj)	Talkative, wordy	The loquacious professor spoke at a million miles an hour and still regularly talked past the scheduled end time of the class.
lucid	(adj)	Clear, easy to understand; rational, sane, clear-headed	After surgery, it'll be at least an hour before she's lucid—it's nothing to worry about, but patients sometimes talk complete nonsense until the anesthesia wears off and their speech becomes lucid again.
lull	(noun, verb)	Soothe or cause to fall asleep (as in a lullaby); quiet down; make to feel secure, sometimes falsely (verb); a period of calm or quiet (noun)	Tisha always tried to be polite. If she had to slip out of class to use the bathroom, she waited for a lull in the action so as not to attract too much attention. / Grandma's singing lulled the baby to sleep—much as, in her work as a spy during World War II, Grandma used her beauty and charm to lull foreign dignitaries into giving up their secrets.
makeshift	(noun, adj)	A temporary, often improvised, substitute (noun); improvised for temporary use (adj)	Lost in the woods for over 24 hours, the children were eventually found sleeping under a makeshift tent made from branches and old plastic bags. / I don't have a ladder, but I can stack up some boxes as a makeshift.
malleable	(adj)	Able to be bent, shaped, or adapted	The more malleable the material, the easier it is to bend into jewelry—and the easier it is to damage that jewelry. / My mother is a little too malleable—she said she liked all the things her first husband liked, and now she says she likes all the things her second husband likes.
maverick	(noun)	Rebel, individualist, dissenter	Most cop movies feature heroes who are maverick police officers, breaking all the rules, blowing things up, and getting their guns confiscated by the chief, but who ultimately save the day.
mendacious	(adj)	Lying, habitually dishonest	She was so mendacious that, when she broke the television, she blamed it on her little brother, even though he was in a wheelchair and could hardly have tipped over a piece of furniture. Her mendacity knows no bounds!
mercurial	(adj)	Quickly and unpredictably changing moods; fickle, flighty	It's tough being married to someone so mercurial. One minute she's happy as a clam; the next, she's inexplicably depressed.

WORD	P.O.S	DEFINITION	USAGE
metamorphosis	(noun)	A complete change or transformation (in biology, a change such as a caterpillar becoming a pupa and then a butterfly)	Many reality show competitions are based on the idea of a contestant undergoing a metamorphosis, such as through dieting, exercise, life coaching, rehab, or plastic surgery—or all of the above.
meticulous	(adj)	Taking extreme care in regards to details; precise, fussy	As a surgeon, of course Mom needs to be highly meticulous in her work—she gets things right down to a fraction of a millimeter. But this also means that when it's her night to cook, she's sometimes a little too meticulous—no one really needs a meatloaf to be sculpted into an absolutely perfect rectangular prism.
mitigate	(verb)	Make less severe; lessen or moderate (damage, grief, pain, etc.)	Sadly, his illness could not be cured, but the nurses made every effort to mitigate the symptoms.
modest	(adj)	Humble; simple rather than showy; decent (esp. "covering up" in terms of dress); small, limited	The reporter was surprised that the celebrity lived in such a modest house, one that looked just like every other plain, two-story house on the block. / Her first job out of college was a rude awakening—her modest salary was barely enough for rent, much less going out and having fun.
mollify	(verb)	Calm or soothe (an angry person); lessen or soften	The cellular company's billing practices were so infuriating to customers that the customer service representatives spent every workday mollifying angry customers.
monotony	(noun)	Sameness or repetitiousness to the point of being boring; lack of variation, uniformity, esp. repetition in sound	The monotony of working on a factory assembly line made her feel as though she would go insane from boredom.
moreover	(adverb)	Besides; in addition to what was just stated	You are fired. Moreover, the police are coming to arrest you for theft.
mores	(noun)	Customs, manners, or morals of a particular group	An American in Saudi Arabia should study the culture beforehand so as to avoid violating deeply conservative cultural mores.
mundane	(adj)	Common, ordinary, everyday	Dominique had been excited to visit France for the first time, but she was soon disappointed at how mundane the stay with her relatives was: they shopped at the market, cooked dinner, chatted with one another, and occasionally went shopping.

WORD	P.O.S	DEFINITION	USAGE
naïve	(adj)	Simple and unsophisticated, unsuspecting, lacking worldly experience and critical judgment	I was a little naïve during the hiring process—the Human Resources rep asked for my acceptable salary range, and I answered honestly. Of course, I got an offer for the very lowest number in the range! Now I know I should have tried to get a number from her first, or named a higher number so I could negotiate down.
nascent	(adj)	Coming into existence, still developing	The violin teacher was always very encouraging with children. All children sound terrible the first couple of years, so she offered plenty of praise to encourage nascent talents.
negate	(verb)	Deny or refute; make void or cause to be ineffective	Darling, if you add "I promise to try to work things out for at least a couple of weeks before giving up" to our wedding vows, it would kind of negate the part where you promise to love, honor, and cherish me "until death do us part." / The debate coach reminded the students that they had to negate each one of their opponents' major points in order to win.
net	(adj, verb)	Remaining after expenses or other factors have been deducted; ultimate (adj); to bring in as profit, or to catch as in a net (verb)	In one day of trading, my portfolio went up $10,000 and down $8,000, for a net gain of $2,000. / All those weeks of working weekends and playing golf with the boss ought to net her a promotion.
nevertheless or nonetheless	(adverb)	However, even so, despite that	While losing the P&G account was a serious blow, we nevertheless were able to achieve a new sales goal this month due to the tireless efforts of the sales team in bringing in three new clients. / I really can't stand working with you. Nonetheless, we're stuck on this project together and we're going to have to get along.
notoriety	(noun)	Ill fame; the state of being well-known for a disgraceful reason	Aiden was notorious for being late to everything; after awhile, his friends just stopped inviting him to the movies. / Some countries ban convicted criminals from capitalizing on their notoriety by writing books from prison or selling rights to movies about their lives.
novel	(adj)	New, fresh, original	You can make your writing better by eliminating clichés and replacing those clichés with more novel turns of speech. / Smoked salmon on a pizza? That's certainly a novel idea.

WORD	P.O.S	DEFINITION	USAGE
nuance	(noun)	A subtle difference in tone, meaning, expression, etc.	People with certain cognitive disabilities cannot understand the nuances of nonliteral speech. For instance, "You can come if you want to, but it's really going to be mostly family" means that you shouldn't try to come.
objective	(adj)	Factual, related to reality or physical objects; not influenced by emotions, unbiased	You cannot be forced to testify against your spouse in a court of law—it's pretty impossible for anyone to be objective about the guilt or innocence of a spouse. / Some philosophers argue that things like "love" and "guilt" don't exist, and that only objective reality—that is, physical matter—is of consequence.
obsequious	(adj)	Servile, very compliant, fawning	An obsequious assistant, Sammy thought he could get ahead by doing everything asked of him, but instead, his boss gave a promotion to someone he viewed as more of a peer; truthfully, he thought Sammy's sucking up was pretty pathetic.
obsolete	(adj)	Out of date, no longer in use	She kept her old laptop so long that it was obsolete — she couldn't sell it on Craigslist, and the local elementary school didn't even want it as a donation. / When you look up a word in the dictionary and see "Archaic" next to a definition, that means that definition is obsolete—people don't use the word that way anymore, although you might want to know that meaning if you're reading old texts.
obstinate	(adj)	Stubborn or hard to control	It's difficult to get an obstinate child to eat food he doesn't want to eat. When Toby realized that his son would rather sit and starve than eat mahi-mahi, he gave in and made him a peanut butter and jelly sandwich.
obviate	(verb)	Prevent, eliminate, or make unnecessary	Adding protective heel taps to your dress shoes can obviate the need to take them to the shoe repair store later, once the heels have worn down.
occult	(noun, adj, verb)	The supernatural (noun); pertaining to magic, astrology, etc.; mysterious, secret or hidden (adj); to hide, to shut off from view (verb)	A group of religious parents demanded that a popular series of young adult vampire novels be banned in schools because it promoted the occult. / During a solar eclipse, the moon occults the sun, and it is momentarily dark in the middle of the day.
offhand	(adj)	Casual, informal; done without preparation or forethought; rude in a short way, brusque	I was pretty happy with my salary until my coworker Deena mentioned offhandedly that she was thinking about buying a house now that she made six figures.

WORD	P.O.S	DEFINITION	USAGE
officious	(adj)	Excessively eager in giving unwanted advice or intruding where one is not wanted; meddlesome, pushy	Natasha's dinner parties are exhausting. She's an officious host who butts in and runs everyone's conversations, keeps an eye on what everyone is eating, and makes sure you finish your vegetables, and even knocks on the bathroom door to make sure you're "okay in there."
offset	(verb, noun)	Counteract, compensate for (verb); a counterbalance (noun)	Property taxes did go up this year, but the hit to our finances was offset by a reduction in fees paid to our homeowners association.
onerous	(adj)	Burdensome, oppressive, hard to endure	Doctors are often faced with the onerous task of telling waiting families that their loved one has died.
opaque	(adj)	Not translucent; not allowing light, heat, etc. to pass through; dark, dull, unclear, or stupid	The school dress code required opaque tights under skirts; the rules specified that sheer stockings were unacceptable. / Rena was tragically opaque. When her boyfriend said "I want to see other people," she thought he meant he needed glasses.
optimal or optimum	(adj)	Best, most desirable or favorable	Many believe that the U.S. Constitution's genius lies in its striking an optimal balance between freedom and order.
orthodox	(adj)	Adhering to a traditional, established faith, or to anything customary or commonly accepted	I appreciate that the new dentist thinks that my oral health can be improved through yoga, but I really prefer a more orthodox approach to dental care.
oscillate	(verb)	Swing back and forth; waver, change one's mind	I wish we had air conditioning, but at least I replaced our old fan with this oscillating one that swings side to side and blows air on the whole room. / Stop oscillating and pick a restaurant! Seriously—Indian or Thai?
outstrip	(verb)	Surpass, exceed; be larger or better than; leave behind	Our sales figures this quarter have outstripped those of any other quarter in the company's history.
overshadow	(verb)	Cast a shadow over, darken; dominate, make to seem less important	She was a straight-A student who excelled at field hockey, but she still felt overshadowed by her older sister, who won a national science competition for her work on cancer in mice, and also had time to become a pole vaulting champion and model who walked in Fashion Week.
paradigm	(noun)	Model or pattern; worldview, set of shared assumptions, values, etc.	Far from being atypically bawdy, this limerick is a paradigm of the form—nearly all of them rely on off-color jokes.
paradox	(noun)	Contradiction, or seeming contradiction that is actually true	Kayla was always bothering the youth minister with her paradoxes, like "If God is all-powerful, can He make a burrito so big He can't eat it?"

MANHATTAN
PREP

WORD	P.O.S	DEFINITION	USAGE
pariah	(noun)	Social outcast, untouchable	After the schoolteacher was fired for participating in what some called a "hate rally," he became a pariah in his own town—even his longtime barber refused him a haircut.
partial	(adj)	Biased, prejudiced, favoring one over others; having a special liking for something or someone (usually partial to)	Although I grew up in New York, I've always been partial to country music. / His lawyers are appealing on the grounds that the judge was partial to the plaintiff, even playing golf with the plaintiff during the trial.
partisan	(adj, noun)	Devoted to a particular group, cause, etc. (adj.); fervent supporter of a group, party, idea, etc.; guerilla fighter (noun)	It is unconscionable to engage in partisan politics in a time of crisis. People are trapped in the rubble of an earthquake, and you suggest that we vote for your tax bill in exchange for your voting for our relief bill?
patent	(adj, noun)	Obvious, apparent, plain to see (adj); a letter from a government guaranteeing an inventor the rights to his or her invention (noun)	Her résumé was full of patent lies: anyone could check to see that she had never been president of UNICEF.
pathological	(adj)	Relating to or caused by disease; relating to compulsive bad behavior	She thought her skin darkening was simply a result of the sun, but it was actually pathological, the result of a serious disease. / I can't believe you stole from the Make a Wish Foundation—you're a pathological thief!
patronizing	(adj)	Condescending, having a superior manner, treating as an inferior	I'm not surprised that Professor McDougal used to teach kindergarten. His patronizing tone has been driving me crazy.
paucity	(noun)	Scarcity, the state of being small in number	Our school has such a disgraceful paucity of textbooks that the students are sharing, and so cannot even count on being able to take the books home to do homework.
peccadillo	(noun)	Small sin or fault	I'm going to propose to Melinda tomorrow—sure, she has her peccadillos, like anyone, but she's the perfect woman for me.
pedestrian	(adj)	Ordinary, dull, commonplace	It was so amazing when you had us over to dinner and made that rack of lamb! I'm afraid neither of us is a professional chef like you are, though, so we hope you won't mind that we've made something more pedestrian: hot dogs and French fries.
penchant	(noun)	Liking or inclination (usually penchant for)	He seems like a mild-mannered accountant, but twice a year he jets off to Australia to satisfy his penchant for adventure sports.

WORD	P.O.S	DEFINITION	USAGE
perfidious	(adj)	Disloyal, treacherous, violating one's trust	The perfidious soldier sold out his comrades, giving secrets to the enemy in exchange for money and protection.
peripheral	(adj)	Relating to or making up an outer boundary or region; not of primary importance, fringe	My main goal is to get into a good grad school. Whether it has good fitness facilities is really a peripheral concern.
permeate	(verb)	Spread or penetrate throughout	Under the Emperor Constantine, Christianity began to permeate every sector of public life.
pervasive	(adj)	Tending to spread throughout	Poverty is pervasive in our school system; 65% of students receive free or reduced-price lunch.
philanthropy	(noun)	Efforts to improve the well-being of humankind, generally through giving money	Many wealthy people turn to philanthropy as a way to create social good, and many others turn to it as a way to hobnob with the rich and famous.
phony	(adj)	Fake, counterfeit; insincere, not genuine	Phony Louis Vuitton bags are easily purchased in Chinatown, but they are illegal—selling them can land a vendor in jail, and the counterfeit bags are often made with child labor. / She's such a phony person, pretending to befriend people and then talking about them behind their backs.
pious	(adj)	Devout; religiously reverent and dutiful	Some matrimonial websites catering to conservative religious groups contain listings for young women that feature testimonials from a woman's relatives about her piety. Naturally, only similarly pious suitors need apply.
pith	(noun)	Core, essence; significance or weight	I can only stay at this meeting for a minute—can you get to the pith of the issue now, and discuss the details after I leave? / This presentation has no pith—there's no central point and nothing I didn't already know.
placate	(verb)	Satisfy or calm down (an angry or dissatisfied person), esp. by conciliatory gestures	"It's an interesting business model," said the flower shop owner. "Outside of Valentine's Day, our average customer uses our product to placate an angry partner."
placid	(adj)	Peaceful, calm, tranquil	Famed Spanish tenor Placido Domingo has an unusual name—literally it means, "Peaceful Sunday." It's certainly not a coincidence that *Placido* looks so much like *placid*.
plastic	(adj)	Able to be shaped or formed; easily influenced	A young child's mind is quite plastic, and exposure to violent movies and video games can have a much greater effect on children than they typically do on adults.

WORD	P.O.S	DEFINITION	USAGE
plausible	(noun)	Believable; having the appearance of truth	When three doctors treating crash victims were suddenly stricken with what looked like the effects of nerve gas, hospital officials posited "hysteria" as the culprit—hardly a plausible explanation, as emergency room doctors are accustomed to seeing horrific things every day.
plummet	(verb)	Plunge, fall straight down	During the first 60 seconds or so of a skydive, the diver plummets towards Earth in freefall; then, he or she activates a parachute and floats down at what seems like a relatively leisurely pace.
polarized	(adj)	Divided into sharply opposed groups	The school board was used to rationally discussing issues, but when it came to the teaching of evolution in schools, the board was polarized, immediately splitting into two camps, with the discussion devolving into a shouting match within minutes.
ponderous	(adj)	Heavy; bulky and unwieldy; dull, labored	The book assigned by her professor was a ponderous tome, more a reference book than something you could read straight through. She was so bored she thought she would die.
posthumous	(adj)	Happening or continuing after death	Ernest Hemingway died in 1961. His novel *The Garden of Eden* was published posthumously in 1986.
potentate	(noun)	Ruler, person of great power	At 62 year's old, Prince Charles has certainly waited long enough to become potentate of England; his mother, Elizabeth II, has been ruling for his entire life.
pragmatic	(adj)	Practical; dealing with actual facts and reality	Megan and Dave were in love, but Megan decided to be pragmatic—she doubted they'd stay together through a four-year long distance relationship as they attended different colleges, so she figured they might as well end things now.
preamble	(noun)	Introductory statement, preface	The Preamble to the Constitution is a brief introduction that begins, "We the People of the United States, in Order to form a more perfect Union…" / The unusual outfit the pop star wore to her first awards ceremony was a mere preamble to a career of full-blown crazy dressing.
precarious	(adj)	Unstable, insecure, dangerous	Recognizing that his position at the company was precarious, Sanjay requested that his bonus structure be formally written down as a contract, rather than dangled over him as a mere verbal promise.

WORD	P.O.S	DEFINITION	USAGE
precursor	(noun)	Something that comes before, esp. something that also announces or suggests something on its way	We cannot ignore this warning sign—it is clearly a precursor of larger problems to come. / The new CEO decided to do things differently from his precursors.
predisposed	(adj)	Having an inclination or tendency beforehand; susceptible	Some autoimmune disorders don't kill the patient directly, but rather predispose the patient to other, potentially fatal illnesses. / His defense attorney argued that his abusive childhood predisposed him to a life of crime.
preempt	(verb)	Prevent; take the place of, supplant; take before someone else can	The speaker attempted to preempt an excessively long Q&A session by handing out a "Frequently Asked Questions" packet at the beginning of the seminar.
presumptive	(adj)	Based on inference or assumption; providing reasonable grounds for belief	The dictator's favorite nephew is the presumptive heir to power, but anything could happen. / He's the presumptive winner of the election; we haven't counted all the votes, but at this point it's almost mathematically impossible for the other guy to win.
presumptuous	(adj)	Too bold or forward; going beyond that which is proper	I would never date that presumptuous jerk! I mean, I thought he was attractive until he walked up to me and said, "We should go out—I looked up your address on Google and I'll pick you up at 8." The nerve!
pretentious	(adj)	Claiming or demanding a position of importance or dignity, esp. when unjustified; showing off, creating a deceptive, false show of worth	Josie found her date's habit of constantly dropping French phrases into conversation to be incredibly pretentious, especially since he knew she didn't speak French. He sure did sound fancy, though.
principled	(adj)	Having high moral standards	Donna was only an intern, but she was also quite principled—although she knew it would kill her shot at a full-time job, she was the one who alerted the authorities when asked to violate federal law via corrupt accounting practices.
pristine	(adj)	In an original, pure state; uncorrupted	Having grown up in a rural area, Billy had been in plenty of forests where people regularly left beer cans and shotgun shells behind. So it truly took his breath away, after hiking hours through the Himalayas, to visit a pristine forest, seemingly untouched by humans.
probity	(noun)	Honesty, integrity	After losing the last election when its candidate's string of mistresses came to light, the party vowed to only nominate candidates whose probity was beyond any doubt.

WORD	P.O.S	DEFINITION	USAGE
prodigal	(adj)	Wasteful, extravagant; giving abundantly, lavish	If you're going to leave a trust fund for your children, you should raise them not to be prodigal, or they'll blow through all the cash the minute they get their hands on it. / The prodigal land produced larger crops than the people could even consume.
prodigious	(adj)	Extraordinarily large, impressive, etc.	The Great Wall of China consists of a prodigious series of fortifications stretching over 5,000 miles. / If we don't double our sales with this new product, we will have to declare bankruptcy—we have a prodigious task ahead.
profligate	(adj)	Completely and shamelessly immoral, or extremely wasteful	The billionaire software developer was so disgusted with his profligate daughter's spending that he cut her off—she had bought champagne for an entire nightclub full of strangers one too many times.
profound	(adj)	Very insightful, penetrating deeply into a subject; pervasive, intense, "down to the very bottom"; at the very bottom	The philosopher's work was difficult to parse, but profound; it said truly novel things about the nature of reality. / He was profoundly disappointed when the project he had worked on for 15 years failed.
profuse	(adj)	Abundant, extravagant, giving or given freely	It didn't mean anything at all to me, giving my old microwave to the family next door, but the woman's profuse thanks made me think that maybe the family was having some financial troubles. / She came home on Valentine's Day to an apartment decorated with a profusion of flowers.
prohibitive	(adj)	Tending to forbid something, or serving to prevent something	I was admitted to NYU, but it was prohibitively expensive, so I ended up at state school instead. / My parents installed a high fence as a prohibitive barrier against the neighborhood hooligans.
proliferate	(verb)	Increase or spread rapidly or excessively	The book alleged that terrorist cells are proliferating across the United States faster than law enforcement can keep up.
prologue	(noun)	Introductory part to a book, play, etc.	The novel's prologue gives some historical background so that the main story can be better understood in context.
pronounced	(adj)	Distinct, strong, clearly indicated	Aunt Shirley claimed we would never know that her "secret recipe" for brownies involved lots of healthy vegetables, but the brownies had a pronounced asparagus flavor.

WORD	P.O.S	DEFINITION	USAGE
propriety	(noun)	Conforming to good manners or appropriate behavior; justness	The parent questioned the propriety of the punishment meted out to her son—sitting in a corner all day seemed a little harsh for using the pencil sharpener at the wrong time. / Saying the accounting firm was complicit in "financial impropriety" was a rather polite way to refer to the fraud it committed against its investors.
prosaic	(adj)	Dull, ordinary	Finding his friends' bar mitzvahs at the local synagogue a bit prosaic, Justin instead asked his dad to rent out the local laser tag center.
proscribe	(verb)	Prohibit, outlaw; denounce; exile or banish	Plagiarism is proscribed by every college's code of conduct.
prospective	(adj)	Potential, in the future	Everyone had a hard time correctly saying the name of the seminar, "Perspectives for Prospective Doctors." Even the prospective doctors—college students hoping to be admitted to medical school—were a bit confused.
prudent	(adj)	Wise in practical matters, carefully providing for the future	Sophie's friends blew all kinds of money on spring break, but Sophie prudently kept to her usual spending habits.
pugnacious	(adj)	Inclined to fight, combative	Maria had hoped to avoid inviting Uncle Luigi to the wedding, as he was a pugnacious fellow. Sure enough, he managed to start a fistfight with the best man.
qualified	(adj)	Modified, limited, conditional on something else	The scientist gave her qualified endorsement to the book, pointing out that, while it posed a credible theory, more research was still needed before the theory could be applied.
quandary	(noun)	Uncertainty or confusion about what to do, dilemma	He knew it sounded like the plot of a cheesy movie, but he really had accidentally asked two girls to the prom, and now he was in quite a quandary.
quibble	(verb)	Make trivial arguments or criticisms, find faults in a petty way, esp. to evade something more important	Look, I am telling you some of the serious consequences of global warming, as predicted by the scientific establishment—I think you're just quibbling to complain that I said "carbon monoxide" when I meant "carbon dioxide."
quotidian	(adj)	Daily; everyday, ordinary	He was so involved in his quest for spiritual enlightenment that he regularly forgot more quotidian concerns—sure, he meditated for six hours a day, but he would forget to do laundry for weeks!
ranks	(noun)	Personnel; a group of people considered all together	Among the ranks of our alumni are two senators and many famous authors.

MANHATTAN
PREP

WORD	P.O.S	DEFINITION	USAGE
reap	(verb)	Harvest, such as by cutting; gather; get as a result of one's effort	He worked night and day in the strange new country, never stopping to rest, for he knew he would reap his reward when his family greeted him as a hero for all the money he had sent back home.
recluse	(noun)	Person who lives in seclusion	That show about "hoarders" featured a recluse who hadn't left her house in six years.
refute	(verb)	Prove to be false	She's not a very valuable member of the debate team, actually—she loves making speeches, but she's not very good at refuting opponents' arguments.
relegate	(verb)	Send or commit to an inferior place, rank, condition, etc.; exile, banish; assign (a task) to someone else	After the legal associate offended one of the partners, he found himself relegated to working on minor—even unwinnable—cases. / This protest is occurring because we refuse to be relegated to the fringes of society—we demand full inclusion!
remedial	(adj)	Providing a remedy, curative; correcting a deficient skill	After harassment occurs in the workplace, it is important that the company take remedial action right away, warning or firing the offender as appropriate, and making sure the complainant's concerns are addressed. / For those who need remedial reading help, we offer a summer school program that aims to help students read at grade level.
render	(verb)	Give, submit, surrender; translate; declare formally; cause to become	When you render your past due payments, we will turn your phone back on. / Only in her second year of Japanese, she was unable to render the classic poem into English. / The judge rendered a verdict that rendered us speechless.
replete	(adj)	Supplied in abundance, filled, gorged (used with *with*)	This essay is replete with errors—I don't think you even bothered to use spellcheck.
reproach	(noun, verb)	Blame, disgrace (noun); criticize, express disappointment in (verb)	I'm not really enjoying my foreign study program. My host mom reproached me in Spanish; it sounded really harsh, but I couldn't really understand her, and I have no idea what I did wrong!
repudiate	(verb)	Reject, cast off, deny that something has authority	If you receive an erroneous notice from a collections agency, you have 30 days to repudiate the debt by mail. / As part of becoming an American citizen, Mr. Lee repudiated his former citizenship.
requite	(verb)	Reciprocate, repay, or revenge	Ashley felt that her unrequited love for George would surely kill her. George barely noticed her—he cared about nothing but requiting his father's death.

WORD	P.O.S	DEFINITION	USAGE
rescind	(verb)	Annul, repeal, make void	The governor rescinded his proclamation making September 10th "Pastafarian Day" once someone told him it wasn't a real religion.
resolution	(noun)	The quality of being firmly determined; resolving to do something; a formal judgment, esp. decided by a vote	The city government passed a resolution to support the new monorail. / A few setbacks did not dampen her resolution to complete her Ph.D.
resolve	(verb, noun)	Find a solution to; firmly decide to do something; decide by formal vote (verb); firmness of purpose (noun)	She was resolved to find a marrow donor for her son, and led a stunningly successful drive to get people to sign up for a national donor registry. Even when no match was found for her son in the first year, her resolve was undampened.
respectively	(adverb)	In the order given	His poems "An Ode to the Blossoms of Sheffield" and "An Entreaty to Ladies All Too Prim" were written in 1756 and 1758, respectively.
restive	(adj)	Restless; Impatient or uneasy under the control of another	The company was purchased by a larger competitor, and the employees grew restive as the new bosses curtailed their freedoms and put a hold on their projects.
reticent	(adj)	Not talking much; private (of a person), restrained, reserved	She figured that, to rise to the top, it was best to be reticent about her personal life; thus, even her closest colleagues were left speculating at the water cooler about whether her growing belly actually indicated a pregnancy she simply declined to mention to anyone.
retrospective	(adj, noun)	Looking to the past or backward; applying to the past, retroactive (adj); an art exhibit of an artist's work over a long period of time (noun)	The proposed law is retrospective: anyone who violated the law before the law even existed can be prosecuted.
reverent	(adj)	Feeling or expressing very deep respect and awe	Ayn Rand is a controversial figure, but critical views are not welcome at the local Objectivist Club meeting, where everyone expresses a reverent view of the author.
rhetoric	(noun)	The art or study of persuasion through speaking or writing; language that is elaborate or pretentious but actually empty, meaning little	The ancient Greeks used to study rhetoric as a major academic subject. Today, if you want to improve your rhetorical skills, you will probably have to hunt down a public speaking class or join Toastmasters. / The politician's blather is all rhetoric and no substance.
rife	(adj)	Happening frequently, abundant, currently being reported	Reports of financial corruption are rife.

WORD	P.O.S	DEFINITION	USAGE
rudimentary	(adj)	Elementary, relating to the basics; undeveloped, primitive	My knowledge of Chinese is quite rudimentary—I get the idea of characters, and I can order food, but I really can't read this document you've just given me.
rustic	(adj, noun)	Relating to country life, unsophisticated; primitive; made of rough wood (adj); a rural or uncultured person (noun)	For their honeymoon, they eschewed fancy hotels and instead chose a rustic cabin in the woods. / Grandpa was a true rustic—I was happy to have him visit, but not so happy to find him urinating outside in a bucket when we have several perfectly nice bathrooms.
sacrosanct	(adj)	Sacred, inviolable, not to be trespassed on or violated; above any criticism	In our house, family dinners were sacrosanct—if being in the school play meant you would miss dinner, then you just couldn't be in the school play.
sagacious	(adj)	Wise; showing good judgment and foresight	It's important to choose a mentor who is not only successful, but also sagacious—plenty of people are successful through luck and have little insight about how to attack someone else's situation.
salubrious	(adj)	Healthful, promoting health	After spending her twenties smoking and drinking, Jessica recognized the necessity of adopting a more salubrious lifestyle, but found it difficult to cut back.
sanction	(noun, verb)	Permission or approval, something that gives support or authority to something else (noun); to allow, confirm, ratify (verb); a legal action by one or more countries against another country to get it to comply (noun); to place sanctions or penalties on (verb)	Professional boxers may only fight in sanctioned matches—fighting outside the ring is prohibited. / America's sanctions on Cuba mean that it is illegal for Americans to do business with Cuban companies.
sanguine	(adj)	Cheerfully optimistic, hopeful; reddish, ruddy (as in rosy-red cheeks indicting health or vitality)	She had three papers due in three days, but she maintained her typically sanguine attitude. "Things always just work out for me," she said, happily.
sap	(noun, verb)	The inner fluid of a plant or any essential body fluid; energy, vitality; a person taken advantage of (noun); undermine, weaken, tire out (verb)	I really thought that if I clicked on that Facebook ad and entered all my information, I would get a free iPad to test and keep! I feel like such a sap. / In order to make maple syrup, you must drain sap from a sugar maple tree. They call this "sapping" the tree, which I can understand, because I feel pretty sapped doing it! It's tiring work.

WORD	P.O.S	DEFINITION	USAGE
satiate or sate	(verb)	To fully satisfy; to go beyond satisfying to the point of excess (possibly inducing disgust, tiredness, etc.)	I usually just eat a tiny salad or something while I'm at work, but since I had a half day off, I went to the Indian buffet and stayed for a whole hour! I've never been more satiated (or sated) in my life. / To maintain a healthy weight, stop eating before you reach the point of satiety.
saturate	(verb)	Soak or imbue thoroughly; cause a substance to unite with the greatest possible amount of another substance	We got married on a rainy beach, and my dress was saturated. Although the pictures were a bit dark, the photographer was able to increase the saturation in Photoshop, making our wedding photos ultimately look quite vivid. / I simply cannot dissolve any more sugar into this iced tea—it's saturated!
savor	(noun, verb)	A characteristic taste or flavor (usually pleasant) (noun); appreciate fully, taste or smell with pleasure (verb)	As a parent, it's important to take a step back and really savor the special moments—those children will grow up sooner than you think!
scant	(adj)	Not enough or barely enough	The new intern was scant help at the conference—he disappeared all day to smoke and didn't seem to realize that he was there to assist his coworkers. / The soldiers were always on the verge of hunger, complaining about their scanty rations.
scathing	(adj)	Severe, injurious; bitterly harsh or critical (as a remark)	The school superintendant gave a scathing criticism of the education bill, calling it "an attack on our community's children that will surely go down in infamy." / How is it possible that she flew off her bicycle like that and walked away unscathed?
secular	(adj)	Not religious or holy; pertaining to worldly things	Forty years ago, American companies wished their employees "Merry Christmas"—even the employees who didn't celebrate Christmas. Today, the secular phrase "Happy Holidays" is common. / Western governments have grown increasingly secular over the last century; many have laws prohibiting religious expression from being sponsored by the government.
sedulous	(adj)	Persevering, persistent, diligent in one's efforts	Sedulous effort is necessary to improve your GRE verbal score—you need to study vocab in a serious way, nearly every day.
sentient	(adj)	Conscious; experiencing sensation or perceiving with the senses	Tia became a vegan because she refused to eat any sentient creature.
simultaneous	(adj)	At the same time	It is rare in a duel that the two shooters draw their guns simultaneously and both fire.

WORD	P.O.S	DEFINITION	USAGE
skeptic	(adj)	Person inclined to doubting or questioning generally accepted beliefs	I wish you'd be more of a skeptic—I can't believe you spent money on a pet psychic so we can "talk" to our dearly departed shih tzu. / Descartes was a great skeptic, famously declaring that we cannot truly be sure of anything except our own existence—hence, "I think, therefore I am."
skirt	(verb)	Border, lie along the edge of, go around; evade	Melissa spent all of Thanksgiving skirting the issue of whom she was dating and when she might get married and make her mother a grandmother. She was exhausted changing the subject two dozen times! / The creek skirts our property on the west, so it's easy to tell where our farm ends.
slack	(adj, verb, noun)	Loose, negligent, lazy, weak (adj); neglect to do one's duties; loosen up, relax (verb); period of little work (noun)	As the product of slack parenting, I never learned good time management skills—Mom and Dad never checked my homework or made me go to bed at a certain time. / The holidays represent an opportunity for employees to slack a bit.
slew	(noun)	A large number or quantity	As soon as we switched software packages, we encountered a whole slew of problems.
slight	(adj, verb, noun)	Small, not very important, slender or delicate (adj); treat as though not very important; snub, ignore (verb); an act of treating in this way, a discourtesy (noun)	She was very sensitive, always holding a grudge against her coworkers for a variety of slights, both real and imagined. / Actress Natalie Portman has always been slight, but she became even thinner to portray a ballerina in the movie Black Swan. / I felt slighted when my husband told you about his promotion before he told me.
solicitous	(adj)	Concerned or anxious (about another person), expressing care; eager or desirous; very careful	A solicitous host, Derek not only asked each person how he or she was doing, but asked by name about everyone's spouses and kids. / Solicitous of fame, she would do anything to get near celebrities.
soporific	(adj, noun)	Causing sleep; sleepy, drowsy (adj); something that causes sleep (noun)	I was excited to take a class with Professor Baria because I had enjoyed her books, but sadly, she is a better writer than speaker—her lectures are soporific. / I was so distressed after the crash that the doctor gave me a soporific and, sure enough, I was able to think more clearly after sleeping.
sound	(verb)	Measure the depth of (usually of water) as with a sounding line; penetrate and discover the meaning of, understand (usually as sound the depths)	The psychiatrist appointed by the court felt he would need more time to sound the depths of the defendant's tortured mind; clearly, she was mentally ill, but did she know on any level that what she was doing was wrong?

WORD	P.O.S	DEFINITION	USAGE
spartan	(adj)	Very disciplined and stern; frugal, living simply, austere; suggestive of the ancient Spartans	A young soldier in the spartan environment of boot camp can really long for a home-cooked meal or even just a comfortable couch to sit on. / Her apartment was so spartan that she couldn't even serve us both soup—she only had one bowl and one spoon. Instead, we sat in hard-backed chairs and drank water.
spate	(noun)	Sudden outpouring or rush; flood	After a brief spate of post-exam partying, Lola is ready for classes to begin again. / He was so furious that a spate of expletives just flew out of his mouth.
spearhead	(verb)	Be the leader of	Lisa agreed to spearhead the "healthy office" initiative, and was instrumental in installing two treadmills and getting healthy food stocked in the vending machines.
specious	(adj)	Seemingly true but actually false; deceptively attractive	"All squares are rectangles, all candy bars are rectangles, therefore all squares are candy bars" is clearly a specious argument.
spectrum	(noun)	A broad range of nevertheless related qualities or ideas, esp. those that overlap to create a continuous series (as in a color spectrum, where each color blends into the next in a continuous way)	A test showed she was partially colorblind—she did see blues and greens, but was unable to perceive some other colors on the spectrum. / A "dialect continuum" is a spectrum of dialects of a language where speakers in different dialect groups can understand some, but not all, of the other groups; for instance, people in the west can understand people in the middle, and people in the middle can understand people in the east, but people in the west and the east cannot talk to one another.
speculate	(verb)	Contemplate; make a guess or educated guess about; engage in a risky business transaction, gamble	During the Gold Rush, speculators bought up land, sometimes with borrowed funds, expecting to prospect the land for gold and get rich quickly. / She speculated that, in zero gravity, showers would have to exist as closed rooms in which a giant bubble of water formed, and a person got inside it.
sporadic	(adj)	Occasional, happening irregularly or in scattered locations	Her attendance was sporadic at best, so when she flounced into class after a two-session absence, she discovered that not only was everyone working on group projects, but that the professor hadn't even thought to assign her to a group. / "Be seeing you." "Yeah, I hope not sporadically."

WORD	P.O.S	DEFINITION	USAGE
sportive	(adj)	Playful, merry, joking around, done "in sport" (rather than intended seriously)	After Will shot a ball entirely off the pool table, knocking a woman's purse off a bar stool, his friends laughed hysterically and called him "purse-snatcher" all night, but he took it as sportive and bought the next round of drinks.
standing	(noun, adj)	Status, rank, reputation (noun); existing indefinitely, not movable (adj)	As he had feared, his divorce greatly reduced his standing as a relationship expert. / I'm disappointed that you don't want to leave your current job, but I want you to know that you have a standing invitation—as long as I'm the boss, you have a job here anytime you want one. / While the U.S. has a standing army (that is, an army that is not disbanded in times of peace), Costa Rica's constitution actually forbids a standing military.
stark	(adj)	Complete, total, utter; harsh or grim; extremely simple, severe, blunt, or plain	The designer's work is appreciated for its stark beauty, but most people prefer to live in a cozier, more welcoming home—the kind with carpets and pillows, for instance. / She is stark raving mad! / The stark reality is that we will have to begin burning our furniture for warmth if we are to survive.
static	(adj)	Fixed, not moving or changing, lacking vitality	The anthropologist studied a society in the Amazon that had been deliberately static for hundreds of years—the fiercely proud people disdained change, and viewed all new ideas as inferior to the way of life they had always practiced.
status quo	(noun)	Existing state or condition	Many opposed the establishment of a needle-exchange program, but others reasoned that the plan would be an improvement on the status quo, in which disease spread rapidly through certain communities.
stingy	(adj)	Not generous with money, reluctant to spend or give	Billionaire industrialist J. Paul Getty was so famously stingy that he installed pay phones in his mansion for guests to use. When his grandson was kidnapped, he refused to pay ransom and only changed his mind when the kidnappers cut off the boy's ear. This famous cheapskate then demanded that his son (the boy's father) pay him back! What a miser.
stoic or stoical	(adj, noun)	Indifferent to pleasure or pain, enduring without complaint; person indifferent to pleasure or pain (noun)	Della was not only calm but positively stoic, facing the measles vaccination without a single yelp, in spite of her terrible fear of needles.

WORD	P.O.S	DEFINITION	USAGE
stolid	(adj)	Unemotional, showing little emotion, not easily moved	Dad is so stolid that we can't get a rise out of him no matter what we do—Jody got a tattoo, Max declared himself a communist, and Helen won a Rhodes Scholarship. No response! Dad just nodded and said "Alright, then."
stymie or stymy	(verb, noun)	Block, hinder, or thwart (verb); an obstacle (noun)	Celine feared that her learning disability would stymie her success in college, but the support services offered were excellent, and she was fine academically; the thing that really stymied her college career was poor time management.
subjective	(adj)	Existing in the mind or relating to one's own thoughts, opinions, emotions, etc.; personal, individual, based on feelings	Naturally, anyone's experience of a movie is subjective, and some will enjoy this picture despite its flaws; however, it is an objective fact that the cinematography is very bad. / We can give names to colors, but we can never quite convey the subjective experience of them—what if my "red" is different from your "red"?
subside	(verb)	Sink, settle down, become less active; return to a normal level	When her terror subsided, she realized that the house wasn't really haunted. / It is a chronic illness—symptoms will flare up and subside over one's lifetime.
substantiate	(verb)	Support with evidence or proof; give a material existence to	You say you were at home when the crime occurred two towns over—is there anyone who can substantiate your claim? / Your business ideas are interesting, but you never substantiate them—you haven't put a single plan into action.
succeeding	(adj)	Coming after or following	After the sale of the company, you will receive 5% of the profits from the current year, and 1% in all succeeding years. / In 1797, George Washington was succeeded by John Adams.
supersede	(verb)	Replace, take the position of, cause to be disregarded as void or obsolete	Of course, electric washing machines superseded hand-powered ones many decades ago, but my great-grandmother used her hand-cranked washer until she died in the 1990s.
supplicate	(verb)	Pray humbly; ask, beg, or seek in a humble way	She had been estranged from her wealthy father for years, but when she needed money for her daughter's medical care, she supplicated the old man for assistance.
surfeit	(noun)	Excess, excessive amount, overindulgence	The soup kitchen would like to announce that it has a serious surfeit of those cans of jellied cranberries that no one seems to want, but it could still use at least 10 Thanksgiving turkeys.

WORD	P.O.S	DEFINITION	USAGE
surmise	(verb)	Guess, infer, opine	Based on your rather sad attempt to figure out the tip on our restaurant bill, I would surmise that you actually have no idea how percents work.
sycophant	(noun)	Servile flatterer, toady	Stop being such a sycophant. I don't need you to compliment my tie or get me coffee; I just need you to do your job without bothering me.
synchronous	(adj)	Happening at the same time; occurring at the same rate and thus happening together repeatedly	The sound of that bell is a signal for the dancers to make perfectly synchronous entrances from opposite sides of the stage. / The two nearby churches have synchronous church bells—if you stand halfway between the buildings as the bells chime out the hour, it sounds really cool!
table	(verb)	Lay aside to discuss later, often as a way to postpone discussion indefinitely	I see we're not going to agree on whether to scrap our entire curriculum and develop a new one, so let's table that discussion and move on to voting on the budget.
tacit	(adj)	Understood without being said; implied, not stated directly	Her parents never told her she could smoke, but they gave their tacit consent when they didn't say anything about the obvious smell coming from her bedroom.
taciturn	(adj)	Not talking much, reserved; silent, holding back in conversation	Because he felt self-conscious about his stutter, Mike had always been taciturn, but after some very good speech therapy, soon he was much more voluble.
tangential	(adj)	Only slightly relevant, going off-topic	It's hard to get a quick answer out of Noah—ask him any question, and you'll get a wide range of tangential remarks before he gets around to the point.
temperance	(noun)	Moderation, self-control, esp. regarding alcohol or other desires or pleasures; total abstinence from alcohol	After the end of the Civil War, economic change led to an increase in alcohol problems and the birth of the Temperance Movement, which ultimately led to Prohibition. / Grandma is a model of temperance—she drinks red wine every night, but only the one-third of a glass that she read was conducive to preventing heart attacks.
tenuous	(adj)	Flimsy, having little substance; long and thin, slender	Your argument is quite tenuous—it depends on our accepting the results of a 1955 study published in an obscure medical journal not subject to peer review.
timely	(adj)	Well-timed, happening at a suitable time	Your arrival is quite timely—we were just mulling over a question we're sure you can answer. / His timely departure prevented him from having to do any work.
timorous	(adj)	Fearful, timid	The expression describing a timorous person as "quaking in his boots" is a bit of a cliché.

WORD	P.O.S	DEFINITION	USAGE
tirade	(noun)	Bitter, abusive criticism or verbal attack	I hate that television show where that commentator goes on angry tirades about all the liberal conspiracies taking over America. Even my conservative friends find his ranting embarrassing.
torpor	(noun)	Sluggishness, lethargy, or apathy; a period of inactivity	Sam had hoped to be able to play in the game after having his wisdom teeth out, but the anesthesia left him in such torpor that he obviously couldn't play soccer.
torrid	(adj)	Very hot, parching, burning; passionate	They had a torrid love affair in the '80s, but split up because a royal was not permitted to marry a commoner. / The wandering refugees were in serious danger of becoming quickly dehydated in the torrid Sahara.
tractable	(adj)	Easily controlled or managed, docile; easily shaped or molded	He's a tractable fellow; when I asked if we could see a different movie than the one we'd come to see, he shrugged and said "Cool." / The clay had hardened overnight, but adding water made it tractable again.
transitory	(adj)	Temporary, short-lived, not lasting	While a few people marry their high school sweethearts, generally, our teenage years are full of transitory relationships.
trifling or trifle	(adj, noun)	Trivial, not very important; so small as to be unimportant; frivolous, shallow	Luis broke up with Cara because she was always obsessed with some trifling matter—he tried to talk about foreign aid dependency, and she changed the subject to what the actress Katie Holmes dressed her daughter Suri in for a shopping trip. / The young heiress was so wealthy that she considered the salary from her internship a mere trifle, and didn't even notice when her paycheck was days late.
trite	(adj)	Lacking freshness and originality, lacking effectiveness due to overuse, cliché	The topic of your speech is "Children Are the Future"? That's pretty trite. Maybe you should think harder and come up with something original.
ubiquitous	(adj)	Existing everywhere at the same time	Pay phones, which used to be ubiquitous in urban areas, are now nearly impossible to find in operation. / Butterflies seem to be ubiquitous in the habitat; watch any surface for several minutes, and a butterfly is sure to alight on it.

MANHATTAN
PREP

WORD	P.O.S	DEFINITION	USAGE
undermine	(verb)	Weaken, cause to collapse by digging away at the foundation (of a building or an argument); injure or attack in a secretive or underhanded way	Rather than searching impartially for the truth, these pharmaceutical company "scientists" willfully ignored any evidence that undermined the conclusion they were being paid to produce. / You are nice to my face, but you are undermining me behind my back, suggesting to others in the office that I am making mistakes in my work and that you have been fixing them.
underscore	(verb)	Emphasize (or, literally, to underline text)	"You're not going to mess with Otto anymore," said Otto. His new bodyguards stepped forward threateningly, as though to underscore his point.
unearth	(verb)	Dig up, uncover, expose	The ACLU's Prison Project works tirelessly to unearth evidence from old cases that might exonerate innocent people who have spent years or even decades in prison. / The archaeologist unearthed what appears to be the world's oldest known gravesite, showing that the earliest humans cared for their deceased loved ones.
unequivocal	(adj)	Unambiguous, clear, absolute; having only one possible meaning	Although Chuck denied he had a problem, his family was unequivocal in demanding that he check into rehab. Chuck knew there was no getting around it this time. / Jorge equivocated, going back and forth on the issue, but his brother Rafael was unequivocal—he knew what he wanted and went and got it.
unprecedented	(adj)	Never before known or seen, without having happened previously	When Nixon resigned, American bravado was at an all-time low—the resignation of a sitting President was disgraceful and unprecedented.
unseemly	(adj)	Improper, inappropriate, against the rules of taste or politeness	The activist really did want to get the candidate's support for the equal-rights measure, so she did what the candidate's aides asked, but she found it very unseemly that they suggested a specific dollar amount for the "donation" she was asked to make in order to get a meeting.
vacillate	(verb)	Waver in one's mind or opinions, be indecisive	In need of a good used car, I was vacillating between the Ford and the Hyundai until a recommendation from a friend helped me decide.
venerate	(verb)	Revere, regard with deep respect and awe	The boys were utterly crushed when the baseball player they venerated saw them waiting and refused to sign an autograph.
veracity	(noun)	Truthfulness, accuracy; habitual adherence to the truth	I question the veracity of your story. I just don't think you've been to outer space. / She was known for her veracity only because she had no choice—she was a terrible liar.

WORD	P.O.S	DEFINITION	USAGE
verbose	(adj)	Wordy	Twitter's 140-character limit really forces the verbose to go against their natural tendencies and instead write succinctly.
viable	(adj)	Capable of living (or growing, developing, etc.); practical, work-able	I have three screenplay ideas, but the studio head said only one was commercially viable. Apparently, it's important to have a human lead character and a satisfying ending. / Due to leaps forward in technology, premature babies are considered viable earlier and earlier—currently around 24 weeks.
vintage	(adj, noun)	Related to items of high quality from a previous era, old-fashioned, antique (adj); the wine of a particular year (noun)	He didn't want just *any* vintage Darth Vader action figure—he wanted a particular vintage, the 1978 telescoping lightsaber one. / She special-ordered her favorite vintage of the Côtes du Rhône, then turned to her George Clooney–lookalike husband and joked that she liked men of a certain vintage as well.
virtual	(adj)	Existing only in the mind or by means of a computer network; existing in results or in essence but not officially or in name	The Tamagotchi is a handheld virtual pet made in Japan. You have to "care" for it by performing various actions with the device, but in the end, your "pet" still looks very much like a keychain.
vituperate	(verb)	Verbally abuse, rebuke or criticize harshly	All couples fight, but your girlfriend vituperates you so severely that I'm not sure she loves you at all. Verbal abuse is actually a pretty good reason to break up.
volatile	(adj)	Varying, inconstant, fleeting; tending to violence, explosive	Following the sudden revolution, the political environment in the country was so volatile that anything could have started a riot. / Stock prices are by nature volatile. If you want a "safe and steady" investment, try mutual funds.
warranted	(adj)	Justified, authorized (warrant can mean to justify or a justification, but can also mean to vouch for or guarantee)	The pundit's comments don't even warrant a response from our organization—they were mere name-calling, not suitable for public discourse. / Your criticism of Anne is unwarranted; as your assistant, she has done everything you've asked her to do. / He doesn't have his documents with him, but I'll warrant that he is indeed a certified forklift operator.
wary	(adj)	Watchful, motivated by caution, on guard against danger	Be wary of anyone who tells you that "anyone" can get rich with some special plan or scheme.

MANHATTAN
PREP

WORD	P.O.S	DEFINITION	USAGE
whereas	(conjunction)	While on the contrary, considering that	Mr. Katsoulas had always assumed his son would take over the family business, whereas his son had always assumed he would go away to college and never come back. / Whereas peppers and squash are technically fruits, they are typically considered vegetables for culinary purposes.
whimsical	(adj)	Marked or motivated by whims (odd, fanciful ideas); erratic, unpredictable	*Alice in Wonderland* is a famously whimsical story in which a little girl falls down a rabbit hole and finds a strange and at times absurd world. / She enjoyed a whimsical day at the seashore—no plan, just wandering around and making sand castles as the mood struck.
wily or wiles	(adj, noun)	Crafty, cunning, characterized by tricks or artifice	The wily criminal stole eight laptops by simply walking into a branch of a large company, introducing himself as the laptop repairman, and waiting for people to hand him their computers. / She was quite offended when her coworker suggested that she use her "feminine wiles" to make the sale.
zeal	(noun)	Great fervor or enthusiasm for a cause, person, etc.; tireless diligence in furthering that cause; passion, ardor	Whether you agree with their views or not, you have to admit that the employees of PETA have great zeal for animal rights—most work for less than $25,000 a year, and often participate in protests that get them shouted at or even arrested.
zenith	(noun)	High point, culmination	At the zenith of her career, the actress could command $5 million per film. Now, she is mostly seen in made-for-TV movies.

500 Advanced Words for the GRE

The list below contains 500 *advanced* words that you should learn for the GRE. If you have not already studied the *essential* word list, go back and do that now.

This list contains all of the words in the Manhattan Prep 500 Advanced Words for the GRE flash card set (available for purchase on our website, on Amazon.com, and at major bookstores). However, the flash cards contain *much* more information about each word, including synonyms, etymologies, and idiomatic usages. If you already have the flash cards, we suggest using those as your primary study tool, and using this list as an alphabetic reference.

WORD	P.O.S.	DEFINITION	USAGE
abase	(verb)	Degrade or humble; to lower in rank, status, or esteem	After messing up at work, the man faced a thorough abasement from his boss; when he realized he had forgotten his own wedding anniversary, he further abased himself in front of his wife.
abeyance	(noun)	Temporary suspension, inactivity	The baseball player's contract negotiations are in abeyance while doctors try to determine whether his injuries will heal in time for the season.
abreast	(adj)	Side-by-side (with preposition *of*); keeping up with, staying aware of, or remaining equal in progress with.	As the professor walked abreast down the street with her mentor, she was amazed that the old man, long since retired, still kept abreast of all the latest developments in neurobiology.
abscission	(noun)	Cutting off; sudden termination; the separation of leaves, petals, or other parts from a plant or animal	The abscission of leaves from the trees is normal in fall. / An inflamed appendix calls for an immediate surgical abscission.
abscond	(verb)	Depart suddenly and secretively	The robber absconded with stolen goods. / The couple who ate at the table next to me at the restaurant absconded before the bill came.
abyss	(noun)	A deep and vast space or cavity; anything profound or infinite	Walking a tightrope over an active volcano, the acrobat was terrified of falling into the abyss. / Now recovering, the patient remembered her experience with clinical depression as an abyss of hopelessness.
accede	(verb)	Agree, give consent; assume power (usually as "accede to")	While the Englishman was a strong believer in democracy, he had to accede that watching Prince Charles someday accede to the throne would indeed be exciting.
accretion	(noun)	Gradual increase; an added part or addition	Malik enjoyed tracking the slow accretion of money in his retirement account. / Some charitable funds keep the principal in their accounts untouched and use only the accretion for philanthropic purposes.

WORD	P.O.S.	DEFINITION	USAGE
acerbic	(adj)	Sour; harsh or severe	Lemons are acerbic. / Her harsh comments were so acerbic, it felt like she was putting lemon juice on a wound.
acidulous	(adj)	Slightly acid or sour; sharp or caustic	Grapefruit juice is acidulous. / I'm skipping Thanksgiving this year just to avoid my mother's acidulous comments about what she thinks I ought to be doing with my life.
acumen	(noun)	Keen, quick, accurate insight or judgment	His political acumen allowed him to bargain behind the scenes and get bills passed despite being in the minority party.
adulterate	(verb)	Make impure by adding inappropriate or inferior ingredients	Some bars adulterate top-shelf liquor by pouring cheaper brands into the more expensive brands' bottles.
adumbrate	(verb)	Give a rough outline of; foreshadow; reveal only partially; obscure	When I took on the lead role in the movie, I agreed not to give away the plot, but I suppose I could give a brief adumbration of the premise.
aerie	(noun)	Dwelling or fortress built on a high place; the nest of a bird of prey, such as an eagle or hawk, built on a mountain or cliff	The billionaire smoked a cigar out his window and watched the riots in the streets below, safe in the aerie of his penthouse apartment.
albeit	(conjunction)	Although, even though	The village leader was illiterate albeit highly intelligent. / The trip was exciting albeit brief.
aloof	(adj)	Distant physically or emotionally; reserved; indifferent	Perceiving her parents as cold and aloof, the child was naturally drawn to her warm, genial aunt.
amalgamate	(verb)	Blend, merge, or unite	The Amalgamated Transit Union is so called because it contains many local unions of bus operators, subway operators, baggage handlers, etc. / When turning her life story into a memoir, she amalgamated two important relatives into a single character, even amalgamating their names (Mary and Rose) into the character "Aunt Mary Rose."
ameliorate	(verb)	Improve; make better or more bearable	If you spill water on your computer keyboard, you can ameliorate the damage by leaving the keyboard upside down to dry; it may still be ruined, but that's still the best chance you've got of saving it.
amortize	(verb)	Gradually pay off a debt, or gradually write off an asset	A mortgage is a common form of amortized debt—spreading the payments out over as long as 30 years is not uncommon.

WORD	P.O.S.	DEFINITION	USAGE
anachronism	(noun)	Something that is not in its correct historical time; a mistake in chronology, such as by assigning a person or event to the wrong time period	The Queen of England is a bit of an anachronism with her old-fashioned pillbox hats. / Did you catch the anachronisms in the latest action blockbuster set in ancient Rome? One of the characters was wearing a wristwatch with his toga!
analgesia	(noun)	Pain relief; inability to feel pain	While natural-birth advocates decline analgesia in childbirth, many women are very eager to take advantage of modern anesthesia. / A disease of the spinal cord can cause analgesia, which can be dangerous because the patient doesn't know when he has injured himself.
annul	(verb)	Make void or null, cancel, abolish (usually of laws or other established rules)	Can we appreciate the art of a murderer? For many, the value of these paintings is annulled by the artist's crimes. / They had the marriage annulled after one week.
anodyne	(noun, adj)	Medicine that relieves pain (noun); soothing, relieving pain (adj)	While aspirin is a nice analgesic, the construction worker argued that, for sore and tired muscles, nothing beat the anodyne effects of a six-pack of beer.
antedate	(verb)	Be older than, precede in time; assign to an earlier date	Dinosaurs antedate the first human beings by about 65 million years. / Jamal didn't get around to writing the "Best Vocabulary Words of 2010" blog post until January 3rd, but he antedated the post for December 31st so at least the infrequent readers wouldn't notice.
antithetical	(adj)	Directly opposed, opposite; involving antithesis (the rhetorical act of placing two phrases opposite one another for contrast, as in *love me or hate me*)	Partying all night, every night, is antithetical to one's academic performance.
apostate	(noun, adj)	Person who deserts a party, cause, religion, etc.	Many people considered "freedom fighters" by some are considered apostates by others. / Some women's rights leaders in very conservative nations receive death threats from religious leaders who consider them apostate.
apostle	(noun)	Pioneer of a reform movement (originally, an early follower of Jesus)	In the 1980s, when low-fat diets were all the rage, Dr. Rubens became an apostle of the Mediterranean diet, which was high in healthy fats, and traveled the world proselytizing to groups of physicians and nutritionists.

WORD	P.O.S.	DEFINITION	USAGE
apposite	(adj)	Highly appropriate, suitable, or relevant	He searched his brain for an apposite word to describe wealthy Americans' addiction to consumer goods, until he discovered the neologism "affluenza."
apprise	(verb)	Inform, give notice to	I can't believe you failed to apprise me that my child was biting the other children in his preschool class. If I had known, I could've addressed this issue before all the other parents threatened to sue.
approbation	(noun)	Praise or approval, especially formal approval	In her speech for class president, she won the approbation of her peers by promising not only to save the prom, but to raise enough money to make it free for everyone.
appropriate	(verb)	Set aside or authorize (such as money) for a particular purpose; take for one's own use	The school board appropriated money for new textbooks. / In putting together the perfect outfit for Career Day at her high school, Mackenzie appropriated her mother's stethoscope and her little brother's stuffed pig, making it clear to everyone that she wanted to be a veterinarian.
arbiter	(noun)	Judge, umpire, person empowered to decide matters at hand	Professional mediators arbitrate disputes. / The principal said, "As the final arbiter of what is and is not appropriate in the classroom, I demand that you take down that poster of the rapper Ice-T and his scantily-clad wife Coco."
ardent or ardor	(adj, noun)	Very passionate, devoted, or enthusiastic	He was an ardent heavy metal lover and became offended anytime someone referred to Poison as a "hair band." / They were so in love that not even meeting each other's awful relatives could dampen their ardor.
arrogate	(verb)	Claim or take presumptuously or without the right to do so	In order to build the oil pipeline, the government arrogated the land of many small farmers who are still fighting for compensation. / The bride's mother arrogated the right to decide on the venue, the food, and even the wedding dress!
ascribe	(verb)	Assign or credit to a certain cause or source	He ascribed his good grades to diligent studying. / The young boy ascribed to his imaginary friend all the powers he wished he had himself—being able to fly, having dozens of friends, and never having to eat broccoli.
aseptic	(adj)	Free from germs	It is very important to perform surgery in an aseptic environment, lest a patient contract sepsis (a systemic infection) and die.

WORD	P.O.S.	DEFINITION	USAGE
asperity	(noun)	Rigor, severity; harshness or sharpness of tone; roughness of surface	Used to a more lax school environment, the freshman at military school was shocked by the asperity of punishments meted out for even the most minor offenses, as well as the asperity with which his drill sergeant bossed him around. / The asperity of her cheap, scratchy sweater made her wish she could afford cashmere.
aspersions	(noun)	Damaging remarks, defamation, slander	He could no longer work with his duplicitous business partner, who acted friendly to his face but then spewed aspersions about him behind his back.
assail	(verb)	Attack violently, assault	One strategy for winning in boxing is to simply assail your opponent with so many blows that he becomes disoriented. / The debate team assailed the opposition with more evidence than they could respond to.
assiduous	(adj)	Persevering, diligent, constant	Through assiduous effort over a substantial period of time, anyone can develop a prodigious vocabulary.
attenuate	(verb)	Weaken or thin out	Sadly, the day care center was so understaffed that the caregivers' efforts were attenuated, and many of the children barely received any attention at all.
attuned	(adj)	In harmony; in sympathetic relationship	Research shows that new mothers are keenly attuned to their babies' cries; even those who were formerly heavy sleepers often find that they now wake up immediately when their babies need attention. / In the sixth week of Melanie's foreign study program, she finally attuned herself to life on a French farm.
augury	(noun)	Telling the future, such as through supernatural means	Value investors such as Warren Buffett (who attempt to buy shares in undervalued companies by analyzing the businesses themselves) consider others' attempts to "time the market" as mere augury, equivalent to trying to predict rain by reading tea leaves.
august	(adj)	Venerable, majestic; inspiring admiration	"I welcome you to this august institution, where presidents and Nobel Prize winners have received the fruits of erudition," said the university president (rather bombastically) to the new crop of first-year students.
avarice	(noun)	Insatiable greed; a miserly desire to hoard wealth	It is hard to fathom the sheer avarice of a company that would fraudulently overcharge a struggling school system for new computers.

WORD	P.O.S.	DEFINITION	USAGE
axiom	(noun)	Self-evident truth requiring no proof; universally or generally accepted principle	Given the last decade of research into the brain—as well as our own experience trying to function while deprived of sleep or food—we must take as axiomatic that the brain is influenced by the body.
balloon	(verb)	Swell or puff out; increase rapidly	During the dot-com bubble, the university's investments ballooned to three times their former value.
banal	(adj)	Lacking freshness and originality; cliché	The drama professor despaired at reading another banal play from his uninspired students. "Oh look," he said sarcastically, "yet another young person has decided to write a play about a young person breaking free of society's constraints. Can you see me yawning?"
bane	(noun)	Something that ruins or spoils	Mosquitoes are the bane of my existence! They just love me, and by "love" I mean ruin my summer! / The closure of the hospital could not have been more baneful to the already strained community.
baying	(adj)	Howling in a deep way, like a dog or wolf	The lonely dog bayed all night.
beneficent	(adj)	Doing good	The billionaire had been a mean and stingy fellow, but after his death, his beneficent widow gave all his money to charity, even accompanying the donations with handwritten notes thanking the charities for all the good work they did
bent	(noun)	Personal inclination or tendency	He had a pedantic bent—he was just naturally inclined to correct people's grammar and otherwise act like an imperious schoolmaster.
besiege	(verb)	Attack, overwhelm, crowd in on or surround	The regiment was besieged by attackers on all sides and finally surrendered. / I cannot go out this weekend—I am besieged by homework!
bevy	(noun)	Group of birds or other animals that stay close together; any large group	The bar owner cringed when a bevy of women in plastic tiaras came in. "Another drunken bachelorette party," he sighed.
bifurcate	(verb, adj)	To fork into two branches or divide into two halves	The medical student carefully bifurcated the cadaver brain, separating it precisely into right and left hemispheres. / The bifurcate tree stood tall, its two massive branches reaching for the sky.
bilk	(verb)	Cheat or defraud	The con artist bilked many elderly people out of their savings, promising to cure illnesses from diabetes to cancer with only 36 monthly payments of $99.99—for which the victims received nothing but useless placebo pills.

WORD	P.O.S.	DEFINITION	USAGE
blight	(noun, verb)	Disease that kills plants rapidly, or any cause of decay or destruction (noun); ruin or cause to wither (verb)	Many potato farmers have fallen into poverty as a result of blight killing their crops. / Gang violence is a blight on our school system, causing innocent students to fear even attending classes. / Violence has blighted our town.
blithe	(adj)	Joyous, merry; excessively care-free (so as to ignore more important concerns)	Delighted about making the cheerleading team, she blithely skipped across the street without looking, and just narrowly avoided being hit by a bus.
bombastic	(adj)	(Of speech or writing) far too showy or dramatic than is appropriate; pretentious	Professor Knutsen's friends joked that he became quite bombastic after a few drinks, once asking a woman in a bar, "Is your daddy an aesthete? Because you are the epitome of ineffable pulchritude." She replied, "I'm not impressed by your bombast."
bonhomie	(noun)	Friendliness, open and simple good heartedness	By the end of the summer, the campers were overflowing with bonhomie, vowing to remain Facebook friends forever.
brandish	(verb)	Shake, wave, or flourish, as a weapon	The Renaissance Fair ended badly, with one drunken fellow brandishing a sword and refusing to leave the ladies' dressing tent.
brook	(verb)	Suffer or tolerate	"You will do your homework every night before you go anywhere, you will do your chores, and you will be home by 9pm I will brook no disobeying of these rules, young man!"
bucolic	(adj)	Suggesting a peaceful and pleasant view of rural life	City dwellers often idealize a bucolic lifestyle, but once they're actually out in the country, all they do is complain about the bugs and the boredom!
burnish	(verb)	Polish, make smooth and lustrous	Mr. Hoffenstotter replaced all of the rustic wood doorknobs with newer models made of burnished steel. "So shiny," said his delighted wife.
calumny	(noun)	Malicious lie intended to hurt someone's reputation; the act of telling such lies	I've had enough of your calumnious accusations! Admit that you made up all those wicked things about me, or I will see you in court when I sue you for slander!
canard	(noun)	Rumor, a false or baseless story	The idea that we only use 10% of our brains is a tired, old canard; actually, even the dumbest people use all of their brains.
cardinal	(adj)	Chief, most important	The cardinal rule of Fight Club is that you don't talk about Fight Club.

WORD	P.O.S.	DEFINITION	USAGE
catholic	(adj)	Universal, broad-minded	Some precursors to the Constitution (such as documents governing the colonies) enumerated the rights of male property holders only. The U.S. Constitution took a more catholic approach, declaring that "All men are created equal." Today, policy writers would probably catholicize a step further and write "All people."
chicanery	(noun)	Trickery, deception by knowingly false arguments	The defense lawyer's strategy for getting her client acquitted by knowingly misinterpreting words in an obscure precedent was nothing but chicanery.
circumscribe	(verb)	Strictly limit a role, range of activity, or area; in math, to be constructed around so as to touch as many points as possible	Sara's parent circumscribed her after-school activities; she was permitted only to study and to join organizations directly related to academic subjects. / A square circumscribed in a circle has all four of its vertices on the circle's circumference. / Our land is circumscribed by hedges and fences.
circumspect	(adj)	Cautious, prudent; careful to consider the circumstances and consequences	Tiana immediately forked over an initiation fee to become a vitamin distributor, but her more circumspect brother had a list of at least 20 questions he wanted answered before he would consider joining.
clamber	(verb)	Climb awkwardly or with difficulty, scramble	The hiker had spent the last hour plodding lethargically up the side of the mountain, but when she caught sight of the summit, she excitedly began to clamber up even the steepest inclines.
cloying	(adj)	Disgustingly or distastefully sweet	I do like visiting our grandmother, but I can't stand those cloying movies she watches—last time it was some heart-tugging story where an orphan saves a suffering pony. / I do like cake, but I find that honey-covered angel food cake positively cloying.
coagulate	(verb)	Cause a liquid to become solid or semisolid	Hemophilia is a medical condition in which the blood doesn't coagulate, meaning that a hemophiliac can easily bleed to death from a small wound. / When making jam, use pectin to get the fruit to coagulate.
coda	(noun)	Final part of a musical composition; an ending, esp. one that sums up what has come before	"You play this middle section twice, then move to the coda," the music teacher explained to the child. "The coda always comes last." / Dropping my purse in a mud puddle right outside my own front door was a fine coda to a horrible evening.
coffer	(noun)	Chest for storing valuables; financial resources, a treasury	The dishonest employee called it "dipping into the company coffers," but the arresting officer called it "embezzlement."

WORD	P.O.S.	DEFINITION	USAGE
collude	(verb)	Conspire; cooperate for illegal or fraudulent purposes	After two competing software companies doubled their prices on the same day, leaving consumers no lower-priced alternative, the federal government investigated the companies for collusion.
compendium	(noun)	Concise but complete summary; a list or collection	I could hardly bring my whole collection of poetry books on vacation, so instead, I brought a light-weight poetry compendium containing a few selections each from 30 or so poets thought to represent various styles and eras. / This movie review is unusually compendious—although a scant 500 words, it tells every single thing that happens in the entire film.
complaisant	(adj)	Eager to please; cheerfully complying	Coming from a more uptight corporate background, Josiah found the soup kitchen volunteers remarkably complaisant; when he asked the greeters to sweep the floor and the cooks to wash dishes, everyone happily moved to their new positions.
confound	(verb)	Confuse, frustrate; mix up or make worse	He was positively confounded by a map that seemed to show "East Bethlehem" as being to the west of "West Bethlehem." / He was already a little flummoxed in regards to differential equations, but reading an incorrectly edited Wikipedia page on the topic only confounded the problem.
connote	(verb)	Suggest or imply in addition to the precise, literal meaning	The word "titanic" simply means large or majestic, but because of the word's association with the sunken ship, "titanic" has a negative connotation to many people.
contraries	(noun)	Things that are opposing; either of two opposite things	The Machiavellian among us would say that ethics and expedience are contraries—at some point, one must win out over the other.
contrite	(adj)	Remorseful; feeling sorry for one's offenses or sins	He would have punished his son more severely for breaking his car's windshield in a "rock throwing contest," but the boy seemed truly contrite.
contumacious	(adj)	Rebellious; stubbornly disobedient	The psychologist's book *Dealing with Your Contumacious Teenager* would have sold many more copies to parents of rude and rebellious youth if only people knew what *contumacious* meant.
convoke	(verb)	Call together, as to a meeting	The dean has convoked this gathering to discuss the Honor Code.

WORD	P.O.S.	DEFINITION	USAGE
cosset	(verb)	Treat as a pet, pamper	The cosseted toddler was lovingly wrapped up in his snow gear, so much so that he could barely even move his arms enough to make his first snowball.
coterie	(noun)	Close or exclusive group, clique	The pop star never traveled anywhere without a coterie of assistants and managers.
cupidity	(noun)	Greed, great or excessive desire	The doctor's medical license was revoked after it was discovered that, out of sheer cupidity, he had diagnosed people with illnesses they didn't have and pocketed insurance money for performing procedures they didn't need.
curmudgeon	(noun)	Bad-tempered, difficult person; grouch	The college students' party was hampered by constant complaints from a curmudgeonly neighbor who insisted that making noise after 8pm was unreasonable, and called the police over a single beer can on his lawn.
declaim	(verb)	Speak in an impassioned, pompous, or oratorical manner; give a formal speech	After a drink or two, Gabe will declaim all night about campaign finance reform—you won't be able get a word in edgewise in between all his grandstanding and "expertise."
declivity	(noun)	Downward slope	Not just any declivity can serve as a wheelchair ramp—I'm pretty sure this thing is too steep to pass regulations.
delimit	(verb)	Fix, mark, or define the boundaries of	The role of an executive coach is delimited by our code of conduct—we may not counsel people for psychological conditions, for instance.
demagogue	(noun)	A leader who lies and gains power by arousing the passions and especially prejudices of the people	Political demagogues lie and twist the facts, depending more on their natural charisma and ability to determine exactly what their audience wants to hear than any actual understanding or perspicacity.
demur	(verb)	Show reluctance or object, esp. for moral reasons	When asked to name her favorite professor in the department, she demurred because she was pretty sure that, if she said anything, it would come back to haunt her.
desultory	(adj)	Lacking consistency or order, disconnected, sporadic; going off topic	Lulu said she'd been studying for the GRE for a year, but she had been doing so in only the most desultory way—a few vocab words here and there, then nothing for a month, and practice tests whenever she felt like it, which was rarely. / Don't mind my daughter; there's no need to let a toddler's desultory remarks pull an adult conversation off track.

WORD	P.O.S.	DEFINITION	USAGE
diaphanous	(adj)	Very sheer, fine, translucent	The wedding dress was a confection of diaphanous silk, made of at least ten layers of the thin fabric, each layer of which was so fine you could see through it.
dichotomy	(noun)	Division into two parts or into two contradictory groups	There is a dichotomy in the sciences between theoretical or "pure" sciences, such as physics and chemistry, and the life sciences, which often deal more with classifying than with theorizing.
dictum	(noun)	Formal or authoritative pronouncement; saying or proverb	The king's dictum stated that each feudal lord must provide a certain number of soldiers within three weeks' time. / "A stitch in time saves nine" is an old dictum meaning that it's easier to solve a problem before it gets too big.
diffident	(adj)	Lacking confidence, shy	Natasha was so diffident that she never believed her comments could be worth anything in class, even when she knew the answer.
diffuse	(verb, adj)	Spread widely, disseminate (verb); dispersed, widely spread out, or wordy and going off-topic (adj)	It will be very difficult to diffuse the power among the people when transitioning from autocracy to democracy. / The spy attempted to root out the dissenters at the gala, but he was only able to detect a diffuse sense of discontent all around the room.
dilate	(verb)	To become wider or make wider, cause to expand; to speak or write at length, elaborate upon	The doctor gave her eye drops to make her pupils dilate. / These dinners at Professor Hwang's house usually run rather late; after the meal, he'll typically dilate on his latest research for at least an hour.
dilatory	(adj)	Slow, late; procrastinating or stalling for time	Jack was supposed to start his presentation 10 minutes ago and he isn't even here? I'm not surprised—he's a dilatory fellow.
dilettante	(noun)	Person who takes up an art or activity for amusement only or in a superficial way	The "arts center" in the rich neighborhood was populated by dilettantes—a sculpture here, a bit of music appreciation there, or two weeks of painting class until they got bored and quit.
dirge	(noun)	A funeral or mourning song or poem	It was supposed to be a wedding march, but when the organist started playing, the reluctant bride thought the song sounded more like a dirge for her former, carefree life.

WORD	P.O.S.	DEFINITION	USAGE
discomfiting	(adj)	Disconcerting, confusing, frustrating	His fiancée's family said they were comfortable with the fact that he was of a different religion, but he found their constant probing about his beliefs quite discomfiting. / He hates telemarketers so much that he likes to discomfit them by asking them personal questions and suggesting he call them at their homes instead.
discordant	(adj)	Harsh or inharmonious in sound; disagreeing, incongruous	In a graduation ceremony full of hopeful and congratulatory speeches, the salutatorian's address about the terrible economy struck a discordant note.
discrete	(adj)	Separate, distinct, detached, existing as individual parts	Be sure to use quotation marks and citations as appropriate in your paper in order to keep your ideas discrete from those of the experts you are quoting. / The advertising agency pitched us not on one campaign, but on three discrete ideas.
disparage	(verb)	Belittle, put down	An ad hominem attack is a logical fallacy in which the arguer disparages his opponent rather than addressing the opponent's ideas.
disparate	(adj)	Distinct, different	He chose the college for two disparate reasons: the strength of the computer science program, and the excellence of the hip-hop dance squad.
dissemble	(verb)	Mislead, conceal the truth, put on a false appearance of	Roxanne was used to dissembling in job interviews; when asked about the gap on her résumé from 1999–2003, she would say, "Oh, I was out of the workforce fulfilling some obligations"—a somewhat misleading way to describe a prison stint. / He won so much money at pool halls by dissembling inexperience, pretending at first that he had no idea how to even hold a pool cue; once bets were placed, he handily defeated his opponents.
dissolution	(noun)	Dissolving, the state of having been dissolved; breaking bonds or breaking up of a group of people; death, disintegration; sinking into extreme hedonism, vice, and degradation	Alan went from garden-variety hedonism to utter dissolution—his three-day drug benders cost him his job and may land him in jail. / Following the dissolution of the corporation and the liquidation of our assets, each investor will receive a cash payment proportional to his or her shareholding in the company.
distaff	(adj, noun)	Female, esp. relating to the maternal side of the family; women or women's work; a staff that holds wool or flax for spinning	In completing your medical history, please try to remember which illnesses occurred on the distaff side of your family. / Medical studies using all-male study groups may produce results that cannot be replicated in distaff subjects.

WORD	P.O.S.	DEFINITION	USAGE
distend	(verb)	Swell, expand, stretch, bloat	The emergency room doctor constantly saw people who came in with distended bellies, sure that they had appendicitis; usually, it was just gas.
dither	(verb, noun)	Act indecisively (verb); a state of fear or trembling excitement (noun)	"Stop dithering," said the mother to her daughter. "Pick which sweater you want so I can pay for it and we can get out of here." / The haunted house brought the children to a dither from which it was difficult for their parents to calm them down.
diurnal	(adj)	Occurring every day; happening in the daytime (rather than at night)	While many Americans rarely have a sit-down family meal, in many other cultures, dining as a family is a diurnal affair. / Wall Street is a diurnal neighborhood—hectic in the day, but quiet once people pile on the rush hour trains to go home.
doctrinaire	(noun, adj)	Person who applies doctrine in an impractical or rigid and close-minded way (noun); merely theoretical, impractical, or fanatical about other people accepting one's ideas (adj)	The old science professor was so doctrinaire that he refused to even consider any evidence that flew in the face of his own research, and thereby failed to recognize when his graduate students made an exciting new discovery. / Don't be a doctrinaire—try actually considering the views of those you disagree with!
doff	(verb)	Take off (such as clothes), put aside; remove one's hat as a gesture	Before the spring break revelers could consider doffing their clothes, they saw the sign: "No skinny dipping." / In my grandfather's day, it was considered polite to doff your hat when a lady entered the room.
dovetail	(verb)	Join or fit together	When the neuroscientist married an exercise physiologist, neither thought they'd end up working together, but when Dr. Marion Ansel received a grant to study how exercise improves brain function and Dr. Jim Ansel was assigned to her team, the two found that their careers dovetailed nicely.
droll	(adj)	Funny in an odd way	The play was a droll production; not laugh-out-loud hilarious, but funny especially because it was so strange. Who's ever seen a fairy be mistaken for a block of cheese?
dupe	(noun, verb)	Person who is easily fooled or used (noun); to fool or exploit (verb)	The dashing rogue used flattery and lies to dupe several old ladies out of their money. "I feel like a total dupe," said Hazel Rosenbaum. "I thought he and I were going to get married, but he really just wanted my Social Security checks."

WORD	P.O.S.	DEFINITION	USAGE
duplicity	(noun)	Deceit, double-dealing, acting in two different ways for the purpose of deception	The campaign worker's duplicity finally came to light when it was discovered that, despite rising to a trusted position within the local Workers Party, he was actually a registered National Party member and was feeding information back to his cronies.
dyspeptic	(adj)	Grumpy, pessimistic, irritable; suffering from dyspepsia (indigestion)	The dyspeptic professor was so angered by a question from a student who hadn't done the homework that he actually stomped out of class.
ebullient	(adj)	Very enthusiastic, lively, excited; bubbling as though being boiled	The children were so ebullient upon their arrival at Disney World that their parents, while happy to see them so excited, wished that there were a way to forcibly restrain them in case they took off running towards the rides.
echelon	(noun)	A level, rank, or grade; the people at that level	Obtaining a job on Wall Street doesn't guarantee access to the upper echelon of executives, where multimillion-dollar bonuses are the norm. / I'm not sure I'm cut out to analyze poetry; I find it hard to dig beyond the most accessible echelon of meaning.
edify	(verb)	Uplift, enlighten, instruct, or improve in a spiritual or moral way	Look, I'm glad that you're reading, but I really wish you would read something more edifying than that magazine that gives tips for winning at violent video games.
effigy	(noun)	Representation or image of a person, esp. a crude facsimile used to mock a hated person	The dictator was disturbed to look out the palace window and see himself being burned in effigy. "That papier-mâché dummy doesn't even look like me!" he said.
effrontery	(noun)	Shameless boldness	Mr. Hou thought his daughter's boyfriend guilty of the worst effrontery when he asked for her hand in marriage—and, as soon as Mr. Hou gave his blessing, followed up by asking for a job at Mr. Hou's company.
egress	(verb, noun)	An exit or the action of exiting	It is against the fire code to put those boxes there— you can't block a primary or secondary egress from the building.
elegy	(noun)	Song or poem of sorrow, esp. for a deceased person	While composing an elegy is certainly old-fashioned, the poet felt that it was a fitting way for her to honor her father at his funeral.
emaciate	(verb)	Make abnormally thin, cause to physically waste away	After 50 days of floating on a raft at sea, he was quite emaciated; his family was elated that he was alive, but shocked to see a formerly 165-pound man looking skeletal at just 125 pounds.

WORD	P.O.S.	DEFINITION	USAGE
encomium	(noun)	Warm, glowing praise, esp. a formal expression of praise	Just after all the encomia at his retirement party, he received a gold watch. / The first draft of your dissertation is little but an encomium of the works of Christopher Marlowe, whereas I'm afraid that doctoral-level work requires a more nuanced and critical view.
endemic	(adj)	Native, local; natural, specific to, or confined to a particular place	Certain diseases—especially those that require a precise mix of environmental conditions and local plant and animal life to thrive—remain endemic to particular regions.
engender	(verb)	Produce, give rise to, cause to exist; procreate	The television demagogue was blamed for engendering hate and divisiveness. / Having four wives helped the magnate engender 15 children.
epicure	(noun)	Person with cultivated, refined tastes, esp. in food and wine	A true epicure, he served only the finest wines, and bragged about how the pancetta was imported from Italy and the Stilton cheese from the English countryside.
equanimity	(noun)	Composure, evenness of mind; mental or emotional stability, esp. under stress	Having worked for many years in mental hospitals, her equanimity was unparalleled—you could throw a chair or a bowl of spaghetti at her, and she would just say, "Settle down, now."
equivocate	(verb)	Use unclear language to deceive or avoid committing to a position	Not wanting to lose supporters, the politician equivocated on the issue, tossing out buzzwords related to each side while also claiming more study was needed.
ersatz	(adj)	Artificial, synthetic; being an inferior substitute	I hate this health food restaurant! I do not want to eat some ersatz meatballs made of textured vegetable protein!
erstwhile	(adj, adv)	Former, previous (adj); in the past, formerly (adv)	A novelist and erstwhile insurance salesman, he told us his story of the long road to literary success, before he was able to quit his day job.
ethos	(noun)	The character, personality, or moral values specific to a person, group, time period, etc.	At the prep school, the young man happily settled into an ethos of hard work and rigorous athletic competition.
euphemism	(noun)	Substitution of a mild, inoffensive, or indirect expression for one that is considered offensive or too direct	Many euphemisms surround death and disease; rather than "Joe died of cancer," many people feel better saying "Joe's suffering is finally over." / When potty training their children, some parents use hilarious euphemisms for body parts.

WORD	P.O.S.	DEFINITION	USAGE
euphony	(noun)	Pleasing or sweet sound, esp. as formed by a harmonious use of words	Poetry in translation can keep its meaning, but often loses the euphony the poet worked so laboriously to create.
exigent	(adj)	Requiring immediate attention, action, or aid; excessively demanding	My boss said she would take me out to lunch and "mentor" me, but that idea always gets tossed aside in favor of more exigent matters.
exonerate	(verb)	Clear from blame or accusation; free from a responsibility	When the defendant was exonerated after a long trial, his family wept for joy.
expedient	(adj)	Suitable, proper; effective, often at the expense of ethics or other considerations	"I need this report by 2pm, and I don't care what you have to do to make that happen," said the boss. "I expect you to deal with it expediently." / When invited to a wedding you cannot attend, it is expedient to send a gift.
expurgate	(verb)	Censor; remove objectionable or offensive parts	When the girl discovered that her ninth-grade class had been reading an expurgated version of *Romeo and Juliet*, she immediately checked the original out from the library so she could read all the "forbidden" parts.
extemporane-ous	(adj)	Done without preparation (esp. of a speech), or with some preparation but no notes; improvised, done on the spur of the moment	The way the Public Affairs Forum works is that the moderator will announce a topic, and then anyone who wishes may speak extemporaneously on that topic for a few minutes. As you can imagine, our members are very well-read. / Lost in the jungle, the hikers fashioned an extemporaneous shelter from palm leaves.
faction	(noun)	Group or clique within a larger organization; party strife and dissension	The opposition movement was once large enough to have a chance at succeeding, but it has since broken into numerous, squabbling factions, each too small to have much impact. / The caucus began in a spirit of unity but now, sadly, is marked by faction and petty squabbles.
fallow	(adj)	Left unplanted (of land); not in use	Crop yields were increased substantially when the villagers discovered that letting a portion of their fields fallow allowed that unused part of the land to become renewed with minerals. / It is terribly important that we make college affordable for underprivileged students, lest great minds lie fallow, and the world never benefit from their genius.
fastidious	(adj)	Excessively particular, difficult to please; painstaking, meticulous, requiring excessive attention to detail	Steve was a fastidious housekeeper, fluffing his couch pillows at least twice a day and never allowing the tiniest speck of dust to settle on any exposed surface.

WORD	P.O.S.	DEFINITION	USAGE
fatuous	(adj)	Foolish, silly, esp. in a smug or complacent manner	Sadly, every philosophy class seems to have one person who responds to every discussion, from metaphysics to ethics, with the fatuous question, "But what if we don't really exist?"
fawn	(verb)	Show affection or try to please in the manner of a dog; try to win favor through flattery and submissive behavior	Although he was only president of a chain of grocery stores, he was used to being fawned over like a king or rock star. "You are truly king of the low-priced produce world," said the regional manager. "May I wash your car for you?"
fecund	(adj)	Fruitful, fertile; capable of abundantly producing offspring, vegetation, or creative or intellectual work	Rabbits are quite fecund; if you've got two, you'll soon have forty. / While some novelists seem to return to the same themes over and over, Bredlaw's fecund mind produced whole new universes for every story he wrote.
felicitous	(adj)	Admirably appropriate, very well-suited for the occasion; pleasant, fortunate, marked by happiness	"What a felicitous occasion!" said the new grandfather, arriving at the hospital with an "It's a Girl!" balloon. The new father found the balloon remarkably felicitous, especially since the baby's gender had been announced less than an hour ago.
fervid	(adj)	Very hot; heated in passion or enthusiasm	He is a fervid fan of Virginia Tech football, so much so that we've all gotten used to receiving "Go Hokies!" hats and shirts for every birthday.
fetid	(adj)	Stinking; having an offensive smell	I hate doing your laundry—it's always full of fetid gym socks.
fledgling	(noun, adj)	A young bird that has just recently gotten its feathers, an inexperienced person (noun); new or inexperienced (adj)	The zoo's EagleCam will hopefully be able to catch the moment the fledglings fly out of the nest for the very first time. / The Society of Engineers is available for Career Day presentations in elementary schools, where we hope to encourage fledgling talents in the applied sciences.
florid	(adj)	Reddish or rosy; flowery, showy, or excessively fancy	His writing was so florid that it was hard for modern readers to understand, and unintentionally humorous when they did. He once called a woman in a hoop skirt a "confection of gossamer-clad ephemerality, the bounty of her raiment ringing in my turgid heart like the tintinnabulation of so many church bells."
flout	(verb)	Treat with disdain, contempt, or scorn (usually of rules)	He flouted the boarding school's curfew so blatantly that, on his way back from a party that lasted past midnight, he actually stopped by the headmaster's house to say hello to his daughter.

WORD	P.O.S.	DEFINITION	USAGE
fluke	(noun)	Stroke of luck, something accidentally successful	It's amazing that I won the prize during halftime, but I guarantee you, it was just a fluke that I made that basket—if I tried a thousand more times, I'm sure I couldn't do it again.
forage	(verb)	Wander in search of; rummage, hunt, make a raid	It's important to seal your trash cans tightly in this neighborhood, or else you'll get raccoons foraging for food in your backyard.
ford	(noun, verb)	Place where a river or similar body of water is shallow enough to walk or ride a vehicle across (noun); to cross at such a place (verb)	The pioneers made camp near the riverbank, waiting for the rains to die down and the river to become fordable again. A week later, the waters were shallow enough to ford the river with their entire caravan—horses, wagons, and all.
forestall	(verb)	Delay, hinder, prevent by taking action beforehand	Our research has been forestalled by a lack of funding; we're all just biding our time until the university approves our grant proposal.
fortuitous	(adj)	Happening by chance; lucky	It was amazingly fortuitous that the exclusive beach resort had a cancellation for exactly the weekend she had wanted to get married, allowing her to have the perfect wedding after all.
fracas	(noun)	Noisy disturbance or fight; brawl	Rugby is one of the most aggressive of sports; when the players rush to pile on top of the person with the ball, bones can easily be broken in the fracas.
fractious	(adj)	Unruly, troublemaking; irritable	The Students for Progressive Action were a fractious bunch, always fighting with one another over exactly which progressive action should take priority.
frenetic	(adj)	Wildly excited, frantic, distracted	The advice in the expert's time management book struck many as unrealistic, as not everyone can handle the frenetic lifestyle the author espouses: getting up before dawn to begin work before spending quality time with the kids over breakfast, taking conference calls from the treadmill, etc.
fulminate	(verb)	Attack verbally in a vehement, thunderous way; explode, detonate;	Please don't bring up anything related to gun control around my family or my dad will fulminate for hours about the Second Amendment.
furtive	(adj)	Done secretly; stealthy, sly, shifty	As a spokesperson for a popular diet plan, the actress had to be quite furtive about eating junk food, even hiding her M&Ms in a breath mint container lest the paparazzi snap photos of the inside of her car.
gambol	(verb)	Frolic; skip or leap playfully	Watching the children gambol in the park like frisky little lambs, she wondered how they could have so much energy.

WORD	P.O.S.	DEFINITION	USAGE
garner	(verb)	Gather and store; amass, collect	The publisher sent copies of the soon-to-be-published manuscript to reviewers, hoping to garner acclaim and publicity for the book.
gestation	(noun)	Pregnancy; the period from conception until birth of an animal or (metaphorically) of an idea or plan	The gestation period of an elephant is 22 months, more than twice as long as that of humans!
glacial	(adj)	Pertaining to glaciers; cold, icy, slow, unsympathetic	He had wanted to appear in the singing reality competition his whole young life, but he was not encouraged by the judges' glacial response to his audition. The awkward silence was excruciating as he waited for the stony-faced panel to say anything at all.
glower	(verb)	Stare in an angry, sullen way	He couldn't figure out why his girlfriend was glowering at him throughout dinner. "Oh," he finally realized, "Is it your birthday? Oh, and I forgot you hate seafood. Sorry about the fishsticks."
goad	(verb)	Spur on, stimulate, encourage; urge on (as cattle) with a pointed or electrically charged stick	He never forgave his friends for goading him into spray-painting the school with them. While the effect was temporarily hilarious, he lost a scholarship over the incident.
gouge	(noun, verb)	Scooping or digging tool, like a chisel, or a hole made with such a tool (noun); cut or scoop out; force out a person's eye with one's thumb; swindle, extort money from (verb)	I was happy with this new video game console for a day or two, until I saw it advertised all over town for half the price and realized I'd been gouged. / He loves gory horror films, where people's eyes are gouged out and gross stuff like that.
graft	(verb, noun)	Insert part of a plant into another plant, where it continues to grow; join living tissue (such as skin) to part of the body where it will continue to live and grow; attach as if by grafting (verb); the part so grafted (as in a graft of skin); the act of acquiring money or other benefits through illegal means, esp. by abusing one's power (noun)	The part of the book describing the financial crisis is good, but the "What You Can Do" section seems grafted on, almost as though written by a different author. / It's not cool for your boss to pressure you into buying Girl Scout cookies from his daughter. If she were selling something larger, we'd call that graft.
grandiloquent	(adj)	Relating to lofty speech, esp. to the point of being pompous, overblown, bombastic	After memorizing 1,000 vocabulary flashcards for the GRE, Derek couldn't help but become a little grandiloquent, declaring his desire to "abscond from my familial domicile and satisfy my penchant for erudition." "You can do that later," said his mother, "but now it's your turn to do the dishes."

WORD	P.O.S.	DEFINITION	USAGE
grandstand	(verb)	Perform showily in an attempt to impress onlookers	I was really passionate about the candidate when he spoke at our school, but now that I think about it, he was just grandstanding. I mean, who could disagree that young people are the future? And doing a cheer for the environment doesn't actually signify a commitment to change any public policies about it.
grating	(adj)	Irritating; harsh or discordant (of a noise); scraping	Folding jeans at the mall finally became unbearable when her kindly old supervisor was replaced with a young woman whose grating tone made commands like "Fold faster and then clean up this display!" sound like nails on a chalkboard.
grievous	(adj)	Causing grief or suffering; very serious, grave; flagrant, outrageous	While people certainly do injure themselves on hot stoves, such burns rarely compare to the grievous injuries sustained by people who do not observe safety procedures with 12-gallon deep fryers.
grouse	(verb, noun)	Complain or grumble (verb); a reason for complaint (noun)	By the end of the trip, everyone was annoyed by Lena's grousing; the bus ride was too bumpy, the food was too spicy, the air conditioning was too dehydrating, etc. / Don't be offended, but I've got a grouse about the way you're handling this project.
grovel	(verb)	Creep or crawl with one's face to the ground, prostrate oneself as a token of subservience, degrade or abase oneself	Most of the laid-off employees packed their things and left the building—only one was seen groveling, literally on his knees asking his boss not to fire him.
halcyon	(adj)	Calm and peaceful, carefree; prosperous, successful, happy	Installing drywall wasn't the career he'd planned for; every day he reminisced about the halcyon days of his high school football career, when he was treated like a god, and he had not a care in the world other than the next big game.
hallmark	(noun)	A mark indicating quality, purity, genuineness, etc.; any distinguishing characteristic	Signature red soles are the hallmark of Christian Louboutin's shoes.
hand-wringing	(noun)	Grasping, squeezing, etc. of the hands as an expression of nervousness, guilt, etc.; extend debate over what to do about an issue	There has been much hand-wringing (or wringing of hands) over falling test scores, with so-called experts acting as if the world will end if students do 1% worse in math and science.
hapless	(adj)	Unlucky, unfortunate	Hiring this hapless new office manager was a mistake—he's always losing and breaking things, as though bad luck simply follows wherever he goes.

WORD	P.O.S.	DEFINITION	USAGE
harangue	(noun, verb)	Long, intense verbal attack, esp. when delivered publicly (noun); to speak to in a forceful way (verb)	Look, I'll clean the gutters when I get a free weekend—I don't need you to keep haranguing me about it.
harrow	(noun, verb)	Farming tool that breaks up soil (noun); painfully disturb or distress (verb)	Let's start our garden together; you harrow, and I'll follow behind you planting the seeds. / The bus ride across Siberia was a harrowing experience—the roads were all ice, and the ancient, barely heated vehicle seemed to be lacking both headlights and brakes.
hedge	(verb)	Avoid commitment by leaving provisions for withdrawal or changing one's mind; protect a bet by also betting on the other side	While he coaxed and cajoled us all into seeing "the best movie ever," he hedged once we were in the theater: "I don't know if you all like this sort of thing," he said. "I mean, you can make up your own minds."
hegemony	(noun)	Domination, authority; influence by one country over others socially, culturally, economically, etc.	The discovery of oil by a previously poor nation disrupted the larger, richer nation's hegemony in the region—suddenly, the hegemon had a competitor.
hermetic	(adj)	Airtight, sealed, isolated; reclusive; pertaining to alchemy, occult	These packaged meals are hermetically sealed—they'll last years in storage, but once opened, you need to finish the contents within a couple of days. / While writing hundreds of vocabulary flash cards, the GRE instructor lived a hermetic lifestyle, her skin growing pallid and her social network drastically shrinking.
hew	(verb)	Strike, chop, or hack (as with an axe, sword. etc.); make or shape something (such as a statue) with a cutting tool	The pioneer had to hew his own way through the brush in order to proceed westward. / She preferred rustic furniture; her dining room chairs were little more than stumps roughly hewn into stools.
hoary	(adj)	Very old, gray or white as from old age	Hoary with age, his white beard making his age obvious even from the top of the bleachers, the old man surprised everyone when he was able to make a free throw. / Dad, I've heard your hoary old college fraternity stories a hundred times.
homage	(noun)	Honor or respect demonstrated publicly	This structure I built in the backyard is not just a skateboard ramp; it is an homage to my hero Tony Hawk. I have dubbed it the "Tony Hawk Rocks Western Pennsylvania Skateboard Ramp." / I'm not copying Madonna's song—I am referencing it in my own song as an homage to her work.

WORD	P.O.S.	DEFINITION	USAGE
hoodwink	(verb)	Trick, deceive	Pretending to be the building's landlord, the shyster was able to hoodwink 11 people into paying deposits on a vacant apartment, of course, he absconded with the money, leaving the victims without their money or a place to live.
hotly	(adv)	In an intense, fiery, or heated way	The issue of how evolution should be taught in schools was hotly disputed by members of the school board, religious leaders, and parent groups.
husband	(verb)	Manage prudently, sparingly, or economically; conserve	As we are dealing with cutbacks, I am calling on you as the office manager to husband our resources, parceling out office supplies and buying new ones only when absolutely necessary.
iconoclast	(noun)	Attacker of cherished beliefs or institutions	A lifelong iconoclast, Ayn Rand wrote a controversial book entitled *The Virtue of Selfishness*.
idolatry	(noun)	Idol worship; excessive or unthinking devotion or adoration	After a year in an education Ph.D. program, she'd had enough with the idolatry of Howard Gardner and his theory of multiple intelligences. "Gardner isn't a god," she would say, "and you simply can't learn calculus through movement or interpersonal skills."
idyllic or idyll	(adj, noun)	Presenting a positive, peaceful view of rural life (as poetry or prose); pleasant in a natural, simple way (adj); a happy, enjoyable experience (noun)	An action-packed vacation wasn't their style. For their honeymoon, they enjoyed a quiet idyll in a cabin in the woods, just watching the deer and enjoying nature.
ignoble	(adj)	Not noble; having mean, base, low motives; low quality	What you have done may not be illegal, but it surely is ignoble—people who don't read the user agreement surely do not expect that, by clicking "I Agree," they have signed up for a Jelly-of-the-Month club!
imbue	(verb)	Permeate or saturate, as dye in a fabric; influence throughout	After shearing the sheep and spinning the yarn, the next step is to imbue the yarn with dye. / His poems are imbued with a sense of longing for a lost homeland.
immutable	(adj)	Unchangeable	Studies of the brains of stroke patients have shown that our identities are not fixed and immutable; rather, physical injuries to the brain can drastically change our personalities.
impasse	(noun)	Position or road from which there is no escape; deadlock	If the union won't budge on its demands and the transit authority won't raise salaries, then we are at an impasse.

MANHATTAN PREP

WORD	P.O.S.	DEFINITION	USAGE
impassive	(adj)	Not having or not showing physical feeling or emotion	Having been in and out of hospitals all his life, he accepted this latest diagnosis impassively. "Whatever happens, happens," he said.
impecunious	(adj)	Poor, without money	Having grown up with impecunious parents who could barely keep the electricity on in the house, she was now obsessed with wealth and security.
imperious	(adj)	Commanding, domineering; acting like a high-ranking person; urgent	Her friends were peeved by her imperious attitude and talked about her while she was in the ladies' room: "Who does she think she is, not only picking the bar and the meeting time, but also telling us where to sit?"
impermeable	(adj)	Impassable, not allowing passage through (such as by a liquid)	A good raincoat is totally impermeable to water.
imperturbable	(adj)	Calm, not able to be upset or agitated	Having seen pretty much everything, the kindergarten teacher was truly imperturbable: a morning containing a discipline problem, two bathroom accidents, one fight, and one temper tantrum didn't bother her in the least.
impervious	(adj)	Impenetrable, not able to be harmed or emotionally disturbed	The problem with arrogant people is that they are impervious to criticism of their arrogance; anything you say to them just rolls right off.
impetuous	(adj)	Passionately impulsive, marked by sudden, hasty emotion; forceful, violent	Reflecting on her most recent breakup, Camille decided that next time she would like to date someone less impetuous; a man who quits his job on a whim and suggests moving together to Utah and raising llamas was just a little too impulsive for her tastes.
impious	(adj)	Not religious, lacking reverence, ungodly	In religious schools, impious behavior is generally prohibited.
implacable	(adj)	Relentless, unstoppable; not able to be appeased, calmed, or satisfied	A good detective is absolutely implacable—refusing to give up until the culprit in question is behind bars. / After the dog groomer misunderstood and shaved the family Weimaraner totally bald, Mr. Garcia was implacable; neither an offer of a free gift certificate nor a complimentary doggie sweater would reduce his fury.
imprecation	(noun)	Curse; prayer for harm to come to someone	The haunted house features a "wicked witch" chanting imprecations at all who pass through.
impugn	(verb)	Attack the truth or integrity of	I hate to impugn the motives of the volunteers, but I think that some of them are here for personal gain, not to help.

WORD	P.O.S.	DEFINITION	USAGE
impute	(verb)	Credit, attribute; lay blame or responsibility for (sometimes falsely)	The ineffectual CEO was nevertheless a master of public relations—he made sure that all successes were imputed to him, and all of the failures were imputed to others.
incarnadine	(adj, noun)	Blood red or flesh-colored	The police took the body to the morgue; all that was left at the murder scene was an incarnadine stain on a pillow.
inconstancy	(noun)	Fickleness, unreliability; the state of changing without good reason	Old-fashioned poems often praised a lover's constancy; the poet would likely be shocked by any inconstancy from his lady, such as if she were receiving poems from other poets.
inculcate	(verb)	Teach persistently, implant (an idea) in a person	Parents spend years trying to inculcate morality in their children, constantly teaching and correcting them.
indefatigable	(adj)	Untiring, not able to become fatigued	The boxer was indefatigable; round after round, he never lost speed or energy, even after he had thoroughly defatigated his opponent.
indigence	(noun)	Extreme poverty	The city government has several agencies that provide shelter, food, and other assistance to help relieve indigence.
indolent	(adj)	Lazy, slothful	Having worked all his life, the CEO was constantly frustrated with his indolent son, who used his inherited wealth as an excuse to sunbathe and party.
inert	(adj)	Inactive; having little or no power to move	"All of the missiles at the military museum are inert, Timmy," said the tour guide, answering the question children always asked. "They're not going to blow up." / When she saw her father's inert body on the floor, she thought the worst, but fortunately he was just practicing very slow yoga.
inexorable	(adj)	Relentless, unyielding; not moved by pleading	Many people fled Europe in the face of Hitler's inexorable march across the continent.
infallible	(adj)	Incapable of error; certain	No good scientist thinks he or she is infallible—it is fundamental to the scientific method that every theory is open to revision based on new evidence.
ingrate	(noun)	Ungrateful person	You ingrate! I have slaved at this laundromat to pay for your college education, and you quit two weeks before graduation to become a Marxist revolutionary, and then you tell me I'm the enemy of the working class?

WORD	P.O.S.	DEFINITION	USAGE
ingratiate	(verb)	Make an effort to gain favor with	Ryan's attempts to ingratiate himself with the boss were quite transparent; no one really believes that a 25-year-old loves the same cigars, classic rock, and AARP crosswords as the 65-year-old company president.
inimical	(adj)	Hostile, adverse, harmful	Most people think that being shouted at in the freezing rain is inimical to learning; sadly, our boot camp instructor disagreed.
iniquity	(noun)	Injustice, wickedness, sin	The preacher's sermon about loving your neighbor was regarded by some as a welcome departure from his usual fiery homilies railing against iniquity. / Iniquitous corporations, such as those that spill oil into our oceans, must be punished.
inordinate	(adj)	Excessive, not within proper limits, unrestrained	Students taking practice Computer-Adaptive Tests at home often take an inordinate number of breaks. Remember, on the real thing, you can't stop just because you're tired or hungry.
inquest	(noun)	Legal or judicial inquiry, esp. before a jury and esp. made by a coroner into the cause of someone's death; the results of such an inquiry	The family waited nervously for the results of the inquest, which finally returned a verdict of misadventure; that is, their grandfather had not been murdered, but rather died in a freak accident of his own doing.
insensible	(adj)	Incapable of feeling; unconscious, unaware	Very intoxicated people can be insensible to pain, leading to serious problems as they injure themselves and don't realize it. / I cannot believe that, while I was insensible after the operation, you put funny hats on me and took pictures!
insinuate	(verb)	Hint, suggest slyly; introduce (an idea) into someone's mind in a subtle, artful way	"Where's your boyfriend? You didn't leave him home alone, did you?" asked Ming. "Are you insinuating something?" asked Helen. "If you have something to say, just say it."
insipid	(adj)	Dull, stale, lacking taste or interest	This is a university-level poetry class, and your insipid drivel just won't cut it here. "Things that are bad always make me sad"? Really? / The restaurant critic called the dish "insipid." I did think it was bland, but I probably would've been more polite about it.
insular	(adj)	narrow-minded, provincial; pertaining to an island; detached, standing alone	The young actress couldn't wait to escape the insularity of her small town, where life revolved around high school football and Taco Bell was considered exotic, international cuisine.

WORD	P.O.S.	DEFINITION	USAGE
insurrection	(noun)	Rebellion or revolt against a government or similarly established authority	Due to frequent insurrections, the nation has had six governments in just five years. / The principal prepared for insurrection as she announced that all teachers were to spend the rest of the year exclusively preparing for standardized tests.
inter	(verb)	Bury (a dead body) or place in a tomb	After the funeral, the body will be interred in the cemetery. / Occasionally, a criminal investigation requires disinterring, or exhuming, a body for autopsy; this can be upsetting to family members who have already buried their loved one.
interplay	(noun)	Interaction, reciprocal relationship or influence	Bilingual readers will enjoy the interplay of English and Spanish in many of the poems in this anthology of the work of Mexican-American poets.
interregnum	(noun)	A time in between two reigns or regimes during which there is no ruler; a period during which government does not function; any period of freedom from authority or break or interruption in a series	When the king died with no heir, his ministers ruled in the interregnum as the nobles argued over which of the king's nephews should rule next. / In the interregnum between Madonna and Lady Gaga, there was no single female pop star who commanded such titanic audiences.
intransigent	(adj)	Refusing to compromise, inflexible, having extreme attitudes	"Even three detentions and a note home to your parents haven't convinced you to behave yourself in class!" the teacher said to the intransigent child.
inundate	(verb)	Flood, cover with water, overwhelm	As the city was inundated with water, the mayor feared that many evacuees would have nowhere to go. / I can't go out—I am inundated with homework!
inure	(verb)	Toughen up; accustom or habituate to pain, hardship, etc.	Having had over a dozen surgeries before she was 10, spending months at a time in the hospital, she considered herself inured to pain and disappointment.
invective	(noun)	Violent denunciation; accusations, insults, or verbal abuse	Although the money was good, she quit her job after nearly having a nervous breakdown from her boss's invective.
inveigle	(verb)	Entice, lure; get something by flattery, cleverness, or offering incentives	After Mrs. Kim found out that her son's friends had inveigled him into doing something stupid, she gave him a lecture on standing up to peer pressure.
investiture	(noun)	Investing; formally giving someone a right or title	The former dean had her academic robes dry cleaned in preparation for her investiture as university president.
invidious	(adj)	Hateful, offensive, injurious	School bullying has become a serious problem, with ongoing invidious behavior driving students to suicide.

WORD	P.O.S.	DEFINITION	USAGE
irascible	(adj)	Irritable, easily angered	"I spent my entire childhood tiptoeing around so as not to anger my irascible mother," Isaiah told his therapist.
irresolute	(adj)	Wavering, not sure how to proceed, not firm in one's decision making	If we were voting on the bill this moment, we'd have enough votes to pass it. But many of our supporters are irresolute—we're worried that when lobbyists get to them, they'll quickly change their minds.
itinerant	(adj)	Traveling from place to place, esp. as part of a job	In rural areas in the 1940s, it was common that a small town would lack its own doctor, instead being seen by an itinerant family physician who made rounds to many such towns.
itinerary	(noun)	Travel schedule; detailed plan for a journey	Great, that was the Parthenon! What's next on our itinerary?
jettison	(verb)	Discard, cast off; throw items overboard in order to lighten a ship in an emergency	We got so tired while hiking the Appalachian Trail that we jettisoned some of our fancy camping supplies just so we could drag ourselves to a place where we could get medical attention.
jingoism	(noun)	Excessive, loud patriotism and aggressive, warlike foreign policy	He is such a jingoist that he's always yelling at the TV, calling even the most conservative commentators "wimps" for failing to suggest that we simply nuke, burn, pillage, and otherwise extirpate our so-called enemies.
juxtapose	(verb)	Place side by side (either physically or in a metaphorical way, such as to make a comparison)	Making a decision between two engagement rings from two different stores was difficult, he noted—it would be much easier if he could juxtapose them and compare them directly.
kindle	(verb)	Ignite, cause to begin burning; incite, arouse, inflame	It's hard to kindle a campfire when it's so damp out. / Although they were apart, the lovers' passion was only further kindled by the love letters they wrote to one another.
kinetic	(adj)	Pertaining to motion	Marisa told her mother what she had learned in science class: a ball sitting on a table has potential energy, but a ball falling towards the ground has kinetic energy.
knell	(noun, verb)	The sound made by a bell for a funeral, or any sad sound or signal of a failure, death, ending, etc. (noun); to make such a sound (verb)	The Senate minority leader's speech was a death knell for the bill; all hope of bipartisan cooperation was lost.
lachrymose	(adj)	Tearful, mournful	Accustomed to lachrymose occasions, the funeral home kept boxes of tissues near every seat.

WORD	P.O.S.	DEFINITION	USAGE
larceny	(noun)	Theft	The department store employs a security officer whose job it is to prevent larceny.
largess or largesse	(noun)	Generosity, the giving of money or gifts (esp. with the implication that the giver is a bit superior to the recipient)	While I did attend an expensive private school, my parents were actually quite poor—I was at that school through the largesse of my grandfather.
latent	(adj)	Potential; existing but not visible or active	Certain experts believe that some people have a genetic propensity for addiction; however, if such a person never comes into contact with drugs, the propensity for addiction can remain latent for life.
laudable	(adj)	Worthy of praise	"Your loyalty to your friends is laudable," the principal said, "but if you don't start naming names, you'll end up in trouble yourself."
lax	(adj)	Not strict; careless, loose, slack	My parents were really lax about homework—they never checked to see if I did it or not. Sadly, this legacy of laxity is not serving me well while studying for the GRE.
leery	(adj)	Suspicious or wary	You should be leery of any business opportunity that requires a startup fee and a "sponsor"—you might find yourself sucked into a scam.
legerdemain	(noun)	Slight-of-hand (magic as performed by a magician); trickery or deception	The child was astounded when her uncle pulled out a quarter from behind her ear. Of course, she hadn't actually lost a quarter there; it was just a bit of leger demain from an amateur magician.
lethargic	(adj)	Lazy, drowsy, or sluggish	I do love the Golden Corral's reasonably priced buffet, but I feel so lethargic after I eat my weight in mac-and-cheese and hand-carved turkey.
licentious	(adj)	Sexually unrestrained; immoral; ignoring the rules	Why is it so hard for politicians to abstain from licentious behavior until they're out of office?
limpid	(adj)	Clear, transparent; completely calm	Hawaii was amazing! The water was crystal clear—so limpid that when you were scuba diving, you could see ahead for what seemed like miles! / After two years meditating in religious seclusion, he had a totally limpid attitude, affected by nothing from the outside world.
lionize	(verb)	Treat like a celebrity	Being a chef has long been a prestigious profession, but it is only in the last decade or so that "celebrity chefs" have been lionized and given their own television shows.

WORD	P.O.S.	DEFINITION	USAGE
lissome	(adj)	Flexible, supple, agile	The actress exercised and stretched every day, but was ultimately told by the casting director that she wasn't lissome enough to play a ballet dancer. The actress had to agree—"I walk like an ogre," she said.
listless	(adj)	Spiritless, lacking interest or energy	"I'm too tired to care about homework," mumbled the listless child, staring blankly at the wall. "Maybe if someone brought me a glass of milk and a cookie…"
livid	(adj)	Furiously angry, enraged	Diane was livid when she discovered that her daughter had borrowed her wedding dress to wear to an '80s party. "I have never been angrier in my life," she said.
lugubrious	(adj)	Mournful, gloomy (sometimes in an exaggerated way)	Kiara was having a good time at the Irish pub until the Traditional Music Hour started, and the lugubrious tunes made her cry into her Guinness.
lumber	(verb)	Walk in a heavy or clumsy way, sometimes due to being weighed down	Alicia was a model and was accustomed to walking everywhere as though on a catwalk, so she was quite displeased when she broke her leg and had to lumber around in a cast, thumping the ground everywhere she went.
luminous	(adj)	Shining, radiant, well-lit; brilliant or enlightening	Use our new light-reflecting shimmer blush for a luminous complexion. / We are conferring this honorary degree on the author in appreciation for sharing his luminous intellect with the world. He is truly a luminary.
lurid	(adj)	Gruesome or excessively vivid; sensational, shocking, unrestrained	I do like to keep up with what celebrities are doing, but that tabloid is just too lurid for me—just look at the cover: "Worst Cellulite in Hollywood" and "Exclusive Crash Photos." Truly horrible.
machination or machinations	(noun, usually plural)	Crafty schemes or plots	It's cute to think that teen idols became famous because their talent was simply so great that the music industry reached out to them, but usually, any teen idol is the product of intense coaching and parental machinations.
maelstrom	(noun)	Any chaotic, turbulent situation; violent whirlpool	After having been homeschooled her whole life, the first week of college was a maelstrom of social events, orientations, and business. / The Smiths lost their houseboat in a maelstrom, but were at least thankful that they weren't on the boat at the time and thus escaped the violent storm at sea.

WORD	P.O.S.	DEFINITION	USAGE
magnanimous	(adj)	High-minded, noble, lofty; generous in forgiving others, free of resentment	The twins were so different from one another—while Andrea was petty and vengeful and would hold a grudge for years, Marina was quite magnanimous, easily forgiving insults or slights, and simply rising above the petty bickering and cliquish behavior of our high school.
magnate	(noun)	Very important or influential person, esp. in business	Many students pursue MBAs in hopes of becoming wealthy and powerful magnates; some students never quite make it there, instead spending their careers staring at spreadsheets and taking orders from magnates.
malediction	(noun)	A curse	Sheila thought the fortune-teller was her friend, but when she didn't pay her bill, the fortune-teller cast a hex on her, a malediction intended to cause terrible things to befall her.
malinger	(verb)	Pretend to be sick, esp. to get out of work, duties, etc.	Elijah was sick in class on Monday and was sent to the school nurse to sleep it off. The next day, having realized that illness was a good way to get out of class, Elijah said his stomach hurt and spent the afternoon in the nurse's office. By Wednesday, though, the nurse accused him of malingering and sent him back to class.
manifest	(verb, adj)	Obvious, apparent, perceptible to the eye (adj); to show, make clear, or prove (verb)	My superstitious aunt claims that she saw a manifestation of our deceased grandfather, who appeared during a thunderstorm to warn us all about our cousin's fiance. / Lupus is difficult to diagnose, but sometimes manifests as muscular weakness or joint pain.
mannered	(adj)	Having a particular manner, esp. an artificial one	Although he grew up in rural Ohio, sometime before he got his own makeover show on television he adopted a mannered way of speaking, as though he had grown up in some very odd corner of Victorian England.
mar	(verb)	Damage, spoil, ruin	The interior designer's secret was to buy furnishings and fixtures that had been marred on the shop floor and therefore were sold at steep discounts; she would then fix the defects herself or add additional aging effects to the pieces.

WORD	P.O.S.	DEFINITION	USAGE
martinet	(noun)	Person who adheres to rules extremely closely; strict disciplinarian	It was no fun growing up with a military officer for a dad. He was such a martinet he once made me do 20 pushups for being one minute late to bed—even though the reason I was late was that I wanted to kiss him goodnight.
maudlin	(adj)	Excessively sentimental, showing sadness or some other emotion in a foolish or silly way	I had no idea the film was going to be a maudlin affair in which the male lead dies and the female lead has his baby, who then also dies. Half the theater was weeping, and the other half was just shaking their heads at how badly written the movie was.
maxim	(noun)	A general truth or fundamental principle, esp. expressed as a proverb or saying	My favorite maxim is "Seize the day!" How much would it cost to get that on a tattoo? How much more for "Curiosity killed the cat"?
mendicant	(noun)	Beggar, or religious follower who lives by begging	Having joined a mendicant order, the friar had vowed not to own property, and instead to subsist on the donations of the faithful.
meretricious	(adj)	Attractive in a vulgar or flashy way, tawdry; deceptive	The singer performed her concert draped in what looked from far away like precious jewels. Up close, though, the fan could see that the accessories were just meretricious plastic, like what little girls buy at the mall.
metaphysical	(adj)	Concerned with abstract thought, related to metaphysics (branch of philosophy concerned with explaining the nature of being and of the world); very subtle or abstruse	My poetry class has all kinds. In contrast to Gary's poetry about dogs and horses, Neil's poetry is very metaphysical, exploring the relation of mortal humans to a timeless universe. It's a little over Gary's head.
milieu	(noun)	Environment, atmosphere; the environmental setting in which something happens or develops	Becoming a priest in the anything-goes milieu of the 1960s gave Father Bryant an interesting perspective on two contrasting philosophies. / After the fall of the Soviet Union, a milieu of crushing poverty, yet hopeful aspiration, existed in the former satellite state.
militate	(verb)	Have a great effect, weigh heavily (often as militate against)	While his résumé was stellar, his speech impediment militated against his performance in job interviews.
mired	(adj)	Stuck, entangled (in something, like a swamp or muddy area), soiled	Mired in her predecessor's mess and mistakes, the new CEO found it difficult to take the company in a new direction.
mirth	(noun)	Jollity, merriment; amusement or laughter	Nothing could beat the mirth of the office holiday party—once everyone had heard how fat their bonuses would be, the delighted staff formed a conga line and drank and danced the night away.

WORD	P.O.S.	DEFINITION	USAGE
misanthrope or misanthropist	(noun)	Hater of humankind	He is such a misanthrope that when some Girl Scouts going door to door asked if he'd like to sponsor a hungry child overseas, he replied, "The fewer people in the world, the better," and shut the door in their faces!
missive	(noun)	Letter, written message	While Don was overseas fighting in World War II, he lived for the missives from the wife he had left behind.
modicum	(noun)	A little bit or limited quantity	In her first five years in Hollywood, she experienced only a modicum of success as an actress, appearing twice in commercials and once as a waitress on *Desperate Housewives*.
modish	(adj)	Stylish, contemporary	While some sculptors sought to make their work universal and timeless, Dania sculpted modish creations that captured the pop-cultural zeitgeist—for instance, a sculpture of Rihanna with an umbrella, or a three-foot high representation of the latest Alexander McQueen heels.
molt	(verb)	Shed or cast off, esp. to regularly shed skin, feathers, etc. (as a snake)	The translucent cylinder left behind when a snake molts is weirdly beautiful; it looks like a piece of blown glass.
monastic	(adj)	Relating to or resembling a monastery (where monks or nuns live), esp. by being quiet, secluded, contemplative, strict, and/or lacking luxuries	Christine decided that the only way she was going to finish her Ph.D. was to live a monastic lifestyle: she broke up with her boyfriend, cancelled her cable service, left the house only when necessary, and ultimately had a draft of her dissertation a few months later.
morose	(adj)	Gloomy, sullen	She had always been a happy child, but once she hit high school and decided to become a goth, she adopted a morose attitude to match her all-black clothing.
multifarious	(adj)	Diverse, having a lot of variety	Last year's jewelry line was all metal and neutrals, but this year's presents a multifarious array of brilliant colors.
munificent	(adj)	Generous, giving liberally	The elderly titan of industry was notoriously miserly, sometimes called "the cheapest man alive." But his wife was quite munificent, and after his death, she used his fortune to support numerous charities and to buy a house for their longtime maid.

WORD	P.O.S.	DEFINITION	USAGE
myopic	(adj)	Near-sighted; lacking long-term thinking, short-sighted	To raise prices in a time of crisis is both wrong and deeply myopic—our profits would go up in the short term, but our customers' resentment would simmer for decades. / Myron's myopia is so strong that he cannot be helped by contact lenses and has to wear the heavy glasses he has worn for decades.
nadir	(noun)	Lowest point	It was only when Ming reached her absolute nadir—what her recovery program called "rock bottom"—that she admitted she had a problem and checked herself into rehab.
neologism	(noun)	New word or phrase (or a new meaning applied to an existing word or phrase)	You won't find "fauxhawk" in the dictionary—it's a neologism that describes a fake mohawk (faux means fake and is pronounced "foe") created by sculpting the hair into a mohawk-like crest without actually shaving the sides.
neophyte	(noun)	Beginner, novice; person newly converted to a religion	It was totally outrageous of our law firm to send a neophyte into the courtroom to defend our case against a team of experienced attorneys.
nettle	(verb)	Irritate, sting, or annoy	His first year in college, my little brother failed gym. How is that even possible? I always remind him about it just to nettle him. Of course, he usually strikes back by reminding me of that time I crashed an amusement park's go-cart.
noisome	(adj)	Having an extremely offensive smell; disgusting	Aside from the noisome effluence they emit when frightened, skunks are not particularly aggressive or unfriendly animals.
nominal	(adj)	Trivial, so small as to be unimportant; in name only, so-called	A notary public will certify a document for a nominal fee, usually under $3. / The country has a nominal president, but his detractors say he's just a puppet leader for the more powerful countries providing foreign aid.
nontrivial	(adj)	Important or big enough to matter	The chief of staff told the assembled doctors, "We all make mistakes. But this mistake was nontrivial, and there is going to be an investigation."
normative	(adj)	Implying or attempting to establish a norm; expressing value judgments or telling people what to do (rather than merely describing that which is happening)	The reason we are not understanding each other in this argument about grammar is that you are arguing normatively, telling me how people *should* talk, and I am simply reporting and analyzing how people *actually* talk.

WORD	P.O.S.	DEFINITION	USAGE
obdurate	(adj)	Stubborn, hardhearted, hardened in wrongdoing	The first mate reported that there was some fuzzy shape on the horizon, but the captain insisted that the instruments showed no such object, and obdurately sailed straight ahead—right into an iceberg. / This obdurate criminal should never be let out on parole—he simply cannot be reformed.
oblique	(adj)	Slanting or sloping; indirect, misleading, or evasive	After the fifteenth oblique reference that Bella made to George or George made to Bella, everyone in the office figured out that they were dating. / The serial killer loved to talk to interrogators, but gave only oblique answers that were useless in finding the bodies.
occlude	(verb)	Stop up, close, shut in or shut off	This drain guard is here to make sure nothing (like silverware) ends up occluding your garbage disposal.
opine	(verb)	Express an opinion	He was happy to opine on everything from books to wine to politics, unaware that people didn't see him as intelligent enough to be worth listening to.
opprobrium	(noun)	Disgrace and disapproval that result from outrageously shameful actions	Some young starlets seem to think a DUI offense isn't such a big deal, but drunk driving deserves opprobrium—driving under the influence maims and kills innocent people every year.
orotund	(adj)	Full, rich, and clear (of the voice or speaking); pompous, bombastic	The actor James Earl Jones has long been sought after for voiceover work as well as acting jobs because of his dignified, orotund voice.
ossify	(verb)	Become inflexible in attitudes, opinions, etc.; become bone or become hard like bone	I remember having many broad-ranging discussions with him back in college, but since then, his opinions have ossified; sadly, he is now the most close-minded person I know.
ostensible or ostensive	(adj)	Professed, evident, or pretended; outwardly appearing in a certain way	Ostensibly, she came to volunteer out of the goodness of her heart. However, I think she's really here because she has a crush on one of the other volunteers. / He's an ostensive candidate for the job, but we need to check these references before we move further.
ostentatious	(adj)	Pretentious, boastful showiness	Her ostentatious clothing is simply not appropriate in a business environment, in fact, nothing emblazoned with 2,000 Swarovski crystals is.

WORD	P.O.S.	DEFINITION	USAGE
overwrought	(adj)	Overly nervous, agitated, or excited; too ornate, elaborate, or fussy; overdone	By the time her boyfriend met her in the park, she was overwrought, thinking he must have chosen a public place so he could break up with her. As it turned out, he had just invited her to a picnic. / Accustomed to more spare American churches, Father Smith found the churches of South America a bit overwrought, with enormous, flowery, gold altars and gold-plating on everything imaginable.
palatial	(adj)	Suitable for or resembling a palace, magnificent	After a career spent in budget hotels, she was thrilled when the client put her up in a palatial room at a five-star hotel. She raided the minibar and then promptly fell asleep on the 600-thread-count duvet.
palliate	(verb)	Make less serious or severe; relieve symptoms of an illness	The doctors said it would be pointless to subject Uncle Akoni to continued treatments when there was no hope of a cure, so we gave consent for him to be transferred to the palliative care wing where he would be made as comfortable as possible in his final weeks.
pallid	(adj)	Abnormally pale (as skin); lacking color or vitality	When Adolfo left the office mid-day, we knew from the pallor that had overtaken him that he really was getting sick. / We need this blog to really hit hard against the special interest groups ruining our country, and your pallid writing isn't doing it—you're going to bore people to death with this wimpy prose.
panache	(noun)	Flair, style, swagger; a flamboyant or grand way of acting	Not only did he quit, but he did so with panache, actually delivering a PowerPoint presentation that we thought would be about the budget, but which turned out to be quite obscene. He then pulled out a flask, guzzled its contents, and walked out. That guy's kind of a legend.
panegyric	(noun)	Formal or lofty expression of praise	Lincoln enthusiasts were excited that a new biography was to be published, and many hoped that new light would be cast on certain controversies. However, the book was pure panegyric, nothing but heroic tales, uncritically presented.
panoply	(noun)	Splendid, wide-ranging, impressive display or array	Our old cafeteria had only premade salads, but the new cafeteria has a salad bar with a panoply of toppings.

MANHATTAN
PREP

WORD	P.O.S.	DEFINITION	USAGE
paragon	(noun)	Model of excellence, perfect example	Unlike his sister, he was a paragon of responsibility, taking in her three children when she went to jail, and even switching jobs so he could be there to pick them up from school.
pare	(verb)	Peel or cut off the outer layer (such as peeling fruit with a knife), reduce or trim as if cutting off the outer parts	We need to pare down our budget if we're going to survive on unemployment for a while. / She simplified her life by paring commitments from her schedule.
parley	(noun, verb)	Discussion, negotiation, esp. between enemies (noun); to have such a discussion (verb)	The industry trade show is our chance to parley with our competitors. We do go out for drinks together, but really, we're just hoping someone slips up and tells us about their new product line.
parry	(verb)	Deflect or avoid, esp. a blow or attack; skillfully evade (a question)	When asked by a reporter if rumors of his infidelity were true, the candidate parried, answering that he had always supported legislation bolstering the sanctity of marriage.
pastiche	(noun)	Mix of incongruous parts; artistic work imitating the work of other artists, often satirically	The slickly produced boy band's first album was deeply unimaginative, just a pastiche of every other boy-band album ever produced.
pathogenic	(adj)	Capable of producing disease	Many common and legal food additives are pathogenic, known to lead to diabetes or even cancer.
pedant	(noun)	Person who pays excessive attention to book learning and rules, or who uses his or her learning to show off	I hate when pedants interrupt you to correct your grammar, especially if what you're saying is important, and, in my opinion, almost anything is more important than pedantic quibbles over whether it's okay to end a sentence with a preposition.
peddle	(verb)	Travel around while selling; sell illegally; give out or disseminate	After an unsuccessful year spent peddling cutlery door-to-door, he turned to peddling drugs, thus landing himself in jail. / "I don't want these people peddling lies to our children," said Mrs. Mahmood, protesting an event in which fringe political candidates were invited to speak to kids.
pejorative	(adj, noun)	Disparaging, derogatory, belittling (adj); a name or word that is disparaging (noun)	I'm open to constructive criticism, but I think my supervisor's remarks are inappropriately pejorative—it's never okay to call an employee a "sniveling dullard." / Although these insults wouldn't be understood by most, "poetaster" and "mathematicaster" are pejoratives for minor, incompetent poets and mathematicians, respectively.

WORD	P.O.S.	DEFINITION	USAGE
pellucid	(adj)	Transparent, translucent; clear, easy to understand	He decided that the cove's pellucid waters were an excellent place to teach his daughter to swim, reasoning that, if she started to sink, he would easily be able to see where she was.
penitent	(adj, noun)	Regretful, feeling remorse for one's sins or misdeeds (adj); a person who feels this way (noun)	After being "separated" from the college for plagiarism, she wrote a letter to the Dean expressing her deep regret and penitence and hoping to be readmitted.
penumbra	(noun)	Outer part of a shadow from an eclipse; any surrounding region, fringe, periphery; any area where something "sort of" exists	The Constitution doesn't specifically mention a right to privacy, but some experts consider this to exist in the penumbra of the Constitution, as a guarantee of privacy is needed in order to exercise the rights that are enumerated. / The rent in Chicago was too high, so they moved to a suburb in the penumbra of the city.
penury	(noun)	Extreme poverty or scarcity	The young model married an elderly billionaire thinking she'd be set for life, but she ended up living in penury after her husband died and his middle-aged children held up the probate case for years, keeping her from receiving any money whatsoever.
per se	(adverb)	Intrinsically; by itself; in itself	The policy isn't sexist, per se, but it has had a disproportionate impact on women that deserves further study.
peregrinate	(verb)	Travel from place to place, esp. on foot	After college, he took a year off to peregrinate across the country, visiting friends and seeing the 40-odd states he had never before had the chance to see.
perennial	(adj)	Lasting through the years or indefinitely, enduring; recurring	Fighting over the bathroom is a perennial problem in our house—there are eight of us, and we're home-schooled, so we're all pretty much always here.
perfunctory	(adj)	Done superficially, without much care, or merely as routine	She did a really perfunctory job on this PowerPoint. Sure, it has a dozen slides, but most of them just say things like "Sales—Ways to Improve" in Times New Roman on a white background. Maybe she's planning to fill in the details later.
peripatetic	(adj)	Journeying from place to place; traveling on foot	He quit his office job to become a peripatetic musician, traveling from town to town playing in bars and sleeping on couches.
pernicious	(adj)	Very harmful or destructive, deadly	Bullying has a pernicious effect on the learning environment, keeping victims too intimidated to speak up and also silencing others who fear that they could be next.

WORD	P.O.S.	DEFINITION	USAGE
perspicacious	(adj)	Having penetrating insight or good discernment	A good detective is shrewd and perspicacious, judging when someone is lying, noticing things the rest of us would ignore, and making connections that allow an investigation to move forward.
phalanx	(noun)	Formation of soldiers carrying shields close together for defense; any very close group of people	To even enter the embassy, the diplomats had to make their way through a phalanx of protestors.
philistine	(noun)	Person deficient in or hostile to culture	Her date was very handsome, but she decided he was an absolute philistine when he said that documentaries were "boring" and that the "best picture" Oscar should go to *Resident Evil: Afterlife 3D*.
phlegmatic	(adj)	Apathetic, sluggish, not easily excited or made emotional	He had a phlegmatic disposition, refusing to get angry or even noticeably upset when his wife left him for his brother.
platitude	(noun)	A shallow, overused statement; cliché	Everyone who knew my mother knows she was an atheist, so I can't imagine why people at her funeral would think we'd enjoy their soppy platitudes about Mom's "being in a better place now."
plebeian	(adj)	Of the common people	I toured a luxury apartment building, and I laughed when I saw that the apartments had walk-in closets and whirlpool bathtubs, but hilariously tiny ovens. Because, of course, the wealthy would never do something so plebian as cook their own food.
plethora	(noun)	Excess; excessive amount	She had a plethora of excuses, but there is simply no justification for arriving to class drunk.
plucky	(adj)	Brave, spirited	Feminist critics have commented that today's romantic comedies tend to feature passive, helpless female leads, whereas the romantic comedies of the 1940s featured plucky heroines who took the lead in cleverly solving problems.
plutocracy	(noun)	Rule by the wealthy	There have always been rich and poor people, of course, but some argue that the U.S. is becoming a plutocracy, with the richest 10% controlling two-thirds of the nation's wealth and nearly half of our Congressional representatives being millionaires.
polemic	(noun)	Controversial argument, esp. one attacking a specific idea	Laura Kipnis's 2003 book *Against Love: A Polemic* has been called "shocking" and "scathing." Perhaps Kipnis used the word *polemic* in the title to indicate that she's making an extreme argument as a means of starting a debate. After all, who's really against love?

MANHATTAN
PREP

WORD	P.O.S.	DEFINITION	USAGE
politic	(adj)	Shrewd, pragmatic; tactful or diplomatic	Celebrities have to watch what they say, as even an offhand comment can end up splashed across the covers of magazines. When the starlet was asked what she thought of her ex-husband marrying the swimsuit model he left her for, she gave the politic reply, "I wish both of them the best."
polyglot	(noun)	Speaking or composed of many languages (of a person, book, etc.); a person who knows several languages	New York's public service announcements often take the form of polyglot posters in the subway, suggesting in six languages that readers give up their seats for pregnant women or those with disabilities.
posit	(verb)	Presume, suggest, put forward (an idea)	For thousands of years, philosophers have thought of the self as a unified entity, but neuroscientists today posit the existence of a modular brain—a self that is a mix of different brain parts, with no central "coordinator."
prattle	(verb)	Talk in an idle, simple-minded, meaningless, or foolish way; chatter, babble	It was infuriating to listen to the boss prattle on about some new restaurant in town when everyone was just waiting to find out if they'd been laid off.
precipitate	(verb)	Cause to happen suddenly or prematurely; fling, plunge, or hurl down	Mr. and Mrs. Sikos had been considering a move to Florida for years, but the sudden destruction of their house in a hurricane precipitated their decision to finally make the move. / "Stay away from the precipice!" said the mother to her child. "I wouldn't want my darling son to be precipitated to his doom!"
précis	(noun)	Concise summary, abstract	Just as scientific journals publish abstracts of their articles online (and then charge for access to the full version), the entrepreneur decided to publish a précis of her whitepaper online, while charging for access to the full version.
predilection	(noun)	Preference, tendency, or favorability towards	She has completed teacher training allowing her to teach grades K–6, but she discovered that she really has a predilection for teaching kindergarten.
prescient	(adj)	Having foreknowledge or foresight, seeing the future	Mariposa swears she's prescient—she thinks she sees the future in her dreams. / The science fiction novel, published in 1955, was strangely prescient—it pictures the year 2000 as having no flying cars, but a communication system known as the "interconnect," used largely for online shopping and wasting time.

MANHATTAN
PREP

WORD	P.O.S.	DEFINITION	USAGE
preternatural	(adj)	Exceptional, supernatural	While Tiger Woods has been mired in scandal, his preternatural golfing talent is still undeniable. / Dad was convinced that the house was haunted, but I doubted that the strange sounds were due to preternatural causes. As it turned out, we had a raccoon in the basement.
prevaricate	(verb)	Lie, stray from the truth, mislead	Maryanne had been shoplifting. When her mother asked where her new clothes had come from, she prevaricated, vaguely suggesting that a rich friend had bought them for her.
primacy	(noun)	The state of being first or most important	The conservative senator argued that the very fabric of society depended on the primacy of the family, and that legislation was needed to shore up the institution of marriage.
proclivity	(noun)	Inclination, natural tendency	After his therapist pointed out that he had a natural proclivity to judge people prematurely, he tried to work on that by imagining things from the other person's point of view.
prolix	(adj)	Excessively long and wordy (of a person, piece of writing, etc.)	My mother is incredibly verbose. She'll tell a boring, prolix story for five whole minutes, and at the end, it turns out that the point was that she got a 50-cent discount on a box of spaghetti at the store.
propagate	(verb)	Reproduce, spread, increase	Hackers can take down a large computer system in minutes as a virus propagates and infects all of the machines on a network.
propensity	(noun)	Natural inclination or tendency	He was an introvert with a propensity for solitary brooding, and thus was considered a bit strange or unfriendly by the others in his dorm.
prophetic	(adj)	Relating to prophesy, predicting, ominous	While most of the country was consumed with irrational optimism about the economy, this particular journalist possessed an almost prophetic pessimism—not only did she predict the crash, she even predicted the month it actually happened.
propitiate	(verb)	Attempt to reconcile with, satisfy, or reduce the animosity of (a person who is angry, offended, etc.)	The ancient Greeks would often attempt to propitiate angry gods by sacrificing animals to them.
propitious	(adj)	Favorable, giving good signs for the future, likely to work out; kind or forgiving	After having to postpone the game earlier in the week due to rain, the officials were pleased to see the propitious weather forecast. "We'll get this game in after all," one of them exclaimed.

WORD	P.O.S.	DEFINITION	USAGE
providential	(adj)	Lucky, fortunate, or relating to divine care (the idea that a deity has helped or cared for a person)	Every time their religious sister ran out of money, help always arrived! She viewed this as God's providential hand, but her family members viewed it as their always having to bail her out, and it was getting annoying.
proxy	(noun)	Agent, substitute, person authorized to act on behalf of another	She was in the hospital, but certainly didn't want to miss voting on the proposal, so she sent a proxy to the board meeting to vote "yes."
puerile	(adj)	Juvenile, immature	The retiring film critic decried the puerile humor common in so many modern American movies, pointing out that the classic comedies of the '40s were so much smarter and less reliant on jokes about bodily functions.
pugilism	(noun)	boxing, fighting with the fists	Pugilism has been called "the sweet science" by some, but others feel that hitting other people in the head until they can't get up isn't much of a sport.
puissance	(noun)	Power, might	When people asked the 25-year-old bride what had attracted her to her commanding, 60-year-old CEO husband, she replied that she had always been drawn to puissance. That tended to end conversations as people went to go look up "puissance."
pulchritude	(noun)	Physical beauty	Marilyn Monroe's mystique is based not only on her obvious pulchritude, but also on her mysterious death and likely dalliance with President John F. Kennedy.
pungent	(adj)	Having a sharp taste or smell; biting, stimulating, sharp	The new assistant chef received some rather pungent criticism from the head chef for her idea to make feta cheese soup, which the customers found much too pungent.
pusillanimous	(adj)	Cowardly, timid	He was so pusillanimous that not only was he afraid to ask his boss for a raise, he was even afraid to tell the waitress that he didn't like sugar in his tea.
querulous	(adj)	Given to complaining, grumbling	Norma had been happy to be a grandmother, but was somewhat less happy when a querulous child was dropped off on her doorstep: "I don't want to come inside," "I don't like sandwiches," "It's too cold in the bathroom." Would the whining and moaning ever stop?
quiescent	(adj)	Quiet, still	After hours of moaning and shaking from his illness, the child finally exhausted himself and grew quiescent.

MANHATTAN
PREP

WORD	P.O.S.	DEFINITION	USAGE
quixotic	(adj)	Extremely impractical but very romantic, chivalrous, or idealistic; impulsive	Prompted by a lesson their teacher devised for election year, the children shared what they would do if elected president. The plans were adorably quixotic, involving housing all the homeless in floating homes on the ocean, or teaching everyone to be nice to each other.
raconteur	(noun)	Witty storyteller	Miguel was quite the raconteur—the laughing party guests naturally congregated in a cluster around him as he held court.
rarefied	(adj)	Lofty, very high up or elevated (in a metaphorical way); exclusive, select; thin, pure, or less dense (as air at the top of a mountain)	Among the rarefied ranks of conference attendees, she counted two Nobel Prize Winners, a MacArthur Genius Grant winner, and Bill Gates—and that was just at one lunch table!
reactant	(noun)	Something that reacts; a substance that undergoes a change in a chemical reaction	The two men had been rivals since high school; when both were elected to the city council, they became reactants in the worsening deadlock of an already-polarized city government.
recalcitrant	(adj)	Not obedient, resisting authority, hard to manage	As an aspiring kindergarten teacher, she had imagined days filled with giggles and singing songs about friendship—she was not prepared for a roomful of 20 recalcitrant children who wouldn't even sit down, much less learn the words to "Holding Hands around the World."
recant	(verb)	Withdraw, retract, or disavow something one has previously said, esp. formally	For saying that the Sun and not the Earth was the center of the universe, Galileo was brought on trial for heresy and forced to recant. He spent the rest of his life under house arrest. Of course, a forced recantation doesn't say much about whether the person really abjures his former views.
recapitulate	(verb)	Summarize, repeat in a concise way	I'm sorry I had to leave your presentation to take a call—I only have a minute, but can you recapitulate what you're proposing?
recondite	(adj)	Not easily understood, hidden, dealing with an obscure topic	Professor Salazar's office is full of books, every single one of which is more than 400 years old and written in ancient Greek. He deals in some seriously recondite information.
recrudescent	(adj)	Revival, breaking out into renewed activity	The recrudescence of his psoriasis came at the worst possible time. "Oh, great," he said, "now I'm going to be shedding skin flakes all over my new coworkers on the first day of work. "

WORD	P.O.S.	DEFINITION	USAGE
redound	(verb)	To have a good or bad effect, esp. as a result of a person's efforts or actions (usually used with to, on, or upon)	"Cramming" vocabulary words probably won't be very effective, but studying a little every day will redound to your success.
redress	(noun, verb)	Setting something right after a misdeed, compensation or relief for injury or wrongdoing (noun); correct, set right, remedy (verb)	My client was an innocent victim of medical malpractice. As would anyone who had the wrong leg amputated in surgery, he is seeking financial redress.
refractory	(adj)	Stubbornly disobedient, hard to manage	Dennis the Menace is the quintessential refractory child, impossible to control and immune to reform.
refulgent	(adj)	Shining, radiant	Her new engagement ring was refulgent—she was so happy with it. I'll bet she polished it every night.
rejoinder	(noun)	Response or reply, esp. a witty comeback	In retrospect, I could have come up with a better rejoinder than "I know you are, but what am I?" I always think of the perfect witty comeback hours after I actually need it.
rend	(verb)	Tear violently, esp. to tear one's clothing or hair out of grief; pull apart, split, or tear away	Many figures in the Bible rend their clothing from grief at a loved one's death, an event that can surely rend one's heart as well.
repast	(noun, verb)	A meal (noun); to eat or feast (verb)	After a light repast in a country inn, the men got back on their horses and rode away.
repertorial	(adj)	Pertaining to a repertory or repertoire, a stock of available things or a number of theatrical performances presented regularly or in sequence	One theater observer noted that repertorial community theater can tie together different plays for a repeat audience: seeing the same actor as Hamlet one night and Romeo another prompts interesting parallels between the two plays.
repose	(noun)	The act or state of resting; peacefulness, tranquility; lying dead in a grave	Thousands of people lined up to see the prime minister's body lying in repose in the capital building. / After working the last two weekends, Myrna was perfectly happy spending her day off in repose in her living room armchair with a cup of tea and a good book.
reprobate	(noun, adj)	Disreputable, unprincipled, or damned person (noun); shameless, depraved (adj)	The police joked that they had so many mug shots of the old reprobate that they could assemble them into a photography book called, *Faces of Petty Crime, 1976–2011*.
resurgent	(adj)	Having a revival, renewing, rising or surging again	Burlesque has experienced a resurgence in the last decade, as young women dress in old-fashioned finery and perform routines appropriate for the vaudeville halls or nightclubs of previous decades.

MANHATTAN
PREP

WORD	P.O.S.	DEFINITION	USAGE
revamp	(verb, noun)	Renovate, redo, revise (verb); a restructuring, upgrade, etc. (noun)	I have my whole room decorated in *Twilight: Eclipse* paraphernalia. When *Breaking Dawn* comes out, I will surely have to revamp my decor.
ribald	(adj)	Using or relating to obscene or vulgar humor	The movie's humor was so ribald that a PG-13 rating was assigned, and Joey's mother covered up his eyes nearly every time a woman was on the screen.
ridden	(adj)	Dominated or burdened by	The neighborhood was ridden with crime. / In this corruption-ridden nation, you simply have to pay bribes if you want anything to get done.
rift	(noun)	A gap or fissure (such as in rock), a break in friendly relations	Olaf's Swedish family was offended when he married a Norwegian girl—so offended that it caused a rift that lasted for decades. / The hikers considered the rift in their path, wondering if it would be possible to leap across.
rococo	(adj)	Very elaborate and ornate (in decorating or metaphorically, as in speech and writing); relating to a highly ornate style of art and architecture in 18th-century France	Although Dot Von Derian was born in Ohio as Melissa Worshowski, she insisted on being called "Madame Von D," and bought herself a mansion she furnished in the most rococo style imaginable—it was gilded cherubs and gold leafing as far as the eye could see.
rue	(noun, verb)	Regret, remorse (noun); to feel regret or remorse (verb)	Movie or cartoon villains sometimes say, "You'll rue the day!" What they mean is, "I will make you regret that you did what you just did." / The couple broke up in high school for a foolish reason, and each hastily married another person. Twenty years later, they were still full of endless rue over having lost each other.
ruminate	(verb)	Turn over in the mind, reflect on; chew cud (as a cow)	Oh, I just don't know about that. Let me ruminate on it for a few days and I'll get back to you.
salient	(adj)	Obvious, standing out; projecting, protruding, jutting out	The attack on our organization was mostly just partisan bickering, but it did have a few salient points that I think we should respond to. / The windowless prison's side wall had only one salient feature: a sculpture of the state bird jutting out from the building.
sardonic	(adj)	Scornfully or ironically mocking, cynically derisive	A sardonic movie critic is one thing, but a sardonic film professor is another—I really wish Professor Dahl wouldn't sarcastically cut down his students the way he does cheesy horror films. / Dorothy Parker wrote sardonically, "If you want to know what God thinks about money, just look at the people he gave it to."

WORD	P.O.S.	DEFINITION	USAGE
savant	(noun)	Learned person, scholar, someone admitted to membership in a scholarly field; a person with amazing mental abilities despite having a cognitive difference or disability	The TED conferences feature savants and newsmakers speaking on topics of great importance to the world.
scintilla	(noun)	A tiny bit or trace	With not one scintilla of food in the house, the pioneer woman resorted to desperate means, boiling weeds and even shoe leather to feed her children.
scurvy	(adj)	Contemptible, mean	Our neighbor is so scurvy that he deliberately broke my little brother's bicycle because, as he said, "You kids are too loud!"
searchingly	(adv)	In a searching or penetrating manner; while examining closely or probing for answers	"I'm fired?" asked Ron, looking searchingly at his boss. "I thought I was like a son to you."
secrete	(verb)	Produce and release a substance from a cell or gland of the body for a functional purpose	When threatened, skunks secrete an odor that humans consider horrible.
sedition	(noun)	Inciting rebellion against a government, esp. speech or writing that does this	Amnesty International regularly fights for the release of political prisoners imprisoned for sedition. While inciting violence is illegal in most of the world, what is considered sedition under many restrictive governments is what Americans consider a normal exercise of freedom of speech, such as writing a letter to the editor of a newspaper criticizing the government's policies.
semantic	(adj)	Relating to the different meanings of words or other symbols	Hector said plastic surgery should be covered under the health care plan, and Marion said it shouldn't, but it turns out that their disagreement was purely semantic—what Hector meant was reconstructive surgery and what Marion meant was cosmetic surgery.
seraphic	(adj)	Like an angel; serene, spiritually carried off or transported	The gospel choir looked seraphic in their shimmering white robes.
sinecure	(noun)	A job or position that pays while requiring little or no work	It's a wealthy university; it's sort of understood that professors who relocate to campus are rewarded with sinecures for their spouses, whether those spouses have any qualifications or not. / In medieval times, a sinecure was a paying position for a priest but without an attachment to a parish where he would actually have to show up and do something.

MANHATTAN
PREP

WORD	P.O.S.	DEFINITION	USAGE
skittish	(adj)	Shy, fickle, uncertain, or prone to act suddenly due to nervousness; lively in a restless or excessive way	After his first experience working with a skittish horse who nervously jerked around and ended up stepping on his foot, Ernest learned to wear steel-toed boots. / The band began with an audience of 80 college students but could see that they were skittish—there was a whole festival going on outside, and the students were ready to head for the door if the band wasn't that great.
slake	(verb)	Satisfy, esp. thirst, cool, or refresh; make less active	Having been lost for hours, the weary hikers were more than willing to slake their thirst in a mountain stream. / The teacher's harsh, demanding attitude soon slaked the girls' enthusiasm for the ballet class.
sobriquet	(noun)	A nickname	James Brown, often referred to with the sobriquet "The Godfather of Soul," scored numerous smash hits and was also known for his feverish dancing.
solecism	(noun)	Nonstandard use of grammar or words; mistake, esp. in etiquette	"I could care less" is a solecism—what the speaker really means to say is "I couldn't care less." / Apparently, Libby had committed a solecism by asking a man if he wanted to dance. "In Lubbock, Texas," said her friend, "we keep things traditional."
solidarity	(noun)	Fellowship in interests, feelings, responsibilities, etc., such as among a group of people or among classes, nations, etc.	The governor attempted to outlaw collective bargaining by unions, but backed down once he was made aware of the union's solidarity with churches and community groups across the state.
somatic	(adj)	Of the body	While some depression is caused by outside forces (the death of a loved one, for instance), many cases of depression have a somatic cause; for instance, postpartum depression can be related to hormones and physical changes associated with pregnancy and childbirth.
squalid	(adj)	Disgusting, filthy, foul, extremely neglected	Social Services removed the children from the home due to the squalid conditions, including rats running freely in the kitchen and spoiled food all over the house.
squelch	(verb)	Crush, squash; suppress or silence; walk through ooze or in wet shoes, making a smacking or sucking sound	The repressive government squelched the rebellion immediately. / Ew, I just squelched a slug in my bare feet!
stasis	(noun)	Equilibrium, a state of balance or inactivity, esp. caused by equal but opposing forces	Edie felt that her career was in stasis: her boss made it clear she wasn't getting promoted, but she also couldn't leave because of her health insurance situation.

WORD	P.O.S.	DEFINITION	USAGE
steeped	(adj)	Immersed (in), saturated (with)	A person steeped in classic literature probably thinks about almost everything in terms of old, famous books. / The Met's new campaign seeks to answer affirmatively the question of whether music lovers steeped in hip-hop and pop can learn to love opera.
stem	(verb)	To branch out from, originate from, or be caused by; To stop, hold back, or limit (the flow of something)	Her interest in applying quantitative methods to social problems stems from her lifelong love of math. / If the struggling city can't stem the tide of violence, further flight to the suburbs is inevitable.
stentorian	(adj)	Very loud and powerful (generally of a human voice)	The substitute teacher had a hard time calling the rowdy class to order. He poked his head into the hallway and flagged down the football coach walking by, who shut down the chaos immediately with a stentorian "Sit down and shut up!"
stigma	(noun)	Mark of disgrace, a figurative stain or mark on someone's reputation	In the 1950s, bearing a child out of wedlock was severely stigmatized, but today in many social circles, there is no stigma whatsoever on unmarried parents having a child.
stint	(noun, verb)	Period of time spent doing something, or a specific, limited amount of work (noun); to be frugal, to get by on little (verb)	After a stint in combat, Jared was used to eating whatever he was given, and being sparing with the few condiments available. After watching him stint on ketchup, his wife said, "Honey, seriously, here you can use all you want!"
stipulate	(verb)	Specify; make an open demand, esp. as a condition of agreement	Before taking the job, Bertram stipulated in his contract that he would be able to leave early on Fridays to attend religious services.
stratagem	(noun)	Military maneuver to deceive or surprise; crafty scheme	The party's stratagem was to dig up a scandal on their candidate's opponent, and then release the photos the day before the election, leaving the opponent no time to defend himself before voters took to the polls.
stratum	(noun)	One of many layers (such as in a rock formation or in the classes of a society)	From overhearing his rich and powerful passengers' conversations, the chauffeur grew to despise the upper stratum of society. / I love this dish! It's like a lasagna, but with strata made of bread, eggs, and pancetta! Oh, look at the menu—it's actually called a strata! That makes perfect sense.
strut	(noun)	A structural support or brace	Looking out the window of the small biplane, Elena could see the struts, the vertical connectors between the lower and upper sets of wings.

WORD	P.O.S.	DEFINITION	USAGE
sublime	(adj)	Lofty or elevated, inspiring reverence or awe; excellent, majestic	She loved visiting Gothic churches, which truly filled even a nonbeliever with a sense of the sublime. / This dinner is sublime! I will leave a glowing review on Yelp!
subpoena	(verb, noun)	A court order requiring a person to appear in court and give testimony	Yana was served with a subpoena requiring her to testify against her former colleague.
sully	(verb)	Make dirty, stain, tarnish, defile	The senator did win his campaign for reelection, but his reputation was sullied when he was photographed shaking hands with the tobacco executives who apparently bankrolled his campaign.
supplant	(verb)	Take the place of, displace, esp. through sneaky tactics	In the 1950s, many people took cod liver oil as a health supplement. Today, fish oil capsules and flaxseed oil have supplanted the smelly old standby our grandparents used. / He did achieve his dream of becoming CEO, but only after supplanting our previous CEO by wresting control while she was battling cancer.
supposition	(noun)	Assumption, hypothesis, something that has been supposed	In order to test our supposition that customers will buy our product if they associate it with celebrities, let's send free samples to some popular young starlets, track mentions in the press, and see if our sales increase accordingly.
surly	(adj)	Bad-tempered, hostile, unfriendly, or rude	This diner is terrible. My eggs are overcooked, and our surly waitress actually told me, "If you don't like it, scram."
surrogate	(noun, adj)	Substitute, person who acts for another (noun); acting as a replacement (adj)	A study found that baby monkeys, once separated from their mothers, preferred a surrogate mother made of cloth to a less comforting, rigid monkey doll, even when induced with treats to change their behavior.
sybarite	(noun)	Person devoted to pleasure and luxury	The reality show about Beverly Hills "housewives" portrayed wealthy sybarites who actually seemed to be pursuing champagne and Pilates full-time.

WORD	P.O.S.	DEFINITION	USAGE
symbiosis	(noun)	Mutually dependent relationship between two organisms, people, groups, etc.	In biology, one example of symbiosis is when a small creature feeds off bugs that live on a larger creature, thus protecting the larger creature from discomfort and possibly disease. / Although some celebrities complain about paparazzi, many have a symbiotic relationship with those same intrusive photographers—the paparazzi need to get paid, and the celebs need the photos to stay in the news.
synoptic	(adj)	Relating to a synopsis or summary; giving a general view	The movie studio had interns read screenplays and write up synoptic outlines for the executives to review.
syntax	(adj)	The rules governing grammar and how words join to make sentences (or how words and symbols join in writing computer code), the study of these rules, or any system or orderly arrangement	Now that my linguistics class is studying syntax, it makes a little more sense when my computer flashes "SYNTAX ERROR" at me. / Anyone learning a language is bound to make syntactical mistakes; even if he or she knows the appropriate vocabulary, it is still difficult to assemble the words perfectly.
tawdry	(adj)	Gaudy, cheap or cheap looking; indecent	Tara modeled her prom look after something she saw in a Pussycat Dolls video. Her mom didn't care for it, but her grandmother found it downright tawdry.
tendentious	(adj)	Marked by a strong point of view, biased	It's hard to become absorbed in the world of a fantasy novel when the author is so tendentious—the planet of Xerxon is clearly meant to mimic the United States, and the author's politics intrude on the story on every page.
terrestrial	(adj)	Relating to the Earth or to land; worldly	Some astronauts have said that it's difficult to focus on mundane, terrestrial issues after spending time in space.
terse	(adj)	Concise, brief and to the point (sometimes to the point of rudeness)	Hoping to talk to her doctor at length about her condition, she was disappointed to be treated so tersely by a doctor who simply renewed her prescription and disappeared.
toady	(noun)	Someone who flatters or acts in a servile manner for self-serving reasons	Look at that toady, sucking up and offering to do the boss's Christmas shopping for his kids. Gross.

MANHATTAN
PREP

WORD	P.O.S.	DEFINITION	USAGE
token	(noun, adj)	Sign, symbol, mark, badge; souvenir, memento; coin-like disk used as currency for subways, arcade games, etc.; sample, or person, thing, idea taken to represent an entire group (noun); of very little or merely symbolic value (adj)	I am starting to realize that this law firm hired me to be its token woman. There I am, smiling in all the ads, but I never actually get to work on important cases. / I am giving you this "Best Friends Forever" necklace as a token of our friendship.
tome	(noun)	Large or scholarly book; one of the volumes in a set of several books	When she discovered that the books she needed for her paper were in the university's online system, she ended up lugging some truly impressive tomes back from the library. She actually had to stop and rest twice on the way home.
tortuous	(adj)	Twisting, winding, complex; devious, not straightforward	If I can follow your tortuous logic, you're saying that people who want the new law protecting the environment are actually hurting the environment because the majority of people deliberately do the opposite of laws? What? / The children found the tortuous path of the roller coaster both terrifying and exciting.
transgression	(noun)	Violation of a law, moral rule, order, etc.; sin	His transgression was so serious that his family disowned him: no one would be visiting him in prison.
travesty	(noun)	Exaggerated, debased, or grotesque imitation	That *Saturday Night Live* sketch was a pretty good travesty of the election scandal. / You call that a sales presentation? What you just did in front of our clients was a travesty! I can't believe you lost what was supposed to be an easy sale.
treacherous	(adj)	Betraying trust, not faithful or trustworthy; not dependable; dangerous or deceptive	Betraying one's country for money is the most base of acts—his treachery cost the lives of several soldiers whom he had pledged to fight alongside. / The small boat was capsized in the treacherous waters.
trenchant	(adj)	forceful or vigorous, effective, keen; caustic, sharp	The school's trenchant new antitruancy policy immediately increased class attendance by a noticeable margin. / Claudia would have gone on making excuses for hours had Juan not trenchantly stepped in and asked, "You want to quit, right?" "Yes!" she said, quite relieved.
truculent	(adj)	Fierce, cruel, savage; belligerent	That guy is too truculent to work in customer service; when the customers are already angry, the last thing this store needs is someone prone to blow up at any moment!

WORD	P.O.S.	DEFINITION	USAGE
tumultuous	(adj)	Riotous, violently agitated, marked by disturbance or uproar; noisy, chaotic	Poland's tumultuous history includes a Nazi invasion, a period of Soviet rule, and, well before that, over 120 years during which it was partitioned by Russia, Prussia, and Austria and simply didn't exist. / She had been enjoying the game, but lost her hat, left earring, and keys in the tumult that resulted when fans went crazy over a referee's call.
turgid	(adj)	Swollen, inflated; metaphorically "inflated," such as in overblown, pompous speech	His prose was so turgid he used the phrase "synchronous repast" to mean a lunch break. / Terry carefully carried the turgid water balloons to the balcony, ready for a serious splash attack on members of the rival fraternity.
turpitude	(noun)	Depravity, baseness of character, corrupt or depraved acts	Worried about her grandson's turpitude—as evinced by his constant detentions and a three-day stay in a juvenile jail—Mrs. Worthington offered to pay for military school.
tyro	(noun)	Beginner	Kenneth felt called to work as a missionary, but he was really a tyro in the field, and was unprepared for many of the questions people asked him.
umbrage	(noun)	Offense or annoyance (usually as "take umbrage," meaning become offended or annoyed)	With 30 years' experience in the field and quite recent successes on a variety of projects, the executive understandably took umbrage when a coworker suggested that he was good to have around to remind others of "ancient history."
unconscionable	(adj)	Not guided by conscience; morally wrong, unjust, unreasonable	It is unconscionable that you would deny your sister a bone marrow transplant knowing that you're the only person in the family who's a match.
unsparing	(adj)	Unmerciful, harsh (as in not sparing any criticism); generous, lavish (as in not sparing any help or gifts to others)	The mother was unsparing in praising her son, so he was in for quite a shock when his new teacher told him his work was substandard.
untempered	(adj)	Not toned down; not moderated, controlled, or counterbalanced	The report was an untempered condemnation of the company's practices—the investigators didn't have a single good thing to say.
upbraid	(verb)	Find fault with, criticize or scold severely	I'm not surprised they got divorced—you can't upbraid someone every time he forgets to put a water glass in the sink and then expect him to stick around.

MANHATTAN
PREP

WORD	P.O.S.	DEFINITION	USAGE
usury	(noun)	Charging interest on a loan, esp. charging illegally high or excessive interest	I can't see how that payday lending place is even legal—a person borrowing $100 will end up paying over $150 interest in just a few months! Isn't that usury?
vanguard	(noun)	Leading units at the front of an army; leaders in a trend or movement, people on the "cutting edge"; the forefront of a trend or movement	While Google has won the search engine wars, in 1994, Yahoo was on the vanguard of search technology.
variegated	(adj)	Varied in color, having multicolored patches or spots; diverse	Unusually, the bridesmaids' dresses were boldly variegated, having many different colors. The bride reasoned that the dresses could be worn again. "Rainbow goes with anything!" she said. The bridesmaids privately agreed that they would never again wear those dresses as long as they lived.
verdant	(adj)	Green, such as with vegetation, plants, grass, etc.; young and inexperienced	Having grown up in Ethiopia, Dabir loved the lushness of the verdant forests in rainy Oregon. / The first-year associate was a little too verdant to be assigned to the big case.
verisimilitude	(noun)	The appearance of being true or real	The film manages to retain verisimilitude even though the plot is about a bunch of space aliens coming through a wormhole and enslaving humanity.
vernal	(adj)	Relating to the spring; fresh, youthful	Alma's favorite part of gardening was the vernal reawakening that followed a frozen winter.
vestige	(noun)	Trace or sign of something that once existed	They hadn't officially broken up, but she felt their relationship was running on fumes and that only vestiges of their former affection remained.
vex	(verb)	annoy or bother; puzzle or distress	"Don't vex me," said the nanny. "Behave, or I'll tell your parents." / She was totally vexed by the crossword clue—nine letters, starting with "b," meaning "person whose socks are either scratchy or imbued with magical powers." What?
via	(preposition)	Through, by means of, by way of (by a route that goes through or touches)	We will be flying to Russia via Frankfurt. / Many of the students at our college got here via special programs that assist low-income students in preparing for college.
vicissitude	(noun)	Changes or variations over time, esp. regular changes from one thing to another	While she scrubbed pots and pans, she pondered the vicissitudes of life—she once had a house full of servants, and now was a maid herself.

WORD	P.O.S.	DEFINITION	USAGE
vim	(noun)	Pep, enthusiasm, vitality, lively spirit	"I'm old, not dead!" said Grandpa Enrique, full of vim and ready for his first bungee jump.
virulent	(adj)	Extremely infectious, poisonous, etc.; hateful, bitterly hostile	The virulence of this strain of influenza has the government worried that there won't be enough vaccine to go around. / Discipline in the classroom is one thing, but the teacher's virulence towards misbehaving students was enough to get her suspended from teaching.
viscid or viscous	(adj)	Thick, adhesive, or covered in something sticky	Ugh, what did you spill on this floor? It's too viscous to be absorbed by these paper towels. Is this hair conditioner?
vitriol	(noun)	Something highly caustic, such as criticism (literally, one of a number of chemicals including sulfuric acid)	After another embarrassing loss, the team's shortstop was full of vitriol for the coach who had led them to their worst season in history.
vociferous	(adj)	Noisily crying out, as in protest	He has always been a vociferous opponent of the estate tax, appearing on numerous news programs to rail against "double taxation."
voluble	(adj)	Easily fluent in regards to speech	The journalist's new book is a voluble tome, covering three centuries of history with numerous flowing, almost conversational asides into the scientific discoveries and cultural advances of various time periods.
wan	(adj)	Unnaturally pale or showing some other indication of sickness, unhappiness, etc.; weak, lacking forcefulness	Are you okay? You're looking wan. / Juhn's wan attempt at asking for a raise was easily brushed off by his boss.
wanton	(adj)	Reckless, vicious, without regard for what is right; unjustifiable, deliberately done for no reason at all; sexually unrestrained or excessively luxurious	Kids do like to play pranks on Halloween, but driving an SUV into people's mailboxes isn't a prank—it's wanton destruction of property. / Many hip-hip videos depict a wanton lifestyle that is attractive to some, but unattainable (and possibly illegal!).
welter	(noun, verb)	Confused mass or pile, jumble; confusion or turmoil (noun); roll around, wallow, toss about, writhe (verb)	It said "thrift store," but inside it was just a welter of used clothing, draped everywhere and even lying in piles. / By the time the teacher broke up the fight, it was already pretty much over—the loser was weltering on the floor. / They struggled to keep the sailboat afloat on the weltering sea.

WORD	P.O.S.	DEFINITION	USAGE
whet	(verb)	Stimulate, make keen or eager (esp. of an appetite)	Dinner will take another 20 minutes, but maybe this cheese plate can whet your appetite?
whitewash	(noun, verb)	A substance used to whiten walls, wood, etc. (noun); deception, covering up of wrongs, errors, misdeeds, etc. (verb)	The journalist accused the government of trying to whitewash the scandal in order to protect the vice president's reputation.
winnow	(verb)	Sift, analyze critically, separate the useful part from the worthless part	We got 120 résumés for one job. It's going to take me a while just to winnow this down to a reasonable stack of people we want to interview.
winsome	(adj)	Charming, engaging, esp. in a sweet and innocent way	It's hard for some to believe that Lindsay Lohan, known for her current run-ins with the law, was once the winsome young starlet in *Freaky Friday*.
wizened	(adj)	Withered, shriveled	Fortunately, the wizened heads for sale at the Ecuadorian market weren't really shrunken heads—just plastic souvenirs for tourists. / The wizened old man still possessed a remarkably sharp mind.
xenophobia	(noun)	Fear or hatred of foreigners or that which is foreign	My mother's xenophobia is so great that she refuses to cross the border into Canada, and once told me that she'd rather die than try a mango because those foreign fruits are "sketchy."
yoke	(noun, verb)	A burden or something that oppresses; a frame for attaching animals (such as oxen) to each other and to a plow or other equipment to be pulled (noun); to unite together or to burden (verb)	The speaker argued that humanity had traded the yoke of servitude to kings and tyrants for the yoke of consumerism, which enslaves us just as much in the end.

STUDY ANYWHERE!

WITH MANHATTAN PREP'S GRE FLASH CARDS

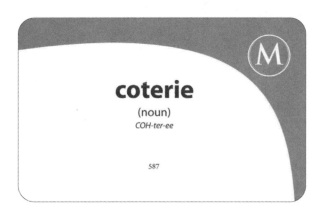

coterie
(noun)
COH-ter-ee

587

Definition: Close or exclusive group, clique

Usage: The pop star never traveled anywhere without a **coterie** of assistants and managers.

Related Words: *Cabal* (conspiracy, group of people who plot), *Entourage* (group of attendants)

More Info: In French, a *coterie* was a group of tenant farmers.

With our flashcards you can study both math and verbal concepts on the go!

Both our 500 Essential Words and a 500 Advanced Words cards go above and beyond providing abstract, out-of-context definitions. Complete with definitions, example sentences, pronunciations, and related words, this two-volume set comprises the most comprehensive vocabulary study tool on the market.

Our GRE Math Flash Cards provide practical exposure to the basic math concepts tested on the GRE.

Designed to be user-friendly for all students, these cards include easy-to-follow explanations of math concepts that promise to enhance comprehension and build fundamental skills.

For the revised GRE*

M

MANHATTAN PREP

GRE® FLASH CARDS

500 Math Flash Cards

✓ Designed specifically for the math question types found on the revised GRE

✓ Cards cover all tested content and include clear, efficient explanations

✓ Want Verbal? Check out our flash card sets *500 Essential Words* & *500 Advanced Words*

*GRE is a registered trademark of the Educational Testing Service (ETS), which neither sponsors nor endorses this test product.

NEED MORE THAN BOOKS ALONE?

TRY OUR GUIDED SELF-STUDY PROGRAM!

With over 27 hours of recorded video lessons, Guided Self-Study is a perfect fit for self-motivated individuals who want full access to all of Manhattan Prep's materials.

Armed with our syllabus and online resources suite, you can get more out of your books. This program is a great fit for students operating under a tight deadline or rigid schedule who may not have the time to take a live prep course.

Check it out at manhattanprep.com/gre/gre-self-study.cfm